Praxis II

Interdisciplinary Early Childhood Education (5023)

Exam Secrets

Study Guide

Dear Future Exam Success Story

First of all, **THANK YOU** for purchasing Mometrix study materials!

Second, congratulations! You are one of the few determined test-takers who are committed to doing whatever it takes to excel on your exam. **You have come to the right place.** We developed these study materials with one goal in mind: to deliver you the information you need in a format that's concise and easy to use.

In addition to optimizing your guide for the content of the test, we've outlined our recommended steps for breaking down the preparation process into small, attainable goals so you can make sure you stay on track.

We've also analyzed the entire test-taking process, identifying the most common pitfalls and showing how you can overcome them and be ready for any curveball the test throws you.

Standardized testing is one of the biggest obstacles on your road to success, which only increases the importance of doing well in the high-pressure, high-stakes environment of test day. Your results on this test could have a significant impact on your future, and this guide provides the information and practical advice to help you achieve your full potential on test day.

Your success is our success

We would love to hear from you! If you would like to share the story of your exam success or if you have any questions or comments in regard to our products, please contact us at **800-673-8175** or **support@mometrix.com**.

Thanks again for your business and we wish you continued success!

Sincerely,
The Mometrix Test Preparation Team

Need more help? Check out our flashcards at:
http://MometrixFlashcards.com/PraxisII

TABLE OF CONTENTS

Introduction

Thank you for purchasing this resource! You have made the choice to prepare yourself for a test that could have a huge impact on your future, and this guide is designed to help you be fully ready for test day. Obviously, it's important to have a solid understanding of the test material, but you also need to be prepared for the unique environment and stressors of the test, so that you can perform to the best of your abilities.

For this purpose, the first section that appears in this guide is the **Secret Keys**. We've devoted countless hours to meticulously researching what works and what doesn't, and we've boiled down our findings to the five most impactful steps you can take to improve your performance on the test. We start at the beginning with study planning and move through the preparation process, all the way to the testing strategies that will help you get the most out of what you know when you're finally sitting in front of the test.

We recommend that you start preparing for your test as far in advance as possible. However, if you've bought this guide as a last-minute study resource and only have a few days before your test, we recommend that you skip over the first two Secret Keys since they address a long-term study plan.

If you struggle with **test anxiety**, we strongly encourage you to check out our recommendations for how you can overcome it. Test anxiety is a formidable foe, but it can be beaten, and we want to make sure you have the tools you need to defeat it.

Secret Key #1 – Plan Big, Study Small

There's a lot riding on your performance. If you want to ace this test, you're going to need to keep your skills sharp and the material fresh in your mind. You need a plan that lets you review everything you need to know while still fitting in your schedule. We'll break this strategy down into three categories.

Information Organization

Start with the information you already have: the official test outline. From this, you can make a complete list of all the concepts you need to cover before the test. Organize these concepts into groups that can be studied together, and create a list of any related vocabulary you need to learn so you can brush up on any difficult terms. You'll want to keep this vocabulary list handy once you actually start studying since you may need to add to it along the way.

Time Management

Once you have your set of study concepts, decide how to spread them out over the time you have left before the test. Break your study plan into small, clear goals so you have a manageable task for each day and know exactly what you're doing. Then just focus on one small step at a time. When you manage your time this way, you don't need to spend hours at a time studying. Studying a small block of content for a short period each day helps you retain information better and avoid stressing over how much you have left to do. You can relax knowing that you have a plan to cover everything in time. In order for this strategy to be effective though, you have to start studying early and stick to your schedule. Avoid the exhaustion and futility that comes from last-minute cramming!

Study Environment

The environment you study in has a big impact on your learning. Studying in a coffee shop, while probably more enjoyable, is not likely to be as fruitful as studying in a quiet room. It's important to keep distractions to a minimum. You're only planning to study for a short block of time, so make the most of it. Don't pause to check your phone or get up to find a snack. It's also important to **avoid multitasking**. Research has consistently shown that multitasking will make your studying dramatically less effective. Your study area should also be comfortable and well-lit so you don't have the distraction of straining your eyes or sitting on an uncomfortable chair.

 The time of day you study is also important. You want to be rested and alert. Don't wait until just before bedtime. Study when you'll be most likely to comprehend and remember. Even better, if you know what time of day your test will be, set that time aside for study. That way your brain will be used to working on that subject at that specific time and you'll have a better chance of recalling information.

Finally, it can be helpful to team up with others who are studying for the same test. Your actual studying should be done in as isolated an environment as possible, but the work of organizing the information and setting up the study plan can be divided up. In between study sessions, you can discuss with your teammates the concepts that you're all studying and quiz each other on the details. Just be sure that your teammates are as serious about the test as you are. If you find that your study time is being replaced with social time, you might need to find a new team.

Secret Key #2 – Make Your Studying Count

You're devoting a lot of time and effort to preparing for this test, so you want to be absolutely certain it will pay off. This means doing more than just reading the content and hoping you can remember it on test day. It's important to make every minute of study count. There are two main areas you can focus on to make your studying count.

Retention

It doesn't matter how much time you study if you can't remember the material. You need to make sure you are retaining the concepts. To check your retention of the information you're learning, try recalling it at later times with minimal prompting. Try carrying around flashcards and glance at one or two from time to time or ask a friend who's also studying for the test to quiz you.

To enhance your retention, look for ways to put the information into practice so that you can apply it rather than simply recalling it. If you're using the information in practical ways, it will be much easier to remember. Similarly, it helps to solidify a concept in your mind if you're not only reading it to yourself but also explaining it to someone else. Ask a friend to let you teach them about a concept you're a little shaky on (or speak aloud to an imaginary audience if necessary). As you try to summarize, define, give examples, and answer your friend's questions, you'll understand the concepts better and they will stay with you longer. Finally, step back for a big picture view and ask yourself how each piece of information fits with the whole subject. When you link the different concepts together and see them working together as a whole, it's easier to remember the individual components.

Finally, practice showing your work on any multi-step problems, even if you're just studying. Writing out each step you take to solve a problem will help solidify the process in your mind, and you'll be more likely to remember it during the test.

Modality

Modality simply refers to the means or method by which you study. Choosing a study modality that fits your own individual learning style is crucial. No two people learn best in exactly the same way, so it's important to know your strengths and use them to your advantage.

For example, if you learn best by visualization, focus on visualizing a concept in your mind and draw an image or a diagram. Try color-coding your notes, illustrating them, or creating symbols that will trigger your mind to recall a learned concept. If you learn best by hearing or discussing information, find a study partner who learns the same way or read aloud to yourself. Think about how to put the information in your own words. Imagine that you are giving a lecture on the topic and record yourself so you can listen to it later.

For any learning style, flashcards can be helpful. Organize the information so you can take advantage of spare moments to review. Underline key words or phrases. Use different colors for different categories. Mnemonic devices (such as creating a short list in which every item starts with the same letter) can also help with retention. Find what works best for you and use it to store the information in your mind most effectively and easily.

Secret Key #3 – Practice the Right Way

Your success on test day depends not only on how many hours you put into preparing, but also on whether you prepared the right way. It's good to check along the way to see if your studying is paying off. One of the most effective ways to do this is by taking practice tests to evaluate your progress. Practice tests are useful because they show exactly where you need to improve. Every time you take a practice test, pay special attention to these three groups of questions:

- The questions you got wrong
- The questions you had to guess on, even if you guessed right
- The questions you found difficult or slow to work through

This will show you exactly what your weak areas are, and where you need to devote more study time. Ask yourself why each of these questions gave you trouble. Was it because you didn't understand the material? Was it because you didn't remember the vocabulary? Do you need more repetitions on this type of question to build speed and confidence? Dig into those questions and figure out how you can strengthen your weak areas as you go back to review the material.

Additionally, many practice tests have a section explaining the answer choices. It can be tempting to read the explanation and think that you now have a good understanding of the concept. However, an explanation likely only covers part of the question's broader context. Even if the explanation makes perfect sense, **go back and investigate** every concept related to the question until you're positive you have a thorough understanding.

As you go along, keep in mind that the practice test is just that: practice. Memorizing these questions and answers will not be very helpful on the actual test because it is unlikely to have any of the same exact questions. If you only know the right answers to the sample questions, you won't be prepared for the real thing. **Study the concepts** until you understand them fully, and then you'll be able to answer any question that shows up on the test.

It's important to wait on the practice tests until you're ready. If you take a test on your first day of study, you may be overwhelmed by the amount of material covered and how much you need to learn. Work up to it gradually.

On test day, you'll need to be prepared for answering questions, managing your time, and using the test-taking strategies you've learned. It's a lot to balance, like a mental marathon that will have a big impact on your future. Like training for a marathon, you'll need to start slowly and work your way up. When test day arrives, you'll be ready.

Start with the strategies you've read in the first two Secret Keys—plan your course and study in the way that works best for you. If you have time, consider using multiple study resources to get different approaches to the same concepts. It can be helpful to see difficult concepts from more than one angle. Then find a good source for practice tests. Many times, the test website will suggest potential study resources or provide sample tests.

Practice Test Strategy

If you're able to find at least three practice tests, we recommend this strategy:

UNTIMED AND OPEN-BOOK PRACTICE

Take the first test with no time constraints and with your notes and study guide handy. Take your time and focus on applying the strategies you've learned.

TIMED AND OPEN-BOOK PRACTICE

Take the second practice test open-book as well, but set a timer and practice pacing yourself to finish in time.

TIMED AND CLOSED-BOOK PRACTICE

Take any other practice tests as if it were test day. Set a timer and put away your study materials. Sit at a table or desk in a quiet room, imagine yourself at the testing center, and answer questions as quickly and accurately as possible.

Keep repeating timed and closed-book tests on a regular basis until you run out of practice tests or it's time for the actual test. Your mind will be ready for the schedule and stress of test day, and you'll be able to focus on recalling the material you've learned.

Secret Key #4 – Pace Yourself

Once you're fully prepared for the material on the test, your biggest challenge on test day will be managing your time. Just knowing that the clock is ticking can make you panic even if you have plenty of time left. Work on pacing yourself so you can build confidence against the time constraints of the exam. Pacing is a difficult skill to master, especially in a high-pressure environment, so **practice is vital**.

Set time expectations for your pace based on how much time is available. For example, if a section has 60 questions and the time limit is 30 minutes, you know you have to average 30 seconds or less per question in order to answer them all. Although 30 seconds is the hard limit, set 25 seconds per question as your goal, so you reserve extra time to spend on harder questions. When you budget extra time for the harder questions, you no longer have any reason to stress when those questions take longer to answer.

Don't let this time expectation distract you from working through the test at a calm, steady pace, but keep it in mind so you don't spend too much time on any one question. Recognize that taking extra time on one question you don't understand may keep you from answering two that you do understand later in the test. If your time limit for a question is up and you're still not sure of the answer, mark it and move on, and come back to it later if the time and the test format allow. If the testing format doesn't allow you to return to earlier questions, just make an educated guess; then put it out of your mind and move on. 

On the easier questions, be careful not to rush. It may seem wise to hurry through them so you have more time for the challenging ones, but it's not worth missing one if you know the concept and just didn't take the time to read the question fully. Work efficiently but make sure you understand the question and have looked at all of the answer choices, since more than one may seem right at first.

Even if you're paying attention to the time, you may find yourself a little behind at some point. You should speed up to get back on track, but do so wisely. Don't panic; just take a few seconds less on each question until you're caught up. Don't guess without thinking, but do look through the answer choices and eliminate any you know are wrong. If you can get down to two choices, it is often worthwhile to guess from those. Once you've chosen an answer, move on and don't dwell on any that you skipped or had to hurry through. If a question was taking too long, chances are it was one of the harder ones, so you weren't as likely to get it right anyway.

On the other hand, if you find yourself getting ahead of schedule, it may be beneficial to slow down a little. The more quickly you work, the more likely you are to make a careless mistake that will affect your score. You've budgeted time for each question, so don't be afraid to spend that time. Practice an efficient but careful pace to get the most out of the time you have.

Secret Key #5 – Have a Plan for Guessing

When you're taking the test, you may find yourself stuck on a question. Some of the answer choices seem better than others, but you don't see the one answer choice that is obviously correct. What do you do?

The scenario described above is very common, yet most test takers have not effectively prepared for it. Developing and practicing a plan for guessing may be one of the single most effective uses of your time as you get ready for the exam.

In developing your plan for guessing, there are three questions to address:

- When should you start the guessing process?
- How should you narrow down the choices?
- Which answer should you choose?

When to Start the Guessing Process

Unless your plan for guessing is to select C every time (which, despite its merits, is not what we recommend), you need to leave yourself enough time to apply your answer elimination strategies. Since you have a limited amount of time for each question, that means that if you're going to give yourself the best shot at guessing correctly, you have to decide quickly whether or not you will guess.

Of course, the best-case scenario is that you don't have to guess at all, so first, see if you can answer the question based on your knowledge of the subject and basic reasoning skills. Focus on the key words in the question and try to jog your memory of related topics. Give yourself a chance to bring the knowledge to mind, but once you realize that you don't have (or you can't access) the knowledge you need to answer the question, it's time to start the guessing process.

It's almost always better to start the guessing process too early than too late. It only takes a few seconds to remember something and answer the question from knowledge. Carefully eliminating wrong answer choices takes longer. Plus, going through the process of eliminating answer choices can actually help jog your memory.

Summary: Start the guessing process as soon as you decide that you can't answer the question based on your knowledge.

How to Narrow Down the Choices

The next chapter in this book (**Test-Taking Strategies**) includes a wide range of strategies for how to approach questions and how to look for answer choices to eliminate. You will definitely want to read those carefully, practice them, and figure out which ones work best for you. Here though, we're going to address a mindset rather than a particular strategy.

Your odds of guessing an answer correctly depend on how many options you are choosing from.

Number of options left	5	4	3	2	1
Odds of guessing correctly	20%	25%	33%	50%	100%

You can see from this chart just how valuable it is to be able to eliminate incorrect answers and make an educated guess, but there are two things that many test takers do that cause them to miss out on the benefits of guessing:

- Accidentally eliminating the correct answer
- Selecting an answer based on an impression

We'll look at the first one here, and the second one in the next section.

To avoid accidentally eliminating the correct answer, we recommend a thought exercise called **the $5 challenge**. In this challenge, you only eliminate an answer choice from contention if you are willing to bet $5 on it being wrong. Why $5? Five dollars is a small but not insignificant amount of money. It's an amount you could afford to lose but wouldn't want to throw away. And while losing

$5 once might not hurt too much, doing it twenty times will set you back $100. In the same way, each small decision you make—eliminating a choice here, guessing on a question there—won't by itself impact your score very much, but when you put them all together, they can make a big difference. By holding each answer choice elimination decision to a higher standard, you can reduce the risk of accidentally eliminating the correct answer.

The $5 challenge can also be applied in a positive sense: If you are willing to bet $5 that an answer choice *is* correct, go ahead and mark it as correct.

Summary: Only eliminate an answer choice if you are willing to bet $5 that it is wrong.

Which Answer to Choose

You're taking the test. You've run into a hard question and decided you'll have to guess. You've eliminated all the answer choices you're willing to bet $5 on. Now you have to pick an answer. Why do we even need to talk about this? Why can't you just pick whichever one you feel like when the time comes?

The answer to these questions is that if you don't come into the test with a plan, you'll rely on your impression to select an answer choice, and if you do that, you risk falling into a trap. The test writers know that everyone who takes their test will be guessing on some of the questions, so they intentionally write wrong answer choices to seem plausible. You still have to pick an answer though, and if the wrong answer choices are designed to look right, how can you ever be sure that you're not falling for their trap? The best solution we've found to this dilemma is to take the decision out of your hands entirely. Here is the process we recommend:

Once you've eliminated any choices that you are confident (willing to bet $5) are wrong, select the first remaining choice as your answer.

Whether you choose to select the first remaining choice, the second, or the last, the important thing is that you use some preselected standard. Using this approach guarantees that you will not be enticed into selecting an answer choice that looks right, because you are not basing your decision on how the answer choices look.

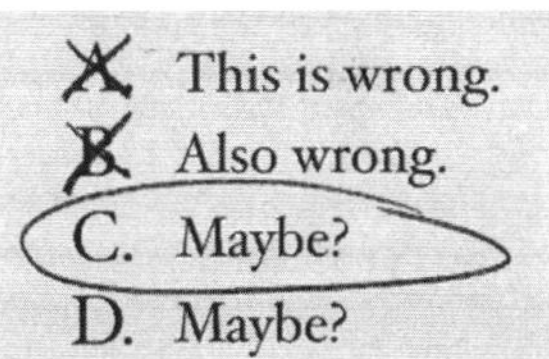

This is not meant to make you question your knowledge. Instead, it is to help you recognize the difference between your knowledge and your impressions. There's a huge difference between thinking an answer is right because of what you know, and thinking an answer is right because it looks or sounds like it should be right.

Summary: To ensure that your selection is appropriately random, make a predetermined selection from among all answer choices you have not eliminated.

Test-Taking Strategies

This section contains a list of test-taking strategies that you may find helpful as you work through the test. By taking what you know and applying logical thought, you can maximize your chances of answering any question correctly!

It is very important to realize that every question is different and every person is different: no single strategy will work on every question, and no single strategy will work for every person. That's why we've included all of them here, so you can try them out and determine which ones work best for different types of questions and which ones work best for you.

Question Strategies

ⓥ READ CAREFULLY

Read the question and the answer choices carefully. Don't miss the question because you misread the terms. You have plenty of time to read each question thoroughly and make sure you understand what is being asked. Yet a happy medium must be attained, so don't waste too much time. You must read carefully and efficiently.

ⓥ CONTEXTUAL CLUES

Look for contextual clues. If the question includes a word you are not familiar with, look at the immediate context for some indication of what the word might mean. Contextual clues can often give you all the information you need to decipher the meaning of an unfamiliar word. Even if you can't determine the meaning, you may be able to narrow down the possibilities enough to make a solid guess at the answer to the question.

ⓥ PREFIXES

If you're having trouble with a word in the question or answer choices, try dissecting it. Take advantage of every clue that the word might include. Prefixes can be a huge help. Usually, they allow you to determine a basic meaning. *Pre-* means before, *post-* means after, *pro-* is positive, *de-* is negative. From prefixes, you can get an idea of the general meaning of the word and try to put it into context.

ⓥ HEDGE WORDS

Watch out for critical hedge words, such as *likely, may, can, sometimes, often, almost, mostly, usually, generally, rarely,* and *sometimes.* Question writers insert these hedge phrases to cover every possibility. Often an answer choice will be wrong simply because it leaves no room for exception. Be on guard for answer choices that have definitive words such as *exactly* and *always.*

ⓥ SWITCHBACK WORDS

Stay alert for *switchbacks.* These are the words and phrases frequently used to alert you to shifts in thought. The most common switchback words are *but, although,* and *however.* Others include *nevertheless, on the other hand, even though, while, in spite of, despite,* and *regardless of.* Switchback words are important to catch because they can change the direction of the question or an answer choice.

⊘ Face Value

When in doubt, use common sense. Accept the situation in the problem at face value. Don't read too much into it. These problems will not require you to make wild assumptions. If you have to go beyond creativity and warp time or space in order to have an answer choice fit the question, then you should move on and consider the other answer choices. These are normal problems rooted in reality. The applicable relationship or explanation may not be readily apparent, but it is there for you to figure out. Use your common sense to interpret anything that isn't clear.

Answer Choice Strategies

⊘ Answer Selection

The most thorough way to pick an answer choice is to identify and eliminate wrong answers until only one is left, then confirm it is the correct answer. Sometimes an answer choice may immediately seem right, but be careful. The test writers will usually put more than one reasonable answer choice on each question, so take a second to read all of them and make sure that the other choices are not equally obvious. As long as you have time left, it is better to read every answer choice than to pick the first one that looks right without checking the others.

⊘ Answer Choice Families

An answer choice family consists of two (in rare cases, three) answer choices that are very similar in construction and cannot all be true at the same time. If you see two answer choices that are direct opposites or parallels, one of them is usually the correct answer. For instance, if one answer choice says that quantity x increases and another either says that quantity x decreases (opposite) or says that quantity y increases (parallel), then those answer choices would fall into the same family. An answer choice that doesn't match the construction of the answer choice family is more likely to be incorrect. Most questions will not have answer choice families, but when they do appear, you should be prepared to recognize them.

⊘ Eliminate Answers

Eliminate answer choices as soon as you realize they are wrong, but make sure you consider all possibilities. If you are eliminating answer choices and realize that the last one you are left with is also wrong, don't panic. Start over and consider each choice again. There may be something you missed the first time that you will realize on the second pass.

⊘ Avoid Fact Traps

Don't be distracted by an answer choice that is factually true but doesn't answer the question. You are looking for the choice that answers the question. Stay focused on what the question is asking for so you don't accidentally pick an answer that is true but incorrect. Always go back to the question and make sure the answer choice you've selected actually answers the question and is not merely a true statement.

⊘ Extreme Statements

In general, you should avoid answers that put forth extreme actions as standard practice or proclaim controversial ideas as established fact. An answer choice that states the "process should be used in certain situations, if…" is much more likely to be correct than one that states the "process should be discontinued completely." The first is a calm rational statement and doesn't even make a definitive, uncompromising stance, using a hedge word *if* to provide wiggle room, whereas the second choice is far more extreme.

⊘ Benchmark

As you read through the answer choices and you come across one that seems to answer the question well, mentally select that answer choice. This is not your final answer, but it's the one that will help you evaluate the other answer choices. The one that you selected is your benchmark or standard for judging each of the other answer choices. Every other answer choice must be compared to your benchmark. That choice is correct until proven otherwise by another answer choice beating it. If you find a better answer, then that one becomes your new benchmark. Once you've decided that no other choice answers the question as well as your benchmark, you have your final answer.

⊘ Predict the Answer

Before you even start looking at the answer choices, it is often best to try to predict the answer. When you come up with the answer on your own, it is easier to avoid distractions and traps because you will know exactly what to look for. The right answer choice is unlikely to be word-for-word what you came up with, but it should be a close match. Even if you are confident that you have the right answer, you should still take the time to read each option before moving on.

General Strategies

⊘ Tough Questions

If you are stumped on a problem or it appears too hard or too difficult, don't waste time. Move on! Remember though, if you can quickly check for obviously incorrect answer choices, your chances of guessing correctly are greatly improved. Before you completely give up, at least try to knock out a couple of possible answers. Eliminate what you can and then guess at the remaining answer choices before moving on.

⊘ Check Your Work

Since you will probably not know every term listed and the answer to every question, it is important that you get credit for the ones that you do know. Don't miss any questions through careless mistakes. If at all possible, try to take a second to look back over your answer selection and make sure you've selected the correct answer choice and haven't made a costly careless mistake (such as marking an answer choice that you didn't mean to mark). This quick double check should more than pay for itself in caught mistakes for the time it costs.

⊘ Pace Yourself

It's easy to be overwhelmed when you're looking at a page full of questions; your mind is confused and full of random thoughts, and the clock is ticking down faster than you would like. Calm down and maintain the pace that you have set for yourself. Especially as you get down to the last few minutes of the test, don't let the small numbers on the clock make you panic. As long as you are on track by monitoring your pace, you are guaranteed to have time for each question.

⊘ Don't Rush

It is very easy to make errors when you are in a hurry. Maintaining a fast pace in answering questions is pointless if it makes you miss questions that you would have gotten right otherwise. Test writers like to include distracting information and wrong answers that seem right. Taking a little extra time to avoid careless mistakes can make all the difference in your test score. Find a pace that allows you to be confident in the answers that you select.

Panicking will not help you pass the test, so do your best to stay calm and keep moving. Taking deep breaths and going through the answer elimination steps you practiced can help to break through a stress barrier and keep your pace.

Final Notes

The combination of a solid foundation of content knowledge and the confidence that comes from practicing your plan for applying that knowledge is the key to maximizing your performance on test day. As your foundation of content knowledge is built up and strengthened, you'll find that the strategies included in this chapter become more and more effective in helping you quickly sift through the distractions and traps of the test to isolate the correct answer.

Now that you're preparing to move forward into the test content chapters of this book, be sure to keep your goal in mind. As you read, think about how you will be able to apply this information on the test. If you've already seen sample questions for the test and you have an idea of the question format and style, try to come up with questions of your own that you can answer based on what you're reading. This will give you valuable practice applying your knowledge in the same ways you can expect to on test day.

Good luck and good studying!

Growth and Development of Young Children Across the Spectrum of Development

Childhood Development Stages

JEAN PIAGET'S THEORY OF COGNITIVE DEVELOPMENT

Jean Piaget's theory of cognitive development theorizes that children will learn more effectively if they are allowed to actively adapt to the world around them through play and exploration rather than being taught skills and knowledge by others. Piaget's theory suggests that there are four major stages that children will go through as they begin to acquire new skills that will aid their ability to learn and process information independently. The four stages of cognitive development that Piaget identifies are the sensorimotor stage, which spans from ages zero to two; the preoperational stage, spanning from ages two to seven; the concrete operational stage for ages seven to 11; and the formal operational stage for ages 11 and up. Piaget's theory is important to the study of child development because it was the first theory that recognized that children can actively and effectively learn on their own rather than being dependent on another person for learning to occur.

SENSORIMOTOR STAGE OF PIAGET'S THEORY OF COGNITIVE DEVELOPMENT

From birth until about 2 years of age, infants are in what Piaget termed the sensorimotor stage of cognitive development. They learn through environmental input they receive through their senses, motor actions they engage in, and feedback they receive from their bodies and the environment about their actions. For example, a baby kicks his legs, sees his feet moving, and reaches for them. He sees objects, reaches for them, and grasps them. Eventually, babies learn they can make some objects move by touching or hitting them. They learn through repeated experiences that when they throw objects out of their cribs, their parents retrieve them. They will seem to make a game of this, not to annoy parents, but as a way of learning rules of cause and effect by repeating actions to see the same results. They also enjoy their ability to be causal agents and their power to achieve effects through their actions.

FIRST THREE SUBSTAGES OF THE SENSORIMOTOR STAGE

From birth to 1 month old, infants learn to comprehend their environment through their inborn reflexes, such as the sucking reflex and the reflex of looking at their surroundings. From 1–4 months old, babies begin to coordinate their physical sensations with new schemas, which are mental constructs and concepts they form to represent elements of reality. For example, an infant might suck her thumb by chance and feel pleasure from the activity; in the future, she will repeat thumb-sucking because the pleasure is rewarding. Piaget called this second substage "primary circular reactions." In the third substage, around 4–8 months, which he called "secondary circular reactions," children also repeat rewarding actions, but now they are focused on things in the environment that they can affect, rather than just the child's own person. For example, once a baby learns to pick up an object and mouth it, he or she will repeat this. Thus, babies learn an early method of environmental exploration through their mouths, an extension of their initial sucking reflex.

LAST THREE SUBSTAGES OF THE SENSORIMOTOR STAGE

According to Piaget, babies about 8–12 months are in the "coordination of reactions" substage of the sensorimotor stage. Having begun repeating actions purposely to achieve environmental effects during the previous substage of secondary circular reactions, in coordination of reactions, infants begin further exploring their surroundings. They frequently imitate others' observed behaviors, more obviously demonstrate intentional behaviors, and become able to combine schemas (mental constructs) to attain certain results. They develop object permanence, the understanding that unseen objects still exist, and they learn to associate certain objects with their properties. For example, once a baby realizes a rattle makes a noise when shaken, he or she will deliberately shake it to produce the sound. In "tertiary circular reactions," at about 12–18 months, children begin experimenting through trial-and-error. For instance, a child might test various actions or sounds for getting parents' attention. From 18–24 months, in the substage of "early representational thought," children begin representing objects and events with symbols. They begin to understand the world via not only actions but mental operations.

OBJECT PERMANENCE

One of the landmarks of infant cognitive development is learning that concrete objects are not "out of sight, out of mind"; in other words, things still continue to exist even when they are out of our sight. Babies generally develop this realization around 8–9 months old, though some may be earlier or later. Some researchers after Piaget have found object permanence in babies as young as 3.5 months. Younger infants typically attend to an object of interest only when they can see it; if it is removed or hidden, they are upset or confused at its disappearance and/or shift their attention to something else. A sign that they have developed object permanence is if they search for the object after it is moved or hidden. Babies only become interested in "hide and seek" types of games once they have developed this understanding that the existence of objects and people persist beyond their immediate vision or proximity. Another example of emerging object permanence is the delight babies begin to take in "peek-a-boo" games.

SCHEMA DEVELOPMENT IN INFANTS

Piaget proposed we form mental constructs or concepts that he called schema, representing elements of the environment, beginning in infancy. A schema does not represent an individual object but a category or class of things. For example, a baby might form a schema representing "things to suck on," initially including her bottle, her thumb, and her pacifier. Piaget said assimilation is when we can fit something new into an existing schema: the child in this example assimilates "Daddy's knee" into her schema of things she can suck on when she discovers this action. When something new cannot be assimilated into an existing schema, we either modify that schema or form a new schema, which both constitute accommodation. The baby in our example, becoming a toddler, might modify her schema of things to suck to include straws, which require a different sucking technique. Piaget said assimilation and accommodation combined constitute the process of adaptation, adjusting to our environment through interacting with it.

PIAGET'S SCHEMA EXAMPLES
SCENARIO

A toddler on an airplane sees a nearby stranger who is male, about 5'8", with white hair and eyeglasses. Both of his grandfathers have these same general appearances. He murmurs to himself, "Hi, Granddaddy." Explain this according to Piaget's concept of the schema in his cognitive-developmental theory.

EXPLANATION

The toddler in this example did not actually mistake a complete stranger for either one of his grandfathers. Notice that he did not directly address the stranger as "Granddaddy" with conversational loudness, but murmured it to himself. He recognized this man was not someone he knew. However, he recognized common elements with his grandfathers in the man's appearance. According to Piaget's theory of cognitive development, the explanation for this is that the child had formed a schema to represent men about 5'8" with white hair and eyeglasses, based initially on his early knowledge of two such men he knew, his grandfathers, and then extending to include other similar-appearing men, through the process of assimilation of new information into an existing schema. His description did not mean he thought the stranger was named Granddaddy. Rather, the word *Granddaddy* was not only the name he called one grandfather, but also the word he used to label his schema for all men who appeared to fit into this category.

SCENARIO

A toddler sees a large brown dog through the window and says, "Moo." Explain this according to Piaget's theory of cognitive development.

EXPLANATION

In this example, the toddler had seen cows in picture books, photos, or on a farm, and learned to associate the sound "Moo" with cows, reinforced by the teaching of toys, books, and adults. She had formed a schema for large, brown, four-legged, furry animals. Because the dog she saw fit these properties, she assimilated the dog into her cow schema. If she were then told this was a dog that says "Bow-wow," she would either form a new schema for dogs, or, if she had previously only seen smaller dogs, accommodate (modify) her existing dog schema to include larger dogs.

PREOPERATIONAL STAGE OF PIAGET'S THEORY OF COGNITIVE DEVELOPMENT

Children between roughly 2 and 6 years old are in Piaget's preoperational stage of cognitive development. Having begun to use objects to represent other things (symbolic representation) near the end of the previous sensorimotor stage, children now further develop this ability during pretend/make-believe play. They may pretend a broom is a guitar or a horse, or talk using a block as a phone. Toddlers begin to play "house," pretending they and their playmates are the mommy, the daddy, the mailman, the doctor, etc. The reason Piaget called this stage preoperational is that children are not yet capable of performing mental "operations," including following concrete logic or manipulating information mentally. Their thinking is intuitive rather than following logical steps. Piaget termed preoperational children "egocentric" in that they literally cannot adopt another's point of view, even concretely: in experiments, after seeing pictures of a scene as viewed from different positions, children could not match a picture to another person's position, selecting the picture showing the scene from their own viewpoint.

ANIMISM AND MAGICAL THINKING

Piaget found that children in the preoperational stage are not yet able to perform logical mental operations. Their thinking is intuitive during the toddler and preschool years. One characteristic of the thinking of young children is animism, or assigning human qualities, feelings, and actions to inanimate objects. For example, a child seeing an autumn leaf fall off of a tree might remark, "The tree didn't like that leaf and pushed it off of its branch." Or a child with a sunburn might say, "The sun was angry at me and burned me." A related characteristic is magical thinking, which is attributing cause-and-effect relationships between their own feelings and thoughts and environmental events where none exists. For example, if a child says "I hate you" to another person or secretly dislikes and wishes the other gone, and something bad then happens to that person, the child is likely to believe what he or she said, felt, or thought caused the other's unfortunate event. This is related to egocentrism—seeing everything as revolving around oneself.

PIAGET'S EGOCENTRISM AND ANIMISM CONCEPTS OF PREOPERATIONAL CHILDREN

Adults aware of the egocentric nature of preoperational children understand that most two-year-olds, for example, neither want to share with others nor understand why they should. Egocentrism also means being unable to see others' perspectives. Adults who take this ability for granted may not realize the simplicity of both some early childhood problems and their solutions. For example, when a preschooler does something physically or emotionally hurtful to another, adults can guide identification of consequences by saying, "Look at her face now. How do you think she feels?" Adults can then guide perspective-taking: "How would you feel if somebody hit you like you just hit Sally?" This has not occurred to the preschooler, but once he or she is guided to think of it, it can be a revelation. Animism is preoperational children's attributing human qualities to inanimate objects. Many children's books and TV shows accordingly appeal to young children by animating letters, numbers, or objects (e.g., SpongeBob SquarePants).

MAGICAL THINKING CONCEPT OF PIAGET'S THEORY OF COGNITIVE DEVELOPMENT

According to Piaget, magical thinking is the belief that one's thoughts make external events happen. He identified this as a common characteristic of the way children in his preoperational stage think. Piaget said that preschool children have not yet developed the cognitive ability to perform mental operations. Because they cannot follow or apply logical thought processes, their thinking is irrational and intuitive rather than organized and based on real-world, empirical observations. For example, a preoperational child may believe that something good happened because he or she wished hard enough for it. Preschoolers also commonly believe their saying or wishing something bad toward another caused the other's misfortune. They often blame themselves for divorce or death in the family, thinking these happened because they were "bad." Adults should explain to young children that what they wished, thought, felt, or said did not cause good or bad events, and reassign causes external to the child (e.g., "Mommy and Daddy were not getting along with each other," "Grandpa was sick," or "It was an accident, not anybody's fault.")

SALIENT CHARACTERISTICS OF PIAGET'S SECOND STAGE OF CHILD COGNITIVE DEVELOPMENT

Toddlers and preschoolers in the preoperational stage typically begin to recognize rudimentary symbolic representation (i.e., that some objects represent other things). This understanding of symbols allows them to begin using words to represent things, people, feelings, and thoughts. Adults can support early childhood language development by frequently conversing with young children, reading books to them, introducing and explaining new vocabulary words, and playing games involving naming and classifying things. Children in this stage also begin pretend/make-believe play through understanding symbols; adults can encourage and support this play, which develops imagination and planning abilities. Preoperational children's thinking is intuitive, not logical; adults understanding this will not expect them to follow/use logical sequences such as doing arithmetic, as they cannot yet perform mental operations. Adults familiar with Piaget's concept of egocentrism realize preoperational children cannot see others' viewpoints. They thus engage children's attention/interest by beginning from topics related to children's personal selves and activities.

PREOPERATIONAL VERSUS CONCRETE OPERATIONAL STAGES

Piaget called the stage of most children aged 2–6 years preoperational because children these ages cannot yet perform mental operations. At around 6–7 years old, children begin to develop concrete operations. A key aspect of this stage is the ability to think logically. This ability first develops relative to concrete objects and events. Concrete operational children still have trouble understanding abstract concepts or hypothetical situations, but they can apply logical sequences and cause and effect to things they can see, feel, and manipulate physically. For example, concrete operational children develop the understanding that things have the same amount or number regardless of their shape or arrangement, which Piaget termed "conservation." They develop proficiency in inductive logic, drawing generalizations from specific instances. However, deductive logic, predicting specific results according to general principles, is not as well-developed until the later stage of formal operations involving abstract thought. Another key development of concrete operations is reversibility, the ability to reverse an action or operation.

The different thinking found between Piaget's preoperational and concrete operations stages is exemplified in experiments he and others conducted to prove his theory. For example, the absence or presence of the ability to conserve liquid volume across shape and/or appearance has been shown in experiments with differently aged children. A preschooler is shown a tall, thin beaker and a short, wide one. The experimenter also shows the child two identically sized and shaped containers with identical amounts of liquid in each. The experimenter then pours the equal amounts of liquid into the two differently shaped beakers. The preschooler will say either the thin beaker holds more liquid because it is taller or the short beaker holds more because it is wider. Piaget termed this "centration"—focusing on only one property at a time. An older child "decentrates," can "conserve" the amount, and knows both beakers hold identical amounts. Older children also use reversibility and logic (e.g., "I know they are still equal, because I just saw you pour the same amount into each beaker.").

PIAGET'S NEW DEVELOPMENTS OF THE CONCRETE OPERATIONS STAGE VERSUS PREVIOUS PREOPERATIONAL STAGE

Piaget said that while preschoolers are in the preoperational stage and do not think logically because they cannot yet perform mental operations, this ability emerges in the concrete operations stage, which tends to coincide with elementary school ages. Concrete operational children can follow and apply logical sequences to concrete objects they can see and manipulate. This is why they can begin learning mathematical concepts and procedures like addition and subtraction, and grammatical paradigms like verb conjugations. While preoperational children "centrate" or focus on one attribute of an object, like its appearance, concrete operational children "decentrate," accommodating multiple attributes, and can perform and reverse mental operations. Piaget found elementary school-age concrete operational children develop conservation—the understanding that an object or substance conserves, or retains, its essential properties despite changes in appearance or configuration. For example, a preoperational child can count pennies but not understand ten pennies spread into a long row equal ten pennies clustered together. Children in concrete operations, instead of focusing on appearance, will use logic and simply count the pennies, showing that each group has the same number regardless of how they look.

CONSERVATION

Conservation is the cognitive ability to understand that objects or substances retain their properties of numbers or amounts even when their appearance, shape, or configuration changes. Piaget found from his experiments with children that this ability develops around the age of five years. He also found children develop conservation of number, length, mass, weight, volume, and quantity, respectively, at slightly different ages. One example of a conservation experiment is with liquid volume: the experimenter pours the same amount of liquid into a short, wide container and a tall, thin one. Children who have not developed conservation of liquid volume typically say one container has more liquid, even though they saw both amounts were equal, based on one container's looking fuller. Similarly, children who have not developed conservation of number, shown equal numbers of beads, usually say a group arranged in a long row has more beads than a group clustered together. Children having developed conservation recognize the amounts are the same regardless of appearance. A universal phenomenon is that after developing conservation, we take it for granted and cannot remember or believe our earlier preoperational thinking.

ABILITIES IN PERCEPTUAL DEVELOPMENT OCCURRING IN INFANCY

In normal development, babies have usually established the ability to see, hear, smell, taste, and feel and also the ability to integrate such sensory information by the age of six months. Additional perceptual abilities, which are less obvious and more complex, continue to emerge throughout the early childhood years. For instance, young children develop increasing precision in recognizing visual concepts like size and shape. This development allows children to identify accurately the shape and size of an object no matter from what angle they perceive it. Infants have these capacities in place but have not yet developed accuracy in using them. For example, a baby might realize that objects farther away occupy less of their visual fields than nearer objects; however, the baby has yet to learn just how much less of the visual field is taken up by the farther object. Young children attain this and similar kinds of learning by actively, energetically exploring their environments. Such activity is crucial for developing accurate perception of size, shape, and distance.

VISUAL PERCEPTUAL ASPECTS OF INTERPRETING PICTURES AND EYE MOVEMENTS

As adults, our ability to look at pictures of people and things in the environment is something we usually take for granted. Researchers have established that 3-year-old children's responses indicate their ability to recognize shading, line convergence, and other cues of depth in two-dimensional pictures. However, scientists have also found that children's sensitivity to these kinds of visual cues increases as they grow older. The eye movements and eye fixation patterns of young children affect their ability to get the most complete and accurate information from pictorial representations of reality. When viewing pictures, adults sweep the entire picture to see it as a whole and use shorter eye movements to focus on specific details. Preschool children differ from adults in using shorter eye movements overall and focusing on small parts of the picture near the center or an edge. They therefore disregard, or do not see, a lot of the picture's available information.

ACTIVITIES ASSISTING CHILDREN DEVELOP COGNITIVE ABILITIES

As shown by Piaget, young children have difficulty reversing operations. To aid in developing this skill, adults can ask children to build block structures, for example, and then dismantle them one block at a time to reverse the construction. They can ask children to retell rhymes or stories backward. They can take small groups of children for walks and ask them if they can return by the same route as they came. Young children often assume causal relationships where none exist. Adults can provide activities to produce and observe results, including pouring water into different containers, knocking over bowling pins by swinging a pendulum, rolling wheeled toys down ramps, and blowing balls through mazes. The adults can then ask them, "What happened when you did this? What would happen if you did this? What could you do to make this happen?" Young children are also often egocentric, seeing everything from their own viewpoint. Adults can help them take others' perspectives through guessing games, wherein they must give each other clues to guess persons or objects, and dramatic role-playing activities, where they pretend to be others.

LEARNING STYLES AND IMPLICATIONS FOR EARLY CHILDHOOD EDUCATION

Young children with normal development learn in the same chronological sequences and learn the same types of skills. Even those with delayed development, as with intellectual disabilities, learn the same things in the same order but simply at a slower rate and hence at later ages, and those with severe/profound impairment may never achieve certain developmental milestones. However, one aspect of learning that varies is learning style. For example, some children approach learning in a primarily visual manner. They focus on what they see and how things look. They learn best given visual stimuli, like colorful objects, pictures, and graphics. They understand abstract concepts and relationships better when these are illustrated visually. Other children approach learning in a primarily haptic or tactile way. They focus on textures and movements, learning through touch and kinesthetic senses. They learn best given concrete things to explore and manipulate, and physical activities to perform. They learn abstract concepts and relationships better through handling materials and engaging in physical movements and actions.

VIKTOR LOWENFELD

Viktor Lowenfeld (1903–1960) taught art to elementary school students and sculpture to blind students. Lowenfeld's acquaintance with Sigmund Freud, who was interested in his work with people with visual impairments, motivated Lowenfeld to pursue scientific research. He published several books on using creative arts activities therapeutically. Lowenfeld was familiar with six stages previously identified in the growth of art. He combined these with principles of human development drawn from the school of psychoanalytic psychology founded by Freud. In his adaptation, he named the six stages reflecting the development of children's art as scribble, preschematic, schematic, dawning realism, pseudorealistic, and period of decision. Lowenfeld identified adolescent learning styles as haptic, focused on physical sensations and subjective emotional experiences, and as visual, focused on appearances, each demanding corresponding instructional approaches. Lowenfeld's book *Creative and Mental Growth* (1947) was the most influential text in art education during the later 20th century. Lowenfeld's psychological emphasis in this text gave scientific foundations to creative and artistic expression and identified developmentally age-appropriate art media and activities.

STAGES OF GROWTH AND DEVELOPMENT IN ART

Austrian and German art scholars established six stages in art.

1. **Scribble stage:** from 2–4 years, children first make uncontrolled scribbles, then controlled scribbling, then progress to naming their scribbles to indicate what they represent.
2. **Preschematic stage:** From ages 4–6, children begin to develop a visual schema. Schema, meaning mental representation, comes from Piaget's cognitive-developmental theory. Without complete comprehension of dimensions and sizes, children may draw people and houses the same height; they use color more emotionally than logically. They may omit or exaggerate facial features, or they might draw sizes by importance (e.g., drawing themselves as largest among people or drawing the most important feature, such as the head, as the largest or only body part).
3. **Schematic stage:** from 7–9 years, drawings more reflect actual physical proportions and colors.
4. **Dawning realism:** from ages 9–11, drawings become increasingly representational.
5. **Pseudorealistic stage:** from ages 11–13, children reflect their ability to reason.
6. **Period of decision stage:** children ages 14+ reflect the adolescent identity crisis.

CHARACTERISTICS IN ART REFLECTING PERCEPTUAL, COGNITIVE, AND MOTOR DEVELOPMENT

Observations of young children find that while a 2½-year-old can grasp a crayon and scribble with it, by the age of 4 years, he or she can draw a picture we recognize as human. The typical 4-year-old drawing of a human being is called the "tadpole person" because it has no body, a large head, and stick limbs. Between the ages of 3 and 4 years, children typically make a transition from scribbling to producing tadpole person drawings. This development is enabled by greater development in motor control and eye-hand coordination, among other variables. Between the ages of 4 and 5 years, children make another transition by progressing from drawing tadpole persons to drawing complete figures with heads and bodies. Howard Gardner, psychologist and author of the theory of multiple intelligences, stated that children achieve a "summit of artistry" by the end of their preschool years. He describes their drawings as "characteristically colorful, balanced, rhythmic, and expressive, conveying something of the range and...vitality associated with artistic mastery." (1980)

INVOLVEMENT OF MUSIC IN THE DEVELOPMENT OF INFANTS AND YOUNG CHILDREN

Long before they can speak, and before they even comprehend much speech, infants respond to the sounds of voices and to music. These responses are not only to auditory stimulation but moreover to the emotional content in what they hear. Parents sing lullabies to babies; not only are these sounds pleasant and soothing but they also help children develop trust in their environment as secure. Parents communicate their love to children through singing and introduce them to experiences of pleasure and excitement through music. As children grow, music progresses to be not only a medium of communication but also one of self-expression as they learn to sing and play musical sounds. Music facilitates memory, as we see through commercial jingles and mnemonic devices. Experiments find music improves spatial reasoning. Children's learning of perceptual and logical concepts like beginning and ending, sequences, cause-and-effect, balance, harmony and dissonance, and mathematical number and timing concepts is reinforced by music. Music also promotes language development. Children learn about colors, counting, conceptual relationships, nature, and social skills through music.

ENHANCING THE EMOTIONAL, SOCIAL, AESTHETIC, AND SCHOOL READINESS SKILLS WITH MUSIC

Young children who are just learning to use spoken language often cannot express their emotions very well verbally. Music is a great aid to emotional development in that younger children can express happiness, sadness, anger, and more through singing and/or playing music more easily than they can with words. Children of preschool ages not only listen to music and respond to what they hear, but they also learn to create music through singing and playing instruments together with other children. These activities help them learn crucial social skills for their lives, like cooperating with others, collaborating, and making group or team efforts to accomplish something. When children are given guided musical experiences, they learn to make their own judgments of what is good or bad music; this provides them with the foundations for developing an aesthetic sense. Music promotes preliteracy skills by enhancing phonemic awareness. As growing children develop musical appreciation and skills, these develop fundamental motor, cognitive, and social skills they need for language, school readiness, literacy, and life.

PREMATHEMATICAL LEARNING EXPERIENCES

Preschool children do not think in the same ways as older children and adults do, as Piaget observed. Their thinking is strongly based upon and connected to their sensory perceptions. This means that in solving problems, they depend mainly on how things look, sound, feel, smell, and taste. Therefore, preschool children should always be given concrete objects that they can touch, explore, and experiment with in any learning experience. They are not yet capable of understanding abstract concepts or manipulating information mentally, so they must have real things to work with to understand premath concepts. For example, they will learn to count solid objects like blocks, beads, or pennies before they can count numbers in their heads. They cannot benefit from rote math memorization or "sit still and listen" lessons. Since young children "centrate" on one characteristic, object, person, or event at a time, adults can offer activities encouraging decentration/incorporating multiple aspects (e.g., not only grouping all triangles but grouping all red triangles separately from blue triangles).

Salient Aspects of Typical Early Childhood Physical Development

Early childhood physical growth, while significant, is slower than infant growth. From birth to 2 years, children generally grow to four times their newborn weight and 2/3 their newborn length and height. From 2–3 years, however, children usually gain only about 4 lb. and 3.5 inches. From 4–6 years, growth slows more; gains of 5–7 lb. and 2.5 inches are typical. Due to slowing growth rates, 3- and 4-year-olds appear to eat less food but do not; they actually just eat fewer calories per pound of body weight. Brain growth is still rapid in preschoolers: brains attain 55 percent of adult size by 2 years, and 90 percent by 6 years. The majority of brain growth is usually by 4–4.5 years, with a growth spurt around 2 years and growth rates slowing significantly between 5 and 6 years. Larger brain size indicates not more neurons but larger sizes, differences in their organization, more glial cells nourishing and supporting neurons, and greater myelination (development of the sheath protecting nerve fibers and facilitating their efficient intercommunication).

Nature-Nurture Interaction in Early Childhood Physical Development

The physical development of babies and young children is a product of the interactions between genetic and environmental factors. Also, a child's physical progress is equally influenced by environmental and psychological variables. For the body, brain, and nervous system to grow and develop normally, children must live in healthy environments. When the interaction of hereditary and environmental influences is not healthful, this is frequently reflected in abnormal patterns of growth. Failure to thrive syndrome is a dramatic example. When children are abused or neglected for long periods of time, they actually stop growing. The social environments of such children create psychological stress. This stress makes the child's pituitary gland stop releasing growth hormones, and growth ceases. When such environmental stress is relieved and these children are given proper care, stimulation, and affection, they begin growing again. They often grow rapidly enough to catch up on the growth they missed earlier. Normal body and brain growth—as well as psychological development—depend upon the collaboration of nature and nurture.

Signs of Progress in Typical Motor Development

Genetics, physiological maturation, nutrition, and experience through practice combine to further preschoolers' motor skills development. Newborns' reflexive behaviors progress to preschoolers' voluntary activities. Also, children's perception of the size, shape, and position of the body and body parts becomes more accurate by preschool ages. In addition, increases in bilateral coordination of the body's two sides enhance preschoolers' motor skills. Motor skills development entails both learning new movements and gradually integrating previously learned movements into smooth, continuous patterns, as in learning to throw a ball with skill. Both large muscles (for gross-motor skills like climbing, running, and jumping) and small muscles (for fine-motor skills like drawing and tying knots) develop. Eye-hand coordination involves fine-motor control. Preschoolers use visual feedback, seeing whether they are making things go where and do what they want them to, in learning to manipulate small objects with their hands and fingers.

Gender Differences in Motor Development

On average, preschool boys have larger muscles than preschool girls, so they can run faster, climb higher, and jump farther. Boys at these ages tend to be more muscular physically. Preschool girls, while less muscular, are on the average more mature physically for their ages than boys. While boys usually exceed girls in their large-muscle, gross-motor abilities like running, jumping, and climbing, girls tend to surpass boys in small-muscle, fine-motor abilities like buttoning buttons, using scissors, and similar activities involving the manipulation of small tools, utensils, and objects. While preschool boys exhibit more strength in large-muscle, gross-motor actions, preschool girls are more advanced than preschool boys in large-muscle, gross-motor skills that do not demand strength so much as coordination, like hopping, balancing on one foot, and skipping. While these specific gender differences in preschoolers' physical and motor development have been observed consistently in research, it is also found that preschool girls' and boys' physical and motor development patterns are generally more similar than different overall.

BASIC TEMPERAMENT TYPES INFLUENCING PERSONALITIES OF CHILDREN

Psychologists studied the behavior of infants and classified their characteristics into three types of temperaments: easy, difficult, and slow-to-warm-up. The majority of infants are easy babies. When they cry from hunger, needing changing, being tired, feeling discomfort, needing cuddling, or needing attention, they are easily soothed by having these needs met. They typically sleep well. While they experience normal negative emotions, their predominant mood is good. Other than normal stranger anxiety at applicable ages, they respond positively to meeting people. In contrast, difficult babies are more likely to cry longer and be much harder to soothe. It is often hard to get them to sleep, and they may sleep fitfully, with many interruptions and/or for shorter times. They are more easily frightened by new people and things and are more easily upset overall. Slow-to-warm-up babies can initially seem difficult by not being as immediately responsive to people other than their parents like easy babies. However, given some time to adjust, they eventually "warm up" to new people and situations.

SELF-CONCEPT AND SELF-ESTEEM

Young children's self-concepts are founded on observable, readily defined, mainly concrete factors. Many young children also experience much adult encouragement. Because their self-concepts are more simple and concrete than those of older children and adults, and because they typically receive abundant encouragement and positive reinforcement, preschoolers often have fairly high self-esteem (i.e., judgment regarding their own value). In general, young children tend to have positive, optimistic attitudes that they can learn something new, finish tasks, and succeed if they persist in their attempts. Self-esteem related specifically to one's ability to perform a given task is sometimes called "achievement-related attribution." Albert Bandura called it "self-efficacy." Young children derive self-esteem from multiple sources, including their relationships with their parents, their friendships, their abilities and achievements in tasks involving playing and helping others, their physical/athletic abilities, and their achievements in preschool and school.

INTERNAL VARIABLE INFLUENCING SELF-CONCEPTS, SELF-ESTEEM, AND SELF-EFFICACY

One major internal influence on self-concept is a child's basic temperament. Easy, difficult, and slow-to-warm-up temperaments in babies continue into early childhood (and throughout life). For example, children having easy temperaments are better prepared for coping with challenges and frustration. When they encounter difficulty attempting new tasks, they do not give up as easily and are more persistent. They are thus more likely to develop self-concepts of being good, valuable, and successful and hence have higher self-esteem. Since they experience more success through persistence, they develop greater self-efficacy. Children with more difficult temperaments become frustrated more easily, after fewer attempts, and give up trying in discouragement or require extra help to perform new or challenging tasks. They are more at risk for believing they cannot succeed and hence are not valuable, leading to their developing lower self-esteem. This also affects self-efficacy: they are more likely to doubt their ability to perform a specific proposed task.

EXTERNAL VARIABLES INFLUENCING SELF-CONCEPTS, SELF-ESTEEM, AND SELF-EFFICACY

The way young children see themselves is affected by the feedback they receive from other people. When adults like parents, caregivers, and teachers give young children positive responses to their efforts—whether they succeed initially or not—the children are more likely to develop positive self-concepts, engendering higher self-esteem and greater self-efficacy. On the other hand, when adults frequently give punitive, judgmental, indifferent, or otherwise negative responses to young children's efforts, children develop poorer self-images. They feel they are not valued, good, important, or worthy. They develop lower self-esteem, and their self-efficacy is weaker; they come to expect failure when they attempt tasks and may not even try. Peers also affect young children's self-concepts and self-esteem. When friends and classmates include a child in activities, this promotes a positive self-image and higher self-esteem and self-efficacy. If peers exclude, tease, or bully a young child, this can cause low self-esteem, make their self-concepts more negative, and lower their self-efficacy.

LOCUS OF CONTROL

Psychologist Julian Rotter originated the term and concept of locus of control. It refers to the place (locus) where we attribute causes for outcomes we experience, either externally or internally. An external locus control is something outside of us, such as another person and/or his or her actions, an environmental event, or an unknown but exterior influence, like good or bad luck or random chance. An internal locus of control is something inside of us, such as our native ability, our motivation, or our effort. Blaming another for failing is an example of external locus of control (e.g., "The teacher gave me something too hard" or "The teacher wouldn't help me"). Blaming conditions is also external (e.g., "It was too dark" or "The sun was in my eyes"). Individuals may also attribute successes externally: "The teacher helped me" or "Johnny showed me how" or "I was lucky." Blaming or crediting oneself for failure or success is internal locus of control: "I didn't study the new words" or "I'm stupid" with failures, or "I worked hard" or "I'm smart" with successes.

THE BASIC PERSONALITY STRUCTURES IN FREUD'S DEVELOPMENTAL THEORY

Freud proposed that the personality is governed by three structures or forces: the id, the ego, and the superego. The id, the "pleasure principle," represents the source of our powerful, instinctual urges, such as sexual and aggressive impulses. It is necessary, as it energizes us to act, but it cannot go unrestrained. The ego, the "reality principle," represents our sense of self within reality. It is necessary for telling us what will happen if we act on the id's impulses and knowing how to control them to protect ourselves. The superego, the "conscience," represents our sense of morality. It is necessary when the ego protects ourselves but not others, so we also control our social interactions to be ethical and nonharmful to others. For example, when a young child sees a cookie or a toy belonging to someone else, his id says, "I want that." His ego says, "If I take that and get caught, I will be in trouble." His superego says, "Whether I get caught or not, stealing is wrong."

FIRST STAGE OF FREUD'S PSYCHOANALYTIC THEORY OF PERSONALITY DEVELOPMENT

Freud's orientation toward personality development was psychosexual. He believed the most important factors were the focus of erotic energy, which shifted in each developmental stage, and the child's early relationship with parents. Freud formulated five stages of development: oral, anal, phallic, latency, and genital. He found if infants and children successfully complete each stage, they are well-adjusted; if not, they become fixated on one stage. Freud said infants from birth to 18 months are in the oral stage: their focus of pleasure is on the mouth as they suck to nurse. If a baby's oral need to nurse is met appropriately, he or she will progress to the following stage. However, if an infant's feeding needs are met either inadequately or excessively, he or she can develop an oral fixation. Signs of this in later life include tendencies to overeat, drink too much, smoke, bite one's nails, talk excessively, and other orally focused activities. Oral personalities either become overly dependent and gullible, or, when resisting oral compulsions, become pessimistic and aggressive to others.

SECOND STAGE OF FREUD'S PSYCHOANALYTIC THEORY OF PERSONALITY DEVELOPMENT

Children 18–36 months are in the anal stage. The focus of pleasure sensations is on the anus as they are engaged in toilet training. Society and parents demand they control retaining/expelling waste; they must learn to control anal stimulation. This can be a power struggle between child and parents. Children this age are also learning to assert their individual independence and will, mirroring the battle of wills over toileting. Success contributes to healthy development; when unsuccessful, individuals develop anal fixation. Signs of this in later life take two extremes: those who resisted parental control and asserted personal control by retaining their feces develop anal-retentive personalities, becoming rigid, controlling, and overly preoccupied with neatness and cleanliness. Conversely, those who asserted themselves by expelling their feces develop anal-expulsive personalities, with sloppy, messy, disorganized, defiant behavior.

THIRD STAGE OF FREUD'S PSYCHOANALYTIC THEORY OF PERSONALITY DEVELOPMENT

When children are aged 3–6 years, they are in the phallic stage. Pleasure is focused on the genitals as children discover these. Freud focused his theory on males, proposing that at this age, boys develop unconscious sexual desires for their mothers and corresponding unconscious rivalries with their fathers for their mother's attention. The rivalry represents aggression toward the father. Therefore, they also unconsciously fear retaliation by the father in the form of castration. Freud named this the Oedipal conflict after the Greek tragic hero Oedipus, who unwittingly slew his father and married his mother. Since these unconscious impulses are socially unacceptable, boys resolve the conflict through a process Freud called "identification with the aggressor." This explains the common behavior of boys around ages 4–5, imitating and wanting to be "just like Daddy." They repress desires for their mother and adopt masculine characteristics. Unsuccessful conflict resolution/fixation leads to later confusion/weakness of sexual identity, and either excessive or insufficient sexual activity.

APPLICATION OF FREUD'S THIRD STAGE OF PSYCHOANALYTIC THEORY

Caregivers and educators who are aware of this stage of development will not be distressed at young children's attention to and manipulation of their genitals and their curiosity and interest in others' genitals, as these are not abnormal (unless excessive). Adults who are also aware of Freud's Oedipal conflict in boys and other neo-Freudian psychologists' corresponding Electra conflict in girls should be neither surprised nor upset when little boys first focus more attention on mothers/female caregivers and later abandon these attentions to focus on imitating fathers/male caregivers. Freud would say they are demonstrating the Oedipal desire for the mother, which includes fear of castration by the father, and then resolving this conflict through identification with the aggressor/father. Neo-Freudians would say little girls are undergoing a similar process in favoring their fathers and subsequently identifying with their mothers. They pointed out how girls at the same ages become "Daddy's girls," often rejecting their mothers, and then around ages 4–5 want to be "just like Mommy," adopting feminine behaviors, paralleling male development. Freud rejected this notion.

FOURTH AND FIFTH STAGES OF FREUD'S PSYCHOANALYTIC THEORY OF PERSONALITY DEVELOPMENT

Freud theorized that children are in the latency stage of development at around the same ages when they begin to attend formal schooling. Since Freud's emphasis on development was psychosexual, he identified an erogenous zone where pleasure was focused in each stage of development. The mouth, anus, and genitals are erogenous zones central to Freud's other developmental stages. However, in the stage he termed latency, there is no erogenous zone of focus. This is because Freud believed that children's sexuality is repressed or submerged during this period. The child's attention is occupied at this time with learning new social and academic skills in the new environment of the school setting. Adults familiar with Freud's basic psychoanalytic concepts realize that children's focus shifts from their relationships with parents to their relationships with friends, classmates, teachers, and other adults during the latency stage. Children are not rejecting/abandoning parents but are responding to widening social environments. They are more able to learn academic concepts and structures and more complex social interactions and behaviors. However, from puberty on, children are in Freud's genital stage, when sexuality reemerges with physical maturation and adolescents are occupied with developing intimate relationships with others.

Ego Defense Mechanisms of Freud's Psychoanalytic Theory of Personality Development

Freud identified and described many ego defense mechanisms in his theory. He said these are ways the ego finds to cope with impulses threatening it, and hence the person. Just a few of these that can be apparent in young children's behavior include the following:

- Regression: A child has received parental attention exclusively for four years, but then the parents introduce a new baby. Not only is parental attention divided between two children, but the baby naturally needs and gets more attention by being a helpless infant. If the child feels displaced and/or threatened by the younger sibling, he or she may regress from normal four-year-old behaviors to more infantile ones in a bid for similar attention.
- Projection: If a child feels threatened by experiencing inner aggressive impulses, such as hating another person, he or she may project these feelings onto that person, accusing, "You hate me!"
- Denial: If a child cannot accept feelings triggered by losing a loved one through divorce or death, he or she may deny reality, saying, "They will come back."

Contribution of Psychoanalytic Theory to Early Childhood Care and Educational Practices

In his development of psychoanalytic theory, Freud identified stages of childhood development according to the particular bodily zones where pleasure is focused during each age period. This identification still regularly informs early childhood care and educational practices. For example, infants are in the oral stage, when nursing provides pleasure as well as nutrition and satisfying hunger. Knowing this, caregivers recognize that babies begin exploring their environments through oral routes. They thus will not punish mouthing of objects, will anticipate and prevent mouthing of unsafe/unsanitary objects, and will provide suitable objects and activities for oral inspection and orally oriented rewards. Toddlers engaged in toilet training are in Freud's anal stage. As they learn to control their bladders and bowels, they also learn to control their impulses and behaviors. Adults knowing this recognize toddlers' willful, stubborn behaviors as normal parts of the process of establishing individual identities and asserting their wishes. Thus, they will not punish these behaviors harshly or inappropriately but strike a balance between permitting exploration and providing limits, guidance, and support.

First Stage in Erikson's Psychosocial Theory of Human Development and Key Differences from Freud's Developmental Theories

Erikson's theory was based on Freud's, but whereas Freud's focus was psychosexual, Erikson's was psychosocial. Both emphasized early parent-child relationships. Freud believed the personality was essentially formed in childhood and proposed five stages through puberty and none thereafter; Erikson depicted lifelong development through nine stages. Each stage centers on a "nuclear conflict" to resolve, with positive and negative outcomes of successful and unsuccessful resolutions.

Erikson's first stage (birth—18 months) is basic trust vs. mistrust. When an infant's basic needs—such as being fed, changed, bathed, held, and cuddled; having discomfort relieved; and receiving attention, affection, and interaction are met sufficiently and consistently, the baby develops basic trust in the world, gaining a sense of security, confidence, and optimism. The positive outcomes are hope and drive; negative outcomes are withdrawal and sensory distortion. If infant needs are inadequately and/or inconsistently met, the baby develops basic mistrust, with a sense of insecurity, worthlessness, and pessimism.

How Erikson's First Stage Informs Early Childhood Caregiving

Caregivers understanding and the first stage of Erikson's theory will feed a baby on a regular schedule and not leave the child crying from hunger for long times. They will change the baby's diaper timely when needed rather than letting him or her experience discomfort and cry too long. Moreover, caregivers will meet infant needs for interaction, especially holding and cuddling. Making care and nurturing predictable for babies establishes optimism. The negative outcome of mistrust is linked to worthless feelings and even suicide.

Second Stage in Erikson's Psychosocial Theory of Human Development

In each of Erikson's developmental stages, a central conflict must be resolved; success/failure dictates outcomes. Babies first develop basic trust or mistrust in the world during the first stage. Toddlers are in Erikson's second stage of autonomy vs. shame and self-doubt. In this stage, children 18 months—3 years are learning muscular control (walking, toilet-training) and developing moral senses of right and wrong. As they gain skills, they want to do more things independently, and they begin to assert their individual wills. Parents are familiar with the associated tantrums, "No!" and other common "Terrible Twos" behaviors. Children receiving appropriate parenting during this stage develop a sense of autonomy through being allowed to attempt tasks realistic for them, to fail and try again, and eventually to master them. Positive outcomes are will/willpower and self-control; negative outcomes are impulsivity and compulsion. Children with parenting at either extreme—being ignored and given no guidance or support, or overly controlled/directed, having everything done for them and never allowed freedom—develop shame, doubting their abilities.

How Erikson's Second Stage Informs Early Childhood Caregiving

Adults appreciating the second stage of Erikson's theory let children express preferences and practice new skills, supplying needed encouragement, support, and positive reinforcement without overly restricting, controlling, or punishing them.

Third Stage in Erikson's Psychosocial Theory of Human Development

In his theory of psychosocial development, Erikson proposed his third stage revolves around the nuclear conflict of Initiative vs. Guilt. Erikson described 3- to 5-year-olds in this stage as being at the "play age." Having developed the ability for make-believe/pretend play, children imitate parents and other adults in their activities. At these ages, children begin taking the initiative to plan and enact scenarios wherein they play roles and use objects to symbolize other things. Through creating situations and stories, they experiment and identify socially with adult roles and behaviors. They are also more actively exploring their environments. Relationships expand from parents to family. The positive outcome/strength of this stage is purpose. Children thwarted in fulfilling their natural goals and desires develop the negative outcome of guilt through adults' punishing them for trying to control their environments and/or adults' controlling them too much. Adults understanding this encourage and support pretend play. They encourage and approve children for initiating activities rather than inhibiting or always directing their actions.

FOURTH STAGE IN ERIKSON'S PSYCHOSOCIAL THEORY OF HUMAN DEVELOPMENT

The fourth stage corresponds to the end of the early childhood years, when children begin formal schooling. Erikson named this stage, which lasts from around ages 5–6 to puberty, industry vs. inferiority. Children in this stage are primarily occupied with learning new academic and social competencies as they attend school, meet more peers and adults, make new friends, and learn to interact in a wider environment. Whereas the focus of Stage 2, autonomy vs. shame and self-doubt, was self-control and parents were the main relationship, and the focus of Stage 3, initiative vs. guilt, was environmental exploration and family was the main relationship, in Stage 4, industry vs. inferiority, the focus is on achievements and accomplishments. Friends, neighbors, school, and teachers are the most important relationships. Children's successful resolutions bring positive outcomes of competence and method; negative outcomes are narrowness of abilities and inertia (lack of activity).

RELATION OF ERIKSON'S FOURTH STAGE TO EARLY CHILDHOOD EDUCATION

Parents and educators who encourage and reinforce children's desires and attempts to learn and practice new skills and perform tasks help them develop senses of method and competence. Unsupportive and punitive adult responses result in restricted competencies and/or lack of motivation.

FUNDAMENTAL PRINCIPLES OF BEHAVIORIST OR LEARNING THEORY

Major principles of behaviorism include these:

- Organisms learn through interacting with the environment.
- Environmental influences shape behavior.
- Environmental stimuli elicit responses from organisms.

Hypothetical constructs like the mind and/or inner physiological changes are unnecessary for scientifically describing behaviors—everything organisms do, including feeling and thinking. Learning and behavior change are achieved through arranging the learner's environment to elicit certain responses, increasing the probability of repeating those responses by rewarding them (positive reinforcement) and decreasing repetition of unwanted behaviors by punishing (positive punishment) or ignoring them (extinction). Just as Thorndike previously found all animals, including humans, learn the same way, Skinner also found his principles applied equally to rats, pigeons, and people. His methods have become so popular that early childhood educators routinely give positive reinforcement—verbal praise, treats, and privileges—for performing new skills and demonstrating socially desirable behaviors; teach young children complex tasks in steps (shaping/chaining/task analysis); take away privileges to punish unwanted behaviors (negative punishment); and remove aversive stimuli for complying (negative reinforcement).

CHILDREN'S DEVELOPMENT OF SEXUAL/GENDER IDENTIFICATION

FREUD'S VIEW OF CHILDREN'S DEVELOPMENT OF SEXUAL/GENDER IDENTIFICATION

While different psychological theories/schools of thought agree that sex as a social identity develops through the process of identification, they have different views and explanations for how children develop their social identities as boys or girls. In Freud's view, gender identity develops through processes of differentiation and affiliation. He said once children observe that certain other people have characteristics in common with themselves, they "endeavor to mold the ego after one that had been taken as a model." In other words, they identify with similar other people and try to attain the same attributes. Freud proposed that boys resolve their Oedipal conflicts through identification with the aggressor (i.e., adopting their fathers' characteristics and suppressing sexual impulses toward their mothers). While he focused exclusively on males in this respect, neo-

Freudian psychologists later proposed a female counterpart, the Electra conflict, wherein girls resolve desires for fathers by identifying with mothers and adopting their characteristics. In either case, children differentiate from their opposite-sex parent and identify or affiliate with their same-sex parent.

EXPLANATION OF SOCIAL LEARNING AND BEHAVIORIST THEORIES

Albert Bandura and other proponents of social learning theory maintain that children learn through a process of observing other people's behavior, observing certain behaviors of others that are rewarded, and then imitating those behaviors to obtain similar rewards. The concept of rewards reinforcing behaviors (i.e., increasing the probability of repeating them) comes from behaviorism or learning theory. Social learning theory is based on behaviorism but includes additional emphasis on the ideas that learning occurs within a social context and that social interactions are primary influences on learning. According to social learning theory, children observe that males and females engage in different behaviors. They additionally observe that boys and girls receive different rewards for their behaviors. Based on these observations, children then imitate the behaviors appropriate to their own sex that they have seen rewarded in others of their sex to obtain the same rewards. Both behaviorist and social learning theories view gender identity development as being environmentally shaped by consequences; social learning theory focuses on the social environment.

KOHLBERG'S COGNITIVE-DEVELOPMENTAL THEORY

Kohlberg had developed a cognitive theory of moral development, based upon and expanding the concepts of morality Piaget included in his theory of cognitive development. Kohlberg also proposed a cognitive-developmental approach to children's acquisition of sex/gender roles. Piaget and Kohlberg discussed classification or categorization as one of the cognitive abilities that children develop. Just as they learn to categorize various things, such as foods, animals, and people, they learn that people include female and male categories. They then learn to categorize themselves as either females or males. When children are around 2 years old, they each begin to develop their distinctive sense of self. Once they have differentiated self from the rest of the world, they also begin to be able to develop complex mental concepts. These abilities enable them to develop self-concepts of gender. According to the cognitive-developmental view, once children have developed concepts of their sex/gender, these are maintained despite social contexts and are difficult to change.

KEY CONCEPTS OF BANDURA'S SOCIAL LEARNING THEORY

Psychologist Alfred Bandura developed the primary theory of social learning. While his theory incorporates elements of behaviorism in that environmental rewards and punishments shape the behaviors and learning of children, Bandura focused more on the social dimension of learning in that he found the context of social interactions the most important medium and influence for learning. Bandura's theory also incorporates elements of cognitive theory by emphasizing the roles played by the cognitive processes of attention, memory, and motivation in learning. Bandura found children learn by observing and imitating the behaviors of models, including adults, older children, and peers. He proposed four conditions required for this learning: attention, retention, reproduction, and motivation. Adults understanding Bandura's theory realize children can learn new behaviors by seeing others be rewarded for performing these, and then imitating them; this greatly expands children's learning potential. Bandura also proved that children viewing violent video content engage in more aggressive behaviors, informing adults of the importance of monitoring and controlling children's exposure to media influences.

HIERARCHY OF NEEDS IN MASLOW'S HUMANISTIC THEORY OF SELF-ACTUALIZATION

Maslow proposed humans are driven by needs, and meeting the most basic needs is a prerequisite to meeting more advanced needs. Maslow's needs hierarchy is depicted as a pyramid, with the most fundamental needs at the base. Its five levels are as follows:

- **Physiological needs:** air, water, sleep, and food necessary for survival
- **Security needs:** shelter and a safe environment
- **Social needs:** feeling loved, receiving affection, and belonging to a family and/or group
- **Esteem needs:** feeling personal value, accomplishment, and social recognition
- **Self-actualizing needs:** achieving optimal personal growth and realizing one's full potential

For example, babies and young children must have clean air to breathe and be fed and rested to survive before other needs can be addressed. Children must have safe places to live, then their needs for love and belonging can be met. Once a child feels loved and part of a family or group, he or she can develop self-esteem through accomplishments and feeling valued by society. After satisfying these, children can self-actualize.

CARL ROGERS' THEORY

Rogers said all organisms naturally pursue a tendency to actualize or make the best of life. Organismic valuing is the natural tendency to value what is healthy (e.g., avoiding bad-tasting foods, which can be poisonous or rotten). Organismic valuing leads to positive regard/esteem, engendering positive self-regard/self-esteem, reflecting what Rogers called the real self—the person one becomes under optimal conditions. Rogers observed society substitutes conditions of worth for organismic valuing, giving us things based not on our needs but on meeting society's required conditions. Children are taught early they will receive something they want on the condition they do what adults want. This establishes conditional positive regard, meaning children only feel esteemed by others on others' conditions; this develops conditional positive self-regard, or self-esteem dependent on others' esteem. This creates an unattainable ideal self based on others' standards rather than the real self. For Rogers, incongruence between real and ideal self causes neurosis. Rogers' required qualities for effective therapists—congruence/genuineness, empathy, and respect—are equally effective in early childhood education.

Rogers believed in actualization, or realizing one's full potential, as did fellow humanist Abraham Maslow. While Maslow applied self-actualization to humans, Rogers applied the "actualization tendency" to all life forms. Rogers gave the name "conditions of worth" to the process he observed whereby others give individuals things based not on need but worthiness. For example, while babies usually receive care based on need, as they grow older, adults establish conditions of worth: children get dessert if they finish dinner or eat their vegetables; they get drinks or snacks after finishing a task, lesson, or class; and most significantly, they often get affection on condition of acceptable/desirable behavior. In behaviorism, this is called contingencies of reinforcement: rewards are given contingent on desired behaviors. Rogers would likely disagree with this practice, which he called conditional positive regard. He felt it makes children do what others want, not what they want or need, and teaches them conditional positive self-regard (i.e., self-esteem dependent on external standards). Rogers' remedy was unconditional positive regard—unconditional love and acceptance.

Factors Influencing Development

EFFECT OF MATURATIONAL FACTORS ON THE DEVELOPMENT AND LEARNING

Many physiological factors affect the development of babies and young children. These dictate which kinds of learning activities are appropriate or ineffective for certain ages. For example, providing a newborn with visual stimuli from several feet away is wasted, as newborns cannot yet focus on distant objects. Adults cannot expect infants younger than about 5 months to sit up unsupported, as they have not yet developed the strength for it. Adults cannot expect toddlers who have not yet attained stable walking gaits to hop or balance upon one foot successfully. It is not coincidental that first grade begins at around 6 years: younger children cannot physically sit still for long periods and have not developed long enough attention spans to prevent distraction. This is also why kindergarten classes feature varieties of shorter-term activities and more physical movement. Younger children also have not yet developed the self-regulation to keep from shouting out on impulse, getting up and running around, etc.—behaviors disruptive to formal schooling but developmentally normal.

NUTRITIONAL FACTORS IN DIET AFFECTING EARLY CHILDHOOD DEVELOPMENT

Babies are typically nourished via the mother's milk or infant formula, and then with baby food; however, young children mostly eat the same foods as adults by the age of 2 years. Though they eat smaller quantities, young children have similar nutritional needs to those of adults. Calcium can be more important in early childhood to support the rapid bone growth occurring during this period; young children should receive 2–3 servings of dairy products and/or other calcium-rich foods. For all ages, whole-grain foods are nutritionally superior for their fiber and nutrients than refined flours, which have had these removed. Refined flours provide "empty calories," causing wider blood-sugar fluctuations and insulin resistance—type 2 diabetes risks—than whole grains, which stabilize blood sugar and offer more naturally occurring vitamins and minerals. Darkly and brightly colored produce are most nutritious. Adults should cut foods into small, bite-sized pieces to prevent choking in young children, who have not yet perfected their biting, chewing, and swallowing skills.

CONSIDERATIONS FOR EARLY CHILDHOOD NUTRITION

Raw or lightly steamed vegetables are best because excess heat destroys nutrients and frying adds fat calories. Fresh, in-season and flash-frozen fruits are more nutritious and less processed than canned. Adults should monitor young children's diets to limit highly processed produce, which can have excessive sugar, salt, or preservatives. Good protein sources include legumes, nuts, lean poultry, and fish. Serving nut butters instead of whole nuts is safer, but spread thinly on whole-grain breads, crackers, or vegetable pieces, because young children can choke on large globs of nut butter as well. Omega-3 fatty acids from salmon, mackerel, herring, flaxseeds, and walnuts control inflammation, prevent heart arrhythmias, and lower blood pressure. Monounsaturated fats from avocados, olives, peanuts, and their oils, as well as canola oil, prevent heart disease, lower bad cholesterol, and raise good cholesterol. Polyunsaturated fats from nuts and seeds and from corn, soy, sesame, sunflower, and safflower oils lower cholesterol. These fats/oils should be served in moderation, and saturated fats should be avoided.

CONSIDERATIONS FOR FEEDING YOUNG CHILDREN

Saturated fats from meats and full-fat dairy should be limited; they can cause health problems like high cholesterol, cardiovascular disease, obesity, and diabetes. Trans fats are produced chemically by hydrogenating normally liquid unsaturated fats and converting them to solid, saturated fats as in margarine and shortening used in many baked goods. These are considered even unhealthier than regular saturated fats and should be avoided. (The words *partially hydrogenated* in the ingredients signal trans fats.) Infants derive enough water from their mother's milk or from formula, but young

32

children should be given plenty of water and/or milk in "sippy cups" to stay hydrated. The common practice of giving young children fruit juice should be avoided. Even without added sugars, fruit juices crowd out room in small stomachs for food nutrients and cause dental cavities and weaken permanent teeth before they erupt. Children can also gain weight, as juice calories do not replace food calories the way actual fruit does with its fiber and solids. Young children should eat two-thirds of adult-sized portions.

CHARACTERISTICS OF YOUNG CHILDREN'S NUTRITIONAL NEEDS

Young children have smaller stomachs than adults and cannot eat as much at one time as teens or adults. However, it is common practice for today's restaurants to provide oversized portions. The historical tradition of encouraging young children to "clean their plates" is ill-advised, considering these excessive portions and the abundance of food in America today. Adults can help young children by teaching them instead to respond to their own bodies' signals and eat only until they are satisfied. Adults can also place smaller portions of food on young children's plates and request to-go containers at restaurants to take leftovers home. Because young children cannot eat a lot at once, they must maintain their blood sugar and energy throughout the day by snacking between meals. However, "snack foods" need not be high in sugar, salt, and unhealthy fats. Cut pieces of fresh fruits and vegetables, whole-grain crackers and low-fat cheeses, and portable yogurt tubes make good snacks for young children.

DEVELOPMENT OF NUTRITIOUS EATING HABITS AND ATTITUDES

Early childhood is an age range often associated with "finicky" eaters. Adults can experiment by substituting different foods that are similar sources of protein or other nutrients to foods young children dislike. Preparing meals to look like happy faces or animals or to have appealing designs can entice young children to eat varied foods. Engaging children age-appropriately in selecting and preparing meals with supervision can also motivate them to consume foods when they have participated in their preparation. Adults should model healthy eating habits for young children, who imitate admired adults' behaviors. Early childhood is when children form basic food-related attitudes and habits and so is an important time for influencing these. Children are exposed to unhealthy foods in advertising, at school, in restaurants, and with friends, so adult modeling and guidance regarding healthy choices are important to counteract these influences. However, adults should also impart the message early that no foods are "bad" or forbidden, allowing some occasional indulgences in small amounts to prevent the development of eating disorders.

RELATIONSHIP OF SLEEP QUALITY TO BLOOD SUGAR CONTROL IN CHILDREN WITH TYPE 1 DIABETES

Researchers find blood sugar stability problematic for many children with type 1 (juvenile) diabetes, despite all efforts by parents and children to follow diabetic health care rules, because of sleep differences. Diabetic children spend more time in lighter than deeper stages of sleep compared to nondiabetic children. This results in higher levels of blood sugar and poorer school performance. Lighter sleep and resulting daytime sleepiness tend to increase blood sugar levels. Sleep apnea is a sleep disorder that causes a person's breathing to be interrupted often during sleeping. These breathing interruptions result in poorer sleep quality, fatigue, and daytime sleepiness. Sleep apnea has previously been associated with type 2 diabetes—historically adult-onset, though now children are developing it, too. It is now known that apnea is also associated with type 1 diabetes in children: roughly one-third of diabetic children studied have sleep apnea, regardless of their weight (being overweight can contribute to apnea). Sleep apnea is additionally associated with much higher blood sugars in diabetic children.

GENERAL SLEEP NEEDS AND BEHAVIORS OF YOUNG CHILDREN

Sleep allows the body to become repaired and recharged for the day and is vital for young children's growth and development. Children aged 2–5 years generally need 10–12 hours of sleep daily. Children 5–7 years old typically need 9–11 hours of sleep. Their sleep schedules should be fairly regular. While occasionally staying up later or missing naps for special events is not serious, overall inconsistent/disorganized schedules cause lost sleep and lethargic and/or cranky children. Some young children sleep fewer hours at night but need long daytime naps, while others need longer, uninterrupted nighttime sleep but seldom nap. Young children are busy exploring and discovering new things; they have a lot of energy and are often excited even when tired. Because they have not developed much self-regulation, they need adult guidance to calm down enough to go to sleep and will often resist bedtimes. Adults should plan bedtime routines. These can vary, but their most important aspect is consistency. Children then expect routines' familiar steps, and anticipating these steps comfort them.

COMPONENTS AND CHARACTERISTICS OF GOOD BEDTIME ROUTINES

Bedtime routines serve as transitions from young children's exciting, adventurous daytime activities to the tranquility needed for healthful rest. Adults should begin routines by establishing and enforcing a rule that daytime activities like rough-and-tumble physical play or TV-watching stop at a specific time. While preschoolers may be less interested in video games than older children, establishing limits early will help parents enforce stopping these activities at bedtime when they are older, too. Bath time is one good way to begin bedtime routines. Toys and games make baths fun, and bath washes with lavender and other soothing ingredients are now available to relax young children. Also, since young children eat smaller meals, healthy bedtime snacks are important. Too much or too little food will disrupt sleep, and too much liquid can cause bedwetting. Adults should plan nighttime snacks appropriately for the individual child. Bedtime reading promotes interest in books and learning and adult-child/family bonding, and calms children. Singing lullabies, hugging, and cuddling also support bonding, relax children, and make them feel safe and secure.

HELPING YOUNG CHILDREN TRANSITION FROM CRIBS TO REGULAR BEDS

One of young children's significant transitions from infancy is moving from a crib to a "big bed." Some become very motivated to escape cribs. For example, some bright, adventurous toddlers and even babies have untied padded crib bumpers, stacked them, and climbed out of the crib. For such children, injury is a greater danger from a crib than a bed. Others, whose cognitive and verbal skills are more developed than motor skills, may stand or jump up and down, repeatedly calling, "Hey, I'm up!" until a parent comes. These children should be moved to regular beds, with guardrails and/or body pillows to prevent rolling and falling-out accidents. If a child is moved to a bed to free the crib for a new baby, this should be done weeks ahead of the infant's arrival if possible, to separate these two significant life events. Most young children are excited about "grown-up" beds. Some, if hesitant, can sleep in the crib and nap in the bed for a gradual transition until ready for the bed full-time.

CONSIDERATIONS IN CHILDREN'S BEDROOMS AND FAMILY BEDS

The majority of early childhood experts think young children should not have adults in their rooms every night while they fall asleep. They believe this can interfere with young children's capacity for "self-soothing" and falling asleep on their own, making them dependent on an adult presence to fall asleep. Parents/caregivers are advised to help children relax until sleepy, and then leave, saying "Good night" and "I love you." Young children frequently feel more comfortable going to bed with a favorite blanket or stuffed animal and/or a night light. Regardless, fears and nightmares are still fairly common in early childhood. "Family beds" (i.e., children sleeping in the same bed or adjacent beds with parents) are subject to controversy. However, this is traditional in many developing countries and was historically so in America. Whatever the individual family choice, it should be consistent, as young children will be frustrated by inconsistent practices and less likely to develop good sleeping habits.

HYGIENE IN EARLY CHILDHOOD
IMPORTANCE OF HAND-WASHING

A major change during early childhood is that hygiene transforms from something adults do for children to something children learn to do themselves. Toddlers are typically learning toilet-training, getting many germs on their hands. Preschoolers today are also often exposed to germs in daycare or school settings. Adults must explain to young children using concrete, easily understood terms how germs spread, how hand-washing removes germs, and when and how to wash their hands. Adults also need to remind children frequently to wash their hands until it becomes a habit. Hand-washing should be required before eating, after toileting, after being outdoors, after sneezing/coughing, and after playing with pets. Because young children have short attention spans and can be impatient, they are unlikely to wash long or thoroughly enough. Adults can encourage this by teaching children to sing "Happy Birthday" or other 15- to 20-second songs/verses while washing, both assuring optimal hand-washing duration and making the process more fun.

BATHING

While infants are bathed by adults, by the time they are toddlers or preschoolers, they generally have learned to sit in a bathtub and wash themselves. However, regardless of their ability to bathe, young children should never be left unsupervised by adults in the bath. Young children can drown very quickly, even in an inch of water; an adult should always be in the bathroom. Also, adults should not let young children run bathwater: they are likely to make it too cold or hot. Adults can prevent scalding accidents by turning down the water heater temperature. The adult should adjust water temperature and test it on his or her own inner arm (an area with more sensitive skin). Parents/caregivers should choose baby shampoos, soaps, and washes that do not irritate young eyes or skin, and keep adult bath products out of children's reach and sight. Very active children may need to bathe daily; others suffering dry, itchy skin should bathe every other day and/or have parents/caregivers apply mild moisturizing lotion.

PROMOTING AND TEACHING DENTAL HYGIENE

Even while young children still have their deciduous teeth ("baby" teeth), dental hygiene practices can affect their permanent adult teeth before they erupt. For example, excessive sugar can weaken adult teeth before they even appear above the gumline. Adults should not only teach young children how important it is to brush their teeth twice and floss once daily at a minimum, they should also model these behaviors. Children are far more likely to imitate parents' dental hygiene practices than do what parents only tell them but do not do themselves. Integrating tooth brushing into morning and bedtime routines promotes the habit. Adults can help motivate resistant children with entertaining toothbrushes that play music, spin, light up, and/or have cartoon illustrations. Young children have not developed the fine motor skills sufficient for flossing independently and will need adult supervision until they are older. Individual flossers are easier for them to use with help than traditional string dental floss.

EXERCISE BENEFITS FOR YOUNG CHILDREN

Young children need daily physical exercise to strengthen their bones, lungs, hearts, and other muscles. Throwing, catching, running, jumping, kicking, and swinging actions develop young children's gross motor skills. Children sleep better with regular physical activity and are at less risk for obesity. Playing actively with other children also develops social skills, including empathy, sharing, cooperation, and communication. Family playtimes strengthen bonding and let parents model positive exercise habits. Outdoor play is fun for youngsters; running and laughing lift children's moods. Pride at physical attainments moreover boosts children's self-images and self-esteem. At least 60 minutes of physical activity most days is recommended for children. This includes jungle gyms, slides, swings, and other playground equipment; family walks, bike-riding, playing backyard catch, baseball, football, or basketball; adult-supervised races or obstacle courses; and age-appropriate community sports activities/leagues. Adults should plan and supervise activities to prevent injuries. They should also provide repeated sunscreen applications for outdoor activities to prevent sunburn and long-term skin damage.

EXPOSURE TO TV/OTHER MEDIA AND OPTIMAL ENVIRONMENTAL CONDITIONS FOR LEISURE ACTIVITIES

Preschool-aged children are not yet cognitively able to distinguish between reality and fantasy. Therefore, overly violent or intense content in TV or other media can frighten them. Additionally, exposure to video violence has been proven to increase aggressive behaviors in young children. Moreover, using TV as a babysitter for long times excludes more cognitively stimulating and interactive pursuits. Parents/caregivers can provide young children with paints, crayons, and modeling clay. They can play board games and simple card games, do puzzles, sing songs, and read stories with young children. Pretend/make-believe play develops during early childhood, so adults can encourage their playing "house," "dress-up," or "auto shop." Park/playground trips afford outdoor play and physical activity/exercise. Visiting local museums, zoos, or planetariums combine education and entertainment with outings. In multiple-child families, it is important for each child to get some one-on-one time with parents regularly, even in unstructured activities like going to the hardware store with Daddy or keeping Mommy company while she washes dishes.

DISADVANTAGES/ADVANTAGES AND RISK/PROTECTIVE FACTORS IN ECONOMICALLY DEPRIVED AND CULTURALLY DIVERSE ENVIRONMENTS

Historically, research on the effects of poverty has been focused on the disadvantages coming from a lack of necessary resources and the presence of risk factors. Due to the lack of resources, children in economically deprived communities commonly have fewer stimulating toys, less diverse verbal interaction, and commonly inadequate nutrition. Other risk factors often include unhealthy family environments, medical illness without treatment, and insufficient social-services, such as education, policing, and medical care. However, more recent research also identifies poverty's advantages, including opportunities for young children to play with peers and older children with little adult intervention, promoting empathy, cooperation, self-control, self-reliance, and sense of belonging; experience with multiple teaching styles, especially modeling, observation, and imitation; and language acquisition within a culturally-specific context through rich cultural traditions of stories, songs, games, and toys. These findings illuminate the resiliency or stress resistance of some children. Recent research also identifies protective factors against risk factors. These protections contribute to child resiliency, including the child's personality traits; having stable, supportive, cohesive family units; and having external support systems promoting positive values and coping skills.

INFLUENCE OF CULTURES AND CULTURAL VALUES ON EARLY CHILDHOOD DEVELOPMENT

The culture in a society influences and determines one's individual values, as do both historical and current social and political occurrences. One's values then influence the ways in which children are valued and raised. American educators can understand the "American" perspective on early childhood better through understanding cultural diversity. Americans tend to fixate on their own culture's beliefs of truth as the only existing reality, but depending on personal histories and values and current conditions, there can actually be multiple right ways of doing things. For example, Western cultures value children's early attainment of independence and individuality, but Eastern cultures value interdependence and group harmony more than individualism. In affluent societies, letting children explore the environment early and freely is valued, but in poor and/or developing societies, parents protect children, keeping them close and even carrying them while working, and thus do not value early freedom and exploration.

Effect of Age, Ethnicity, and Income on Health and School Outcomes

Research traces many variations in well-being and health to early childhood. These differences come from inequities in service access and treatment, congenital health problems, and early exposure to greater familial and community risk factors. Child groups at risk that are overrepresented in the American population include young children, low-income children, and minority children. These risk factors also carry a high correlation with one another as minority groups tend to be overrepresented below the federal poverty level (FPL) and low-income families statistically carry the highest birth rate. Childhood poverty has long-lasting effects on students' developmental, socioeconomic, and academic success. Furthermore, the earlier a student is in poverty, the more likely they are to encounter the adverse effects of poverty, as they may miss certain milestones or lack the support needed to keep up with their peers.

Environment, Social and Emotional Support, Self-Image, and Success

Researchers have recently found that a child's sense of self is significant in predicting success in life. Even when a child's family environment involves multiple stressors, having a good relationship with one parent mitigates a child's psychosocial risks. As a child grows older, a close, supportive, lasting relationship with an adult outside the family can confer similar protection. Such relationships promote self-esteem in a child. Children with positive self-esteem are more able to develop feelings of control, mastery, and self-efficacy to achieve tasks, and they are more able to manage stressful life experiences. Such children demonstrate more initiative in forming relationships and accomplishing tasks. They reciprocally derive more positive experiences from their environments. Children with positive self-concepts pursue, develop, and sustain experiences and relationships that support success. Their positive self-images are further enhanced by these successes, generating additional supportive relationships and experiences. While we often hear about negative cycles of poverty, abuse, or failure, positive cycles of success can be equally as self-perpetuating.

Individualistic Versus Collectivistic Cultures

Anthropologists have classified various world cultures along a continuum of how individualistic or interdependent their structures and values are. Investigating these differences is found to afford much insight and application for early childhood education. The predominant culture in America is considered very individualistic. Children are encouraged to assert themselves and make their own choices to realize their highest potentials, with the ultimate goal of individual self-fulfillment. Collectivistic/sociocentric cultures, however, place the highest importance on group well-being; if collective harmony is disrupted by individual assertiveness, such self-assertion is devalued. Some educators characterize this contrast as the difference between standing out (individualist) and fitting in (collectivist). Researchers note that when asked to finish "I am…" statements, members of interdependent cultures tend to supply a family role, religion, or organization (e.g., "a father/a Buddhist"), whereas members of individualistic cultures cite personal qualities (e.g., "intelligent/hardworking"). Research finds American culture most individualistic, Latin American and Asian cultures most interdependent, and European cultures in the middle.

HEALTH STATISTICS RELATED TO RACE AND ETHNICITY

Children are at higher risk for inadequate development when they are born prematurely or with low birth weights. Recent research found racial and ethnic disparities in these birth conditions. For example, average rates of low birth weights between 2018 and 2020 were almost double for African Americans as for whites (14 percent versus 6.9 percent). Latinos had similar but slightly higher risk than whites for low birth weight (7.5 percent versus 6.9 percent). Native American/Alaska Natives had slightly higher risk than whites (8.1 percent versus 6.9 percent), as did Asian/Pacific Islanders (8.6 percent versus 6.9 percent). The CDC reported that in 2017 and 2018, the prevalence of obesity among different racial groups varied greatly. Non-Hispanic Asians reported the lowest average 17.4 percent of obesity, whereas non-Hispanic White demonstrated a 42.2 percent obesity rate, followed by 44.8 percent for Hispanic and 49.6 percent for Non-Hispanic Black adults. These two statistics demonstrate a sample of correlated health risks present among varied socioeconomic groups.

Language and Literacy Development

COMMUNICATION DEVELOPMENT NORMALLY OCCURRING WITHIN A CHILD'S FIRST FIVE YEARS OF LIFE

Language and communication development depend strongly on the language a child develops within the first five years of life. During this time, three developmental periods are observed. At birth, the first period begins. This period is characterized by infant crying and gazing. Babies communicate their sensations and emotions through these behaviors, so they are expressive; however, they are not yet intentional. They indirectly indicate their needs through expressing how they feel, and when these needs are met, these communicative behaviors are reinforced. These expressions and reinforcement are the foundations for the later development of intentional communication. This becomes possible in the second developmental period, between 6 and 18 months. At this time, infants become able to coordinate their attention visually with other people relative to things and events, enabling purposeful communication with adults. During the third developmental period, from 18 months on, children come to use language as their main way of communicating and learning. Preschoolers can carry on conversations, exercise self-control through language use, and conduct verbal negotiations.

MILESTONES OF NORMAL LANGUAGE DEVELOPMENT BY THE 2 YEARS OLD

By the time most children reach the age of 2 years, they have acquired a vocabulary of about 150 to 300 words. They can name various familiar objects found in their environments. They are able to use at least two prepositions in their speech (e.g., *in*, *on*, and/or *under*). Two-year-olds typically combine the words they know into short sentences. These sentences tend to be mostly noun-verb or verb-noun combinations (e.g., "Daddy work," "Watch this"). They may also include verb-preposition combinations (e.g., "Go out," "Come in"). By the age of 2 years, children use pronouns, such as *I*, *me*, and *you*. They typically can use at least two such pronouns correctly. A normally developing 2-year-old will respond to some commands, directions, or questions, such as "Show me your eyes" or "Where are your ears?"

SALIENT GENERAL ASPECTS OF HUMAN LANGUAGE ABILITIES FROM BEFORE BIRTH TO 5 YEARS OF AGE

Language and communication abilities are integral parts of human life that are central to learning, successful school performance, successful social interactions, and successful living. Human language ability begins before birth: the developing fetus can hear not only internal maternal sounds, but also the mother's voice, others' voices, and other sounds outside the womb. Humans have a natural sensitivity to human sounds and languages from before they are born until they are about 4½ years old. These years are critical for developing language and communication. Babies and young children are predisposed to greater sensitivity to human sounds than other sounds, orienting them toward the language spoken around them. Children absorb their environmental language completely, including vocal tones, syntax, usage, and emphasis. This linguistic absorption occurs very rapidly. Children's first 2½ years particularly involve amazing abilities to learn language, including grammatical expression.

6 MONTHS, 12 MONTHS, AND 18 MONTHS

Individual differences dictate a broad range of language development that is still normal. However, parents observing noticeably delayed language development in their children should consult professionals. Typically, babies respond to hearing their names by 6 months of age, turn their heads and eyes toward the sources of human voices they hear, and respond accordingly to friendly and angry tones of voice. By the age of 12 months, toddlers can usually understand and follow simple directions, especially when these are accompanied by physical and/or vocal cues. They can

39

intentionally use one or more words with the correct meaning. By the age of 18 months, a normally developing child usually has acquired a vocabulary of roughly 5 to 20 words. Eighteen-month-old children use nouns in their speech most of the time. They are very likely to repeat certain words and/or phrases over and over. At this age, children typically are able to follow simple verbal commands without needing as many visual or auditory cues as at 12 months.

THREE YEARS

By the time they are 3 years old, most normally developing children have acquired vocabularies of between 900 and 1,000 words. Typically they correctly use the pronouns *I*, *me*, and *you*. They use more verbs more frequently. They apply past tenses to some verbs and plurals to some nouns. 3-year-olds usually can use at least three prepositions; the most common are *in*, *on*, and *under*. The normally developing 3-year-old knows the major body parts and can name them. 3-year-olds typically use 3-word sentences with ease. Normally, parents should find approximately 75 to 100 percent of what a 3-year-old says to be intelligible, while strangers should find between 50 and 75 percent of a 3-year-old's speech intelligible. Children this age comprehend most simple questions about their activities and environments and can answer questions about what they should do when they are thirsty, hungry, sleepy, hot, or cold. They can tell about their experiences in ways that adults can generally follow. By the age of 3 years, children should also be able to tell others their name, age, and sex.

FOUR YEARS

When normally developing children are 4 years old, most know the names of animals familiar to them. They can use at least four prepositions in their speech (e.g., *in*, *on*, *under*, *to*, *from*, etc.). They can name familiar objects in pictures, and they know and can identify one color or more. Usually, they are able to repeat four-syllable words they hear. They verbalize as they engage in their activities, which Vygotsky dubbed "private speech." Private speech helps young children think through what they are doing, solve problems, make decisions, and reinforce the correct sequences in multistep activities. When presented with contrasting items, 4-year-olds can understand comparative concepts like bigger and smaller. At this age, they are able to comply with simple commands without the target stimuli being in their sight (e.g., "Put those clothes in the hamper" [upstairs]). Four-year-old children will also frequently repeat speech sounds, syllables, words, and phrases, similar to 18-month-olds' repetitions but at higher linguistic and developmental levels.

FIVE YEARS

Once most children have reached the age of 5 years, their speech has expanded from the emphasis of younger children on nouns, verbs, and a few prepositions, and is now characterized by many more descriptive words, including adjectives and adverbs. Five-year-olds understand common antonyms, such as big/little, heavy/light, long/short, and hot/cold. They can now repeat longer sentences they hear, up to about 9 words. When given three consecutive, uninterrupted commands, the typical 5-year-old can follow these without forgetting one or two. At age 5, most children have learned simple concepts of time like today, yesterday, and tomorrow; day, morning, afternoon, and night; and before, after, and later. Five-year-olds typically speak in relatively long sentences and normally should be incorporating some compound sentences (with more than one independent clause) and complex sentences (with one or more independent and dependent clauses). Five-year-old children's speech is also grammatically correct most of the time.

PERSONAL NARRATIVES

Personal narratives are the way that young children relate their experiences to others by telling the stories of what happened. The narrative structure incorporates reporting components such as who was involved, where the events took place, and what happened. Understanding and using this structure is crucial to young children for their communication; however, many young children cannot follow or apply this sequence without scaffolding (temporary support as needed) from adults. Adults can ask young children guiding questions to facilitate and advance narratives. They can also provide learning tools that engage children's visual, tactile (touch), and kinesthetic (body position and movement) senses. This reinforces narrative use, increases the depth of scaffolding, and motivates children's participation. Children learn to play the main character, describe the setting, sequence plot actions, and use words and body language to express emotions. Topic-related action sequences or "social stories" are important for preschoolers to comprehend and express to promote daily transitions and self-regulation. Such conversational skills attainment achieves milestones in both linguistic and emotional-social development.

ACHIEVEMENTS OR PROCESSES ENABLED BY ORAL LANGUAGE SKILLS DEVELOPMENT

Crucial oral language development skills enable children to do the following:

- Communicate by listening and responding to others' speech
- Comprehend meanings of numerous words and concepts encountered in their listening and reading
- Acquire information on subjects they are interested in learning about
- Use specific language to express their own thoughts and ideas

Research finds young children's ability to listen to, understand, and use spoken and written language is associated with their later reading, spelling, and writing literacy achievement. Infants typically begin developing oral language skills, which continue developing through life. Babies develop awareness of and attend to adult speech and soon begin communicating their needs via gestures and speech sounds. Toddlers express emotions and ideas and solicit information via language. They start uttering simple sentences, asking questions, and giving opinions regarding their likes and dislikes. Young preschoolers expand their vocabularies from hearing others' speech and from books. They describe past and possible future events and unseen objects, tell fictional or "make-believe" stories, and use complete sentences and more complex language.

BENEFITS OF PLAY-BASED ACTIVITIES

When young children play, they often enact scenarios. Play scenarios tell stories that include who is involved, where they are, what happens, why it happens, and how the "actors" feel about it. Children engage in planning when they decide first what their playing will be about, which children are playing which roles, and who is doing what. This planning and the thought processes involved reflect narrative thinking and structure. Children who experience difficulties with planning play are more likely to avoid participating or to participate only marginally. Since playing actually requires these thought and planning processes, children who do not play spontaneously can be supported in playing by enabling them to talk about potential narratives/stories as foundations for play scenarios. When conflicts emerge during play, conversation is necessary to effect needed change. Narrative development constitutes gradual plot development; play conflicts are akin to fictional/personal narrative problems and result in changed feelings. Adults can help young children discuss problems, identify the changed feeling they cause, and discuss plans/actions for resolution.

CONVERSATION OF ADULTS WITH YOUNG CHILDREN

Adults should converse with young children so the children get practice with hearing and using rich and abstract vocabulary and increasingly complex sentences, using language to express ideas and ask questions for understanding, and using language to answer questions about past, future, and absent things rather than only about "here-and-now" things. To ensure they incorporate these elements in their conversations, adults can consider whose voices are heard most often and who does the most talking in the home, care setting, or classroom; the child, not the adult, should be talking at least half of the time. Adults should be using rich language with complex structures when conversing with young children. Adults should be talking with, not at children; the conversation should be shared equally rather than adults doing all the talking while children listen to them. Adults should also ask young children questions, rather than just telling them things. Additionally, adult questions should require that children use language to formulate and communicate abstract ideas.

NATURAL VS. INTENTIONAL

Children enjoy conversing with significant adults, including parents, caregivers, and teachers, and they require practice with doing so. Caregivers tend to talk with young children naturally, sometimes even automatically, throughout the day, which helps children develop significant language skills. However, caregivers can enhance young children's oral language development further through intentional conversations. One element of doing this is establishing an environment that gives the children many things to talk about and many reasons to talk. Another element of intentionally promoting oral language skills development is by engaging in shared conversations. When parents and caregivers share storybook reading with young children, this affords a particularly good springboard for shared conversations. Reading and conversing together are linguistic interactions supplying foundations for children's developing comprehension of numerous word meanings. Researchers find such abundant early word comprehension is a critical basis for later reading comprehension. Asking questions, explaining, requesting what they need, communicating feelings, and learning to listen to others talk are some important ways whereby children build listening, understanding, and speaking skills.

ONE-TO-ONE CONVERSATIONS WITH CHILDREN

When parents, caregivers, or teachers converse one-to-one with individual children, children reap benefits not as available in group conversations. Caregivers should therefore try to have such individual conversations with each child daily. In daycare and preschool settings, some good times for caregivers to do this include when children arrive and leave, during shared reading activities with one or two children, and during center time. Engaging in one-to-one talk allows the adult to repeat what the child says for reinforcement and allows the adult to extend what the child said by adding more information to it, like new vocabulary words, synonyms, meanings, or omitted details. It allows the adult to revise what the child said by restating or recasting it. It allows the child to hear his or her own ideas and thoughts reflected back to them when the adult restates them. Moreover, one-to-one conversation allows adults to contextualize the discussion accordingly with an individual child's understanding. It also allows adults to elicit children's comprehension of abstract concepts.

EXTENDED CONVERSATIONS AND TURN-TAKING

When adults engage young children in extended conversations, including taking many "back-and-forth" turns, these create the richest dialogues for building oral language skills. Adults make connections with and build upon children's declarations and questions. Adults model richer descriptive language by modifying/adding to children's original words with new vocabulary, adjectives, adverbs, and varying sentences with questions and statements. For example, a child shows an adult his or her new drawing, saying, "This is me and Gran in the garden," and the adult can build on this/invite the child to continue by saying, "What is your gran holding?" The child identifies what they planted: "Carrot seeds. Gran said to put them in the dirt so they don't touch." The adult can then encourage the child's use of language to express abstract thoughts: "What could happen if the seeds were touching?" The adult can then extend the conversation through discussion with the child about how plants grow or tending gardens. This introduces new concepts, builds children's linguistic knowledge, and helps them learn to verbalize their ideas.

> **Review Video: What is Sensory Language?**
> Visit mometrix.com/academy and enter code: 177314

IN-DEPTH COMPREHENSION OF WORD MEANINGS

To support deeper word-meaning comprehension, teachers can give multiple definitions and examples for the same word and connect new vocabulary with children's existing knowledge. For example, a teacher conducting a preschool classroom science experiment incorporates new scientific concepts with new vocabulary words and conversational practice: Pouring water on a paper towel, the teacher asks children what is happening to the water. A child answers, "It's going into the paper." The teacher asks how. Another child says, "The paper's soaking it up." The teacher confirms this, teaches the word *absorb*, compares the paper to a sponge, and asks how much more water will be absorbed. A child responds probably no more since water is already dripping out. The teacher pours water on a plastic lid, asking if it absorbs. Children respond, "No, it slides off." Confirming, the teacher teaches the word *repel*. This teacher has introduced new science concepts and new vocabulary words, engaged the children in conversation, related new concepts and words to existing knowledge, and added information to deepen comprehension.

ADULTS' NARRATION OF CHILD ACTIVITIES AND ACTIONS

One oral language development technique adults can use is to narrate, or describe what a child is doing as he or she does it. For example, a caregiver can say, "I see you're spreading paste on the back of your paper flower—not too much so it's lumpy, but not too little so it doesn't stick. Now you're pressing the flower onto your poster board. It sticks—good work!" Hence, narration can be incorporated as prelude and segue to verbal positive reinforcement. This promotes oral language development by introducing and illustrating syntaxes. Communicating locations and directionality employs verbs and prepositions. Describing intensity and manner employs adverbs. Labeling objects/actions that are currently present/taking place with new vocabulary words serves immediately to place those words into natural contexts, facilitating more authentic comprehension of word meanings and better memory retention. Caregivers/teachers can narrate children's activities during formal instructional activities and informal situations like outdoor playtime, snack time, and cleanup time, and subsequently converse with them about what they did.

TOPICS THAT YOUNG CHILDREN ENJOY TALKING ABOUT

Personal content is important with young children, who enjoy talking about themselves, such as what their favorite color is or where they got their new shirt; about their activities, like what they are constructing with Legos or shaping with Play-Doh; or about familiar events and things that access their knowledge, like their family activities and experiences with neighbors and friends. Here is an example of how a teacher can make use of children's conversation to reinforce it, expand it, and teach new vocabulary and grammar. The teacher asks a child what he or she is building, and the child answers, "A place for sick animals." The teacher asks, "You mean an animal hospital [or vet clinic]?" and the child confirms. When a child says someone was taken to a hospital "in the siren," the teacher corrects the usage by saying, "They took him to the hospital in the ambulance with the siren was sounding?" This recasts *siren* with the correct word choice, *ambulance*. It incorporates *siren* correctly and extends the statement to a complete sentence.

STORYTELLING

Young children like to communicate about their personal life experiences. When they can do this through narrative structure, it helps them use new words they are learning, organize their thoughts to express them coherently, and engage their imaginative powers. Teachers/caregivers can supply new words they need, model correct syntax for sentences by elaborating on or extending child utterances and asking them questions, and build further upon children's ideas. For example, a teacher asks a child what they did at her sister's birthday party. When the child describes the cake and makes gestures for a word she doesn't know, the teacher supplies "candles," which the child confirms and repeats. When the child then offers, "Mom says be careful with candles," the teacher asks what could happen if you're not careful. The child replies that candles can start a fire. In this way, teachers give young children models of sentence structure, teach vocabulary, and guide children in expressing their thoughts in organized sequences that listeners can follow.

SHARED BOOK READING

When teachers share books with preschoolers, they can ask questions and discuss the content, giving great opportunities for building oral language through conversation. Books with simple text and numerous, engaging illustrations best invite preschoolers to talk about the characters and events in the pictures and the plotlines they hear. Children's listening and speaking skills develop, they learn new information and concepts, their vocabularies increase, and their ability to define words and explain their meanings is enhanced through shared reading. Many children's books include rich varieties of words that may not occur in daily conversation, used in complete-sentence contexts. Teachers should provide preschoolers with fictional and nonfictional books, poetry and storybooks, children's reference books like picture dictionaries/encyclopedias, and "information books" covering single topics like weather, birds, reptiles, butterflies, or transportation whereby children can get answers to questions or learn topical information. Detailed illustrations, engaging content, and rich vocabulary are strong elements motivating children to develop oral language and understand how to form sentences, how to use punctuation, and how language works.

Abstract thought is stimulated by asking young children to think about things not observed and/or current. During/after sharing books, teachers can ask children what else might happen in the story; what they imagine the story's characters could be feeling or thinking—which also engages their imaginations; and ask them the meaning of the story's events using questions necessitating children's use of language to analyze this meaning. Teachers can ask younger children vocabulary words ("What did we call this animal?") and encourage them to use language by asking them to describe story details, like "How do the firemen reach people up high in the building?" Once younger children are familiar with a story, teachers can activate and monitor their retention and recall by saying, "Do you remember what happened to Arthur the day before that?" Teachers can ask older children to predict what they think will happen next in a story, to imagine extensions beyond the story ("What would you do if...?"), and make conclusions regarding why characters feel/behave as they do.

ENHANCING THE EFFECTS OF SHARED READING

According to researchers' findings, the effectiveness of shared reading experiences is related to the ways that adults read with young children. Rather than merely labeling objects or events with vocabulary words, teachers should ask young children to recall the shared reading, which monitors their listening comprehension and retention abilities. They should ask children to predict what will happen next based on what already happened in a book; speculate about what could possibly happen; describe characters, actions, events, and information from the shared reading; and ask their own questions about it. Shared reading with small groups of 1–3 children permits teachers to involve each child in the book by questioning and conversing with them about the pictures and plots. To teach vocabulary, teachers can tell children word meanings; point to illustrations featuring new words; relate new words to words the children already know; give multiple, varied examples of new words; and encourage children to use new words they learn in their conversations.

REPEATING SHARED READING

Young children develop preferences for favorite books. Once they know a story's plot, they enjoy discussing their knowledge. Teachers can use this for extended conversations. They can ask children who the characters are, where the story takes place, and why characters do things and events occur. They can ask specific questions requiring children to answer how much, how many, how far a distance, and how long a time. Teachers can also help children via prompting to relate stories to their own real-life experiences. In a thematic approach, teachers can select several books on the same theme, like rain forests or undersea life. This affords richer extended conversations about the theme. It also allows teachers to "recycle" vocabulary by modeling and encouraging use of thematically related words, which enhances memory and in-depth comprehension of meanings. Teachers can plan activities based on book themes, like painting pictures/murals, sculpting, making collages, or constructing models, which gives children additional motivation to use the new language they learn from shared readings of books.

READING ALOUD

Just before reading a story aloud to young students, the teacher should identify vocabulary words in the story that he or she will need to go over with the children. The teacher can write these words on the board or on strips of paper. Discussing these words before the reading will give the children definitions for new/unfamiliar words and help them understand word meanings within the story's context. Teachers can also give young children some open-ended questions to consider when listening to the story. They will then repeat these questions during and after the reading. Questions should NOT be ones children can answer with yes/no. When discussing vocabulary words, the teacher can also ask the children to relate words to personal life experiences. For example, with the word *fish*, some children may want to talk about going fishing with parents. Teachers can encourage children to tell brief personal stories, which will help them relate the story they are about to hear to their own real-life experience, making the story more meaningful.

Before reading a story aloud, adults should tell young children its title and the author's name. Then they can ask the children what an author does (children should respond "write stories" or something similar). Giving the illustrator's name, the adult also can then ask the children what illustrators do (children should respond "draw pictures" or something similar). Holding up the book, an adult can identify the front, spine, and back and ask the children if we start reading at the front or back (children should respond "at the front"). Adults can show young children the illustration on the front cover of the book and ask them, "From this picture, what do you think is going to happen in this story?" and remind them to answer this question in complete sentences. These exchanges before reading a story aloud activate children's fundamental knowledge regarding print and books, as well as the last example's exercising their imagination and language use.

When a teacher is reading a story aloud to young children, after reading each page aloud, he or she should have the children briefly discuss the picture illustrations on each page and how they relate to what was just read aloud. After reading aloud each plot point, action, event, or page, the teacher should ask the children open-ended (non yes/no) questions about what they just heard. This monitors and supports listening comprehension and memory retention/recall and stimulates expressive language use. When children associate something in the story with their own life experiences, teachers should have them explain the connection. As they read, teachers should stop periodically and ask the children to predict or guess what will happen next before continuing. This promotes abstract thinking and understanding of logical sequences and also exercises the imagination. After reading the story, teachers should ask children whether they liked it and why/why not, prompting them to answer using complete sentences. This helps children to organize their thoughts and opinions and to develop clear, grammatical, complete verbal expression.

ENVIRONMENTAL PRINT

Street signs, traffic signs, store and restaurant names, candy wrappers, food labels, and product logos—all the print we see in everyday life—are environmental print. Just as parents often play alphabetic games with children in the car ("Find something starting with A…with B…" etc.), adults can use environmental print to enhance print awareness and develop reading skills. They can ask children to find letters from their names on colorful cereal boxes. They can select one sign type, such as stop, one-way, or pedestrian crossing, and ask children to count how many they see during a car trip. They can have children practice reading each sign and talk about the phonemes (speech sounds) each letter represents. Adults can take photos of different signs and compile them into a little book for children to "read." By cutting familiar words from food labels, they can teach capitalized and lowercase letters, associate letters with phonemes, have children read the words, and sort words by their initial letters and by categories (signs, foods, etc.).

ALPHABETIC PRINCIPLE

The alphabetic principle is the concept that letters and letter combinations represent speech sounds. Children's eventual reading fluency requires knowing these predictable relationships of letters to sounds, which they can then apply to both familiar and unfamiliar words. Young children's knowing the shapes and names of letters predicts their later reading success: knowing letter names is highly correlated with the ability to view words as letter sequences and to remember written/printed words' forms. Children must first be able to recognize and name letters to understand and apply the alphabetic principle. Young children learn letter names first, via singing the alphabet song and reciting rhymes and alphabetical jump-rope chants ("A my name is Alice, I come from Alabama, and I sell Apples; B my name is Betty…" etc.). They learn letter shapes after names, through playing with lettered blocks, plastic/wood/cardboard letters, and alphabet books. Once they can recognize and name letters, children learn letter sounds after names and shapes and spellings after sounds.

To help young children understand that written or printed letters represent corresponding speech sounds, teachers should teach relationships between letters and sounds separately and in isolation and should teach these directly and explicitly. They should give young children daily opportunities during lessons to practice with letter-sound relationships. These opportunities for practice should include cumulative reviews of sound-letter relationships they have already learned and new letter-sound relationships as well. Adults should begin early in providing frequent opportunities to young children for applying their increasing knowledge and understanding of sound-letter relationships to early experiences with reading. They can do this by providing English words that are spelled phonetically (i.e., spelled the same way that they sound) and have meanings that are already familiar to the young learners.

PRINT AWARENESS

Even before they have learned how to read, young children develop print awareness, which constitutes children's first preparation for literacy. Children with print awareness realize that spoken language is represented by the markings on paper (or computer screens). They understand that the information in printed books adults read comes from the words, not the pictures. Children who have print awareness furthermore realize that print serves different functions within different contexts. They know that restaurant menus give information about the foods available; books tell stories or provide information; some signs show the names of stores, hotels, or restaurants; and other signs give traffic directions or danger warnings. Moreover, print awareness includes knowledge of how print is organized (words are combinations of letters and have spaces in between them). Children with print awareness also know that English print is read from left to right and top to bottom, book pages are numbered, words convey ideas and meaning, and reading's purpose is to understand those ideas and acquire that meaning.

One way in which a teacher can get an idea of whether or to what extent a young child has developed print awareness is to provide the child with a storybook. Then the teacher can ask the child the following: "Show me the front of the book. Show me the back of the book. Show me the spine of the book. Where is the book's title? Where in the book are you supposed to start reading it? Show me a letter in the book. Now show me a word. Show me the first word of a sentence. Can you show me the last word of a sentence? Now will you show me the first word on a page? Please show me the last word on a page. Can you show me a punctuation mark? Can you show me a capital letter? Can you find a small letter/lowercase letter?" The teacher should also praise each correct response, supply the correct answers for incorrect responses, and review corrected answers.

Teachers should show young children the organization of books and the purpose of reading. When they read to them, they should use books with large print, which are more accessible for young children to view and begin to learn reading. Storybook text should use words familiar/predictable to young children. While reading together, teachers should point out high-frequency words like *the*, *a*, *is*, *was*, and *you*, as well as specific letters, words, and punctuation marks in a story. Teachers can use index cards to label objects, areas, and centers in the classroom, pairing pictorial labels with word labels, and direct children's attention to them. They can invite preschoolers to play with printed words by making greeting cards, signs, or "writing" shopping lists and personal letters. They should point out print in calendars, posters, and signs. Also, teachers can have children narrate a story using a wordless picture book, write down their narrative on a poster, and reinforce the activity with a reward related to the story (e.g., eating pancakes after narrating the book *Pancakes*).

SELF-CONCEPT

Self-concept development begins during early childhood. Children come to identify characteristics, abilities, values, and attitudes that they feel define them. From 18–36 months, children develop the categorical self. This is a concrete view of oneself, usually related to observably opposite characteristics such as child versus adult, girl versus boy, short versus tall, and good versus bad. A 4-year-old might say, "I'm shorter than Daddy. I have blue eyes. I can help Mommy clean house!" Young children can also describe emotional and attitudinal aspects of self-concept ("I like playing with Joshua. I'm happy today."). Preschoolers do not usually integrate these aspects into a unified self-portrait, however. Also, many preschoolers do not yet realize one person can incorporate opposite qualities; a person is either good or bad to them, rather than having both good and bad qualities. The remembered self develops with long-term memory, including autobiographical memories and things adults have told them, to comprise one's life story. The inner self is the child's private feelings, desires, and thoughts.

PHONICS INSTRUCTION

Because children display individual differences in their speeds of learning sound-to-letter relationships, instruction should consider this; there is no set rate. Generally, a reasonable pace ranges from two to four sound-letter relationships per week. Relationships vary in utility: many words contain the letters *m*, *a*, *t*, *s*, *p*, and *h*, which are high-utility, but *x* in *box*, *gh* in *through*, *ey* in *they*, and *a* in *want* are lower-utility. High-utility sound-letter relationships should be taught first. Teachers should first introduce consonant relationships using *f*, *m*, *n*, *r*, and *s*, which are continuous sounds children can produce in isolation with less distortion than word-initial or word-medial stops like *p*, *b*, *t*, *d*, *k*, and *g*. Teachers should also introduce similar-sounding letters like *b* and *v* or *i* and *e*, and similar-looking letters like *b* and *d* or *p* and *g*, separately to prevent confusion. Single consonants versus clusters/blends should be introduced in separate lessons. Blends should incorporate sound-letter relationships children already know.

LANGUAGE EXPERIENCE APPROACH (LEA)

The LEA teaches beginning reading by connecting students' personal life experiences with written/printed words. A unique benefit is students using their own language and words, enabling them to interact with texts on multiple levels simultaneously. They thus realize they acquire knowledge and understanding through not just instruction but also their own experiences. The four steps for implementing the LEA with EC groups are as follows:

1. Children and the teacher choose a topic, like an exciting trip, game, or recent TV show, to discuss with teacher guidance
2. Each child takes a turn saying a sentence using his or her own words that advances the discussion/story. The teacher writes the children's words verbatim without corrections, visibly and clearly
3. Every few sentences or several words, the teacher stops and reads the record aloud for children to confirm accuracy
4. The teacher points to each word, they read aloud together, or children repeat after the teacher. The teacher gives children copies of the record for independent review and possible compilation into books of LEA stories

WHOLE LANGUAGE APPROACH

The whole language approach concentrates on children's seeking, finding, and constructing meaning in language. As such, young children's early technical correctness is not the priority. Whole language teachers do not ignore children's errors. However, they do not make correction more important than overall engagement, understanding, and appreciation of reading, writing, and literature. Instead, teachers make formative assessments taking into account the errors each child makes. Then they design learning experiences for children that give them opportunities and assistance in acquiring mechanically correct linguistic forms and structures. While this holistic approach finds analytical techniques that break language down into components like phonemes and alphabet letters less useful, children with language processing/reading problems need to learn phonemic awareness, phonics, and other decoding skills to develop reading fluency. The National Reading Panel conducted a study (1997–2000) to resolve controversy over phonics vs. whole language as the best teaching method, finding that any effective reading instruction program must teach phonemic awareness, phonics, reading fluency, vocabulary development, and reading comprehension.

The whole language approach is based on constructivist philosophy and psychology: children construct their own knowledge through their interactions with their environments. In contrast to analytical approaches like phonics and alphabetic learning, constructivism views learning as an individual's unique cognitive experience of acquiring new knowledge, shaped by the individual's existing knowledge and personal perspective. Whole language instruction emphasizes helping children create meaning from their reading and express meaning in their writing. The whole language philosophy emphasizes cultural diversity, integrating literacy instruction across subject domains, reading high-quality literature, and giving children many opportunities for independent reading, small-group guided reading, and being read to aloud by teachers. Whole language believes children learn to read by writing and vice versa. Realistically purposeful reading and writing are encouraged, as is using texts that motivate children to develop a love for literature. Early grammatical/spelling/technical correctness is not stressed, which can be problematic for children with reading/language processing disorders, who need explicit instruction in decoding skills and strategies.

ADDRESSING EARLY MECHANICAL ERRORS IN LEARNING READING AND WRITING

The basal reader is America's commonest approach, used in an estimated 75–85 percent of K–8th-grade classrooms. The number of publishers offering basal reading series has decreased to about one-fourth of that in the 20th century, decreasing teacher responsibility for investigating/piloting readers for district approval. Using basal readers is a skills-based/bottom-up approach. Teaching smaller-to-larger reading subskills in systematic, rigid sequence assists students' transition from part to whole. Texts graded by reading level contain narration and exposition organized thematically by unit, including children's literature and diverse other genres. Phonics and other specific instructional strands with practice assignments develop skills, which are assessed with end-of-unit tests. For young children, text decoding is enabled through exact control of vocabulary items and word analysis skills, "big [enlarged] books," and word and picture cards. Twentieth-century and older series sacrificed comprehension and enjoyment for vocabulary control and skill acquisition, but 21st-century series vary methods more (like multiple story versions or book excerpts enabling selection sharing), affording children more motivation to read.

DIRECTED READING ACTIVITY (DRA) AND THE DIRECTED READING-THINKING ACTIVITY (DR-TA)

Using basal readers, the DRA comprises the following:

1. The teacher prepares children for reading by stimulating their motivation and introducing new concepts and/or vocabulary
2. Students read silently, guided by teacher questions and statements
3. The teacher develops student comprehension, and students discuss characters, plots, or concepts to further comprehension
4. After silent reading, students read aloud and read answers to teacher questions, known as "purposeful rereading"
5. Students' follow-up workbook activities/practice review comprehension and vocabulary.

Some selections may include enrichment activities relating them to writing, art, drama, or music. The DR-TA approach is designed to develop critical readers through instruction in group comprehension. It requires children's active engagement in reading by processing information, asking questions, and receiving feedback as they read. The first phase of DR-TA is the teacher's direction of student thought processes throughout reading. The second phase involves developing student skills according to their needs as identified in phase 1 and additional extension or follow-up activities.

DIFFERENCES BETWEEN DRA AND DR-TA APPROACHES

- One main difference is that the DR-TA approach gives teachers all the responsibility and greater flexibility for developing lessons. As such, it contains fewer directions than the DRA approach, which contains specific materials and questions to use, specific guidelines, and is more teacher-manual-oriented and materials-oriented. Therefore, DR-TA can be used for not only basal readers but also planning lessons in other curriculum areas involving reading; the DRA approach applies more directly to basal reader programs.
- DRA manuals use mostly literal, factual questions, requiring only convergent thinking for student responses. However, in DR-TA, questions also demand divergent (creative) thinking of students, stimulating higher-level reading comprehension and interpretation.

- New vocabulary is pretaught in the DRA approach before children read. The DR-TA approach excludes preteaching, realistically requiring student decoding of new vocabulary words during reading.
- DRA manuals specify when to teach which skills for reading comprehension. DR-TA approaches do not, requiring more questioning expertise and acceptance of some alternative student responses by teachers.

Educational and Service Requirements for Children with a Range of Abilities and Special Needs

Diversity and Early Childhood Education

EFFECT OF RACIAL/ETHNIC, ECONOMIC, EDUCATIONAL, AND MENTAL HEALTH FACTORS ON THE EMOTIONAL, MENTAL HEALTH, AND SOCIAL OUTCOMES

Proportionately more mothers in minority and low-income groups—up to 40 percent—suffer maternal depression than in other parts of the population. Maternal depression is associated with poor mother-child bonding, lower child scores in language and reading, and higher prevalence of depression and other mental health problems later in children. Low-income and minority families are at higher risk for developmental difficulties and mental health issues. According to US surveys, about one-third, or over 3 million, of young children have two or more health and developmental risk factors. These risk factors include maternal mental health, maternal education, family poverty, and race/ethnicity. Each added risk factor increases the probability of either greater developmental risk or worse health status. Risk increases exponentially with multiple factors. One risk factor doubles risk, two factors more than triple it, three causes almost five times the risk, and four risk factors represent 14 times the risk of developmental delay or poor health.

EFFECTS OF RACIAL, ETHNIC, AND ECONOMIC DISPARITIES UPON PARENTING, HOME SAFETY, AND SCHOOL READINESS

According to the National Survey on Early Childhood Health, significant differences are reported in Latino and African Americans' parenting practices, home routines, and home safety measures. These differences are associated with differing degrees of positive early childhood development. Research studies have also revealed that American children in minority groups, on average, demonstrate lower school readiness levels when they begin formal education than white American children do. The research furthermore shows that most of these differences in school readiness levels are associated with differences in family income. Researchers also comment that disparities among racial and ethnic groups in their school readiness and subsequent academic achievement in school may be additional contributors to discrimination against minority racial and ethnic groups by teachers and other educational personnel.

EFFECTS OF INCOME AND RACE/ETHNICITY UPON HEALTH CARE ASPECTS

Although the disparity in childhood immunizations between white and minority infants and toddlers has decreased, still, fewer minority children are receiving standard immunizations than white children in America. For example, the preschool rates for receiving each major vaccination in America were the lowest among non-Latino black, Native American, and Alaskan Native children. One sign of health service quality and continuity is having a regular health care provider. Recent national surveys have found that while more than 80 percent of children under the age of 5 in economically affluent families are seen at physicians' offices or HMOs for care when sick, not much more than 54 percent of children under age 5 in economically poor families are seen for sick care. The National Survey of Early Childhood Health has found African American and Latino parents report more dissatisfaction with pediatricians and more unmet needs for early childhood development services than white parents. Twice as many Latino as white parents felt providers never or only occasionally understood their individual child's needs.

SOCIOECONOMIC AND RACIAL EFFECTS ON MENTAL, EMOTIONAL, AND SOCIAL HEALTH

According to the National Survey of Child and Adolescent Well-Being, in recent years, over 40 percent of toddlers and over 68 percent of preschoolers who were in contact with the child welfare system had high levels of need, developmentally and behaviorally. Overall, fewer than 23 percent of these children were getting services to address these needs. Thus, young children of socioeconomically disadvantaged families were found to have more developmental and behavioral problems than children in other socioeconomic groups, yet were also less likely to receive help with such problems. Another social and emotional difference related to racial group membership has been reflected by levels of violence in the family. Although the statistics on family violence is difficult to acquire and analyze for cause, it is commonly thought that the cause of most incidents is spousal or parental conflict and is reported at a higher rate among minority groups.

INEQUITY IN HEALTH INSURANCE COVERAGE FOR CHILDREN OF MINORITY GROUPS

Research has demonstrated that after taking health insurance status into account, there are no significant socioeconomic differences in how family organization and doctor/health care practitioner visits are related. Furthermore, research has shown that having health insurance coverage decreases differences in developmental and health outcomes for young children. However, despite these findings, children of minority groups are less likely than their nonminority peers to have either private or public health care coverage. Regarding access to health care services, it has been found that parents whose first language was not English were only half as likely to get preventive health care for their infants as native English-speaking families. This inequity in service delivery was found to be constant across white, African American, and Latino families that had infants, but not in Asian American families having infants.

According to data collected by the National Survey of Early Childhood Health, minority families have less communication and guidance from pediatric health care providers than white families. For example, African American parents were found to make significantly fewer phone calls than white parents to pediatric health care practices. Latino parents made fewer than half the calls that white parents did, while African American parents made fewer than three-fourths of the calls white parents did. This survey also found that pediatricians and other pediatric health care service providers were more likely to emphasize topics of household alcohol and drug use and community violence when they talked with minority patient families than they did in discussions with white patient families. African American children are found far more likely to have special health care needs than white children, yet researchers find that even after controlling for health status, insurance, and other pertinent variables, health care providers are still nearly twice as likely not to refer minority children to specialists and consultants.

EARLY CHILDHOOD COMPREHENSIVE SYSTEMS
DECREASING SOCIOECONOMICALLY AND RACIALLY INFLUENCED HEALTH CARE INEQUITIES

According to the National Center for Children in Poverty, Early Childhood Comprehensive Systems (ECCS) initiatives in each US state have the ability to further methods that can decrease socioeconomically related health care inequities in early childhood, which generates positive impacts for the rest of children's lives. To raise and shape consciousness of health care issues affected by income and race, experts recommend that ECCSs establish connections between projects/programs designed to eradicate poverty and racism and efforts in developing early childhood systems. Another consciousness-raising strategy recommended for ECCS is to work at increasing the general public's awareness of racial, ethnic, and economic disparities in early childhood health care and to work at increasing such awareness in health professionals, educators, early care providers, and other significant stakeholders who regularly provide services to young children. ECCSs can also include racial/ethnic data in performance monitoring; encourage state SCHIP and Medicaid agencies to do the same; analyze state data for disparities in risk, access, and outcomes, including small-area analyses and geocoding; and identify and measure unequal treatment through data analysis.

IMPROVING AND EQUALIZING HEALTH CARE FOR ALL AMERICAN DEMOGRAPHIC GROUPS
ENHANCING COMMUNITY SUPPORT

Experts in early childhood development find that state ECCSs should target their support toward communities with larger populations of minority and low-income families. Inasmuch as local systems have limited resources, some state ECCSs might need to allocate more of these resources to communities having higher risks of adverse outcomes for children. ECCSs can also provide assistance to communities by helping them assess their local assets, strengths, needs, and risk factors. Early childhood development experts emphasize that state ECCSs should focus their efforts on improving the quality of health care services that are available within communities where all or the majority of residents are members of minority groups and/or have low socioeconomic status. Another way in which state ECCSs can strengthen the supports available in communities for citizens who are subject to unequal health care treatment according to their demographic groups is to offer and provide incentives for community development projects that are designed to decrease health care treatment disparities based on racial/ethnic and economic differences.

REDUCING UNEQUAL TREATMENT OF CULTURAL/LINGUISTIC MINORITIES

Early childhood experts advise that each US state's ECCSs should implement strategies designed to monitor health care providers and services for cultural and linguistic competency, and to improve these competencies. One example of such improvement is ensuring that specific training in cultural and linguistic competency and cross-cultural competency is integrated into the training of both health care providers and early childhood educators. ECCSs can also be responsible for seeing that parent education materials and resources in health care are translated into the native languages of local families who are not native English speakers, and supporting interpreter and translator services for communities having families needing these. Experts find that ECCSs can additionally improve child and family health services by supporting various early childhood service settings in employing nonprofessional/community health workers. Moreover, ECCSs can help further equality and consistency of health care across varied demographic groups by applying research evidence-based guidelines regarding health care, family support, early learning, and related services and programs.

BENEFITS OF LEVELING INEQUALITIES IN CARE, HEALTH, AND EDUCATION

Eliminating unequal treatment in early childhood has significant benefits, including lowering overall national rates of poverty, improving overall health and education measures, saving long-term health care costs, decreasing disabilities, and lengthening lives by decreasing mortality rates. The effects of low income and racism on young children and their families are complex, and these influences interact with one another. Therefore, it is impossible or extremely difficult to solve problems generated by one of these social factors without including the other associated influencing factors. Because of the interrelationships of variables, strategies on a system level have the most potential for effectiveness. For example, job training and placement programs that could help parents economically are limited in effectiveness if quality child care is not also available to those parents. Enhancing educational programs could improve academic performance, but not if young students are too hungry to benefit from instruction. The measurement and monitoring of developmental, health, and educational outcomes will not change their disparity unless treatment inequities are resolved.

Involving Families in Their Children's Education

Flexibility and variety are key elements for involving diverse families, with changing situations and needs, in ECE. Adaptable approaches include these: Educators include families in designing children's Individual Family Service Plans (IFSPs) for preschoolers. They ask families to develop their own goals for educational participation. They create volunteer calendars, encouraging parents to collaborate when able. They communicate with families regularly, using speech if written/printed language presents barriers. They establish media libraries for parents/families to browse and check out resources. They facilitate parental meeting attendance and school visits by providing transportation and child care. They adapt to parental work schedules by convening meetings at alternative times of day. They often send families communications about both their children and class content, including information regarding important developmental milestones and methods for nurturing growth and development. They offer families individualized, specific strategies for home use. They recruit interested family members to help in preschool. They also function as clearinghouses to facilitate family access to community supports like local health care agencies, businesses, and universities.

Types of Disabilities and Exceptionalities and their Implications

CAUSES OF INTELLECTUAL DISABILITIES IN BABIES AND YOUNG CHILDREN

INFECTIONS

Congenital cytomegalovirus (CMV) is passed to fetuses from mothers, who may be asymptomatic. About 90% of newborns are also asymptomatic; 5–10% of these have later problems. Of the 10% born with symptoms, 90% will have later neurological abnormalities, including intellectual disabilities. Congenital rubella, or German measles, is also passed to fetuses from unvaccinated and exposed mothers, causing neurological damage, including blindness or other eye disorders, deafness, heart defects, and intellectual disabilities. Congenital toxoplasmosis is passed to fetuses by infected mothers, who can be asymptomatic, with a parasite from raw or undercooked meat that causes intellectual disabilities, vision or hearing loss, and other conditions. Encephalitis is brain inflammation caused by infection, most often viral. Meningitis is inflammation of the meninges, or membranes, covering the brain and is caused by viral or bacterial infection; the bacterial form is more serious. Both encephalitis and meningitis can cause intellectual disabilities. Maternal human immunodeficiency virus (HIV) and acquired immunodeficiency syndrome (AIDS) can be passed to fetuses, destroying immunity to infections, which can cause intellectual disabilities. Maternal listeriosis, a bacterial infection from contaminated food, animals, soil, or water, can cause meningitis and intellectual disabilities in surviving fetuses and infants.

ENVIRONMENTAL, NUTRITIONAL, AND METABOLIC INFLUENCES

Environmental deprivation syndrome results when developing children are deprived of necessary environmental elements—physical, including adequate nourishment (malnutrition); climate or temperature control (extremes of heat or cold); hygiene, like changing and bathing; and so on. It also includes lack of adequate cognitive stimulation, which can stunt a child's intellectual development, and neglect in general. Malnutrition results from starvation; vitamin, mineral, or nutrient deficiency; deficiencies in digesting or absorbing foods; and some other medical conditions. Environmental radiation, depending on dosage and time of exposure, can cause intellectual disabilities. Congenital hypothyroidism (underactive thyroid) can cause intellectual disabilities, as can hypoglycemia (low blood sugar) from inadequately controlled diabetes or occurring independently and infant hyperbilirubinemia. Bilirubin, a waste product of old red blood cells, is found in bile made by the liver and is normally removed by the liver; excessive bilirubin buildup in babies can cause intellectual disabilities. Reye syndrome, caused by aspirin given to children with flu or chicken pox, or following these viruses or other upper respiratory infections, or from unknown causes, produces sudden liver and brain damage and can result in intellectual disabilities.

GENETIC ABNORMALITIES AND SYNDROMES AFFECTING THE NERVOUS SYSTEM

Rett syndrome is a nervous system disorder causing developmental regression, particularly severe in expressive language and hand function. It is associated with a defective protein gene on an X chromosome. Having two X chromosomes, females with the defect on one of them can survive; with only one X chromosome, males are either miscarried, stillborn, or die early in infancy. Rett syndrome produces many symptoms, including intellectual disabilities. Tay-Sachs disease, an autosomal recessive disorder, is a nervous system disease caused by a defective gene on chromosome 15, resulting in a missing protein for breaking down gangliosides, chemicals in nerve tissues that build up in cells, particularly brain neurons, causing damage. Tay-Sachs is more prevalent in Ashkenazi Jews. The adult form is rare; the infantile form is commonest, with nerve damage starting in utero. Many symptoms, including intellectual disabilities, appear at 3 to 6 months, and death occurs by 4 to 5 years. Tuberous sclerosis, caused by genetic mutations, produces tumors damaging the kidneys, heart, skin, brain, and central nervous system. Symptoms include intellectual disabilities, seizures, and developmental delays.

Genetic or Inherited Metabolic Disorders

Adrenoleukodystrophy is an X-linked genetic trait. Some female carriers have mild forms, but it affects more males more seriously. It impairs metabolism of very long-chain fatty acids, which build up in the nervous system (as well as adrenal glands and male testes). The childhood cerebral form, manifesting at ages 4 to 8, causes seizures, visual and hearing impairments, receptive aphasia, dysgraphia, dysphagia, intellectual disabilities, and other effects. Galactosemia is an inability to process galactose, a simple sugar in lactose, or milk sugar. By-product buildup damages the liver, kidneys, eyes, and brain. Hunter syndrome, Hurler syndrome, and Sanfilippo syndrome each cause the lack of different enzymes; all cause an inability to process mucopolysaccharides or glycosaminoglycans (long sugar-molecule chains). Hurler and Sanfilippo (but not Hunter) syndromes are autosomal recessive traits, meaning both parents must pass on the defect. All cause progressive intellectual disabilities. Lesch-Nyhan syndrome, affecting males, is a metabolic deficiency in processing purines. It causes hemiplegia, varying degrees of intellectual disabilities, and self-injurious behaviors. Phenylketonuria (PKU), an autosomal recessive trait, causes lack of the enzyme to process dietary phenylalanine, resulting in intellectual disabilities.

Prescription Drugs, Substances of Abuse, Social Drugs, and Diseases

Warfarin, a prescription anticoagulant drug to thin the blood and prevent excessive clotting, can cause microcephaly (undersized head) and intellectual disabilities in an infant when the mother has taken it during pregnancy. The prescription antiseizure drug trimethadione can cause developmental delays in babies when it has been taken by pregnant mothers. Maternal abuse of solvent chemicals during pregnancy can also cause microcephaly and intellectual disabilities. Maternal crack cocaine abuse during pregnancy can cause severe and profound intellectual disabilities and many other developmental defects in fetuses, which become evident when they are newborns. Maternal alcohol abuse can cause fetal alcohol syndrome, which often includes intellectual disabilities, among many other symptoms. Maternal rubella (German measles) virus can cause intellectual disabilities as well as visual and hearing impairments and heart defects. Maternal herpes simplex virus can cause microcephaly, intellectual disabilities, and microphthalmia (small or no eyes). The varicella (chicken pox) virus in pregnant mothers can also cause intellectual disabilities as well as muscle atrophy in babies.

Characteristics of Infants and Young Children with Intellectual Disabilities

Newborns with intellectual disabilities, especially of greater severity, may not demonstrate normal reflexes, such as rooting and sucking reflexes, necessary for nursing. They may not show other temporary infant reflexes such as the Moro, Babinski, swimming, stepping, or labyrinthine reflexes, or they may demonstrate weaker versions of some of these. In some babies, these reflexes will exist but persist past the age when they normally disappear. Babies with intellectual disabilities are likely to display developmental milestones at later-than-typical ages. The ages when they do display milestones vary according to the severity of the disability and by individual. Young children with intellectual disabilities are likely to walk, self-feed, and speak later than normally developing children. Those who learn to read and write do so at later ages. Children with mild intellectual disabilities may lack curiosity and have quiet demeanors; those with profound intellectual disabilities are likely to remain infantile in abilities and behaviors throughout life. Intellectually disabled children will score below normal on standardized IQ tests and adaptive behavior rating scales.

POTENTIAL VARIABLES CAUSING LEARNING DISABILITIES

LDs are basically neurological disorders. Though they are more specific to particular areas of learning than global disorders like intellectual disabilities, scientific research has found correlations between LDs and many of the same factors that cause intellectual disabilities, including prenatal influences like excessive alcohol or other drug consumption, diseases, and so on. Once babies are born, glandular disorders, brain injuries, exposure to secondhand smoke or other toxins, infections of the central nervous system, physical trauma, or malnutrition can cause neurological damage resulting in LDs. Hypoxia and anoxia (oxygen loss) before, during, or after birth is a cause, as are radiation and chemotherapy. These same influences often cause behavioral disorders as well as LDs. Another factor is genetic: Both LDs and behavior disorders have been observed to run in families. While research has not yet identified specific genetic factors, heritability does appear to be a component in influencing learning and behavioral disorders.

TYPES OF NEUROLOGICAL DAMAGE FOUND IN CHILDREN WITH LDS AND ADHD

Various neurological research studies have revealed that children diagnosed with LDs and ADHD have at least one of several kinds of structural damage to their brains. Scientists have found smaller numbers of cells in certain important regions of the brains of some children with learning and behavioral disorders. Some of these children are found to have brain cells of smaller than normal size. In some cases, dysplasia is discovered; that is, some brain cells migrate into the wrong area of the brain. In some children with learning and behavioral disorders, blood flow is found to be lower than normal to certain regions in the brain. Also, the brain cells of some children with learning and behavioral disabilities show lower levels of glucose metabolism; glucose (blood sugar) is the brain's main source of fuel, so inadequate utilization of glucose can affect the brain's ability to perform some functions related to cognitive processing, as in LDs, and to attention and impulse control, as in ADHD.

TYPES AND CHARACTERISTICS OF LEARNING DISABILITIES

Dyslexia is the most common subcategory of specific learning disability that primarily affects reading but can also interfere with writing and speaking. Characteristics include reversing letters and words, for example, confusing *b* and *d* in reading and writing; reading *won* as *now*, confusing similar speech sounds like /p/ and /b/, and perceiving spaces between words in the wrong places when reading. Dyscalculia is difficulty doing mathematical calculations; it can also affect using money and telling time. Dysgraphia means difficulties specifically with writing, including omitting words in writing sentences or leaving sentences unfinished, difficulty putting one's thoughts into writing, and poor handwriting. Central auditory processing disorder causes difficulty perceiving small differences in words despite normal hearing acuity; for example, *couch* and *chair* may be perceived as *cow* and *hair*. Background noise and information overloads exacerbate the effects. Visual processing disorders affect visual perception despite normal visual acuity, causing difficulty finding information in printed text or from maps, charts, pictures, graphs, and so on; synthesizing information from various sources into one place; and remembering directions to locations.

ATTACHMENT STYLES IDENTIFIED IN TODDLERS BY MARY AINSWORTH

Mary Ainsworth worked with John Bowlby, discovering the first empirical evidence supporting his attachment theory. From her "strange situation" experiments, she identified secure, insecure and avoidant, insecure and resistant, and insecure and disorganized attachment styles. Securely attached children show normal separation anxiety when their mother leaves and happiness when she returns, avoid strangers when alone but are friendly when their mother is present, and use their mother as a safe base for environmental exploring. Insecure and resistant children show exaggerated separation anxiety, ambivalence, and resistance to their mother upon reuniting, fear strangers, cry more, and explore less than secure or avoidant babies. Insecure and avoidant children show no separation anxiety or stranger anxiety and little interest on reunions with their mother and are comforted equally by their mother or strangers. Insecure and disorganized types seem dazed and confused, respond inconsistently, and may mix resistant and ambivalent and avoidant behaviors. Secure styles are associated with sensitive, responsive caregiving and children's positive self-images and other images, resistant and ambivalent styles with inconsistent caregiving, and avoidant with unresponsive caregivers. Avoidant, resistant, and disorganized styles, associated with negative self-images and low self-esteem, are most predictive of emotional disturbances.

EMOTIONAL DISTURBANCES IN YOUNG CHILDREN CLASSIFIED AS ANXIETY DISORDERS

Anxiety disorders include generalized anxiety disorder (GAD), obsessive-compulsive disorder (OCD), posttraumatic stress disorder (PTSD), panic disorder, social phobia, and specific phobias. All share a common characteristic of overwhelming, irrational, and unrealistic fears. GAD involves excessive worrying about anything or everything and free-floating anxiety. Anxiety may be about real issues but is nonetheless exaggerated and spreads, overtaking the child's life. OCD involves obsessive and preoccupied thoughts and compulsive or irresistible actions, including often bizarre rituals. Germ phobia, constant hand washing, repeatedly checking whether tasks are done or undone, and collecting things excessively are common. PTSD follows traumatic experiences/events. Children have frequent, extreme nightmares, crying, flashbacks wherein they vividly perceive or believe they are experiencing the traumatic event again, insomnia, depression, anxiety, and social withdrawal. Symptoms of panic disorder are panic attacks involving extreme fear and physical symptoms like a racing heart, cold hands and feet, pallor, hyperventilation, and feeling unable to move. Children with social phobia develop fear and avoidance of day care, preschool, or other social settings. Specific phobias are associated with specific objects, animals, or persons and are often triggered by traumatic experiences involving these.

FACTORS CONTRIBUTING TO EMOTIONAL DISTURBANCES

Researchers have investigated emotional disturbances but have not yet established known causes for any. Some disturbances, for example, the major mental illness schizophrenia, seem to run in families and hence include a genetic component; childhood schizophrenia exists as a specific diagnosis. Factors contributing to emotional disturbances can be biological or environmental but more often are likely a combination of both. Dysfunctional family dynamics can often contribute to emotional disorders in children. Physical and psychological stressors on children can also contribute to the development of emotional problems. Some people have attributed emotional disturbances to diet, and scientists have also researched this but have not discovered proof of cause and effect. Bipolar disorder is often successfully treated with the chemical lithium, which affects sodium flow through nerve cells, so chemical imbalance may be implicated as an etiology. Pediatric bipolar disorder, which has different symptoms than adult bipolar disorder, correlates highly with histories of bipolar and other mood disorders or alcoholism in both parents.

SYMPTOMS OF PEDIATRIC BIPOLAR DISORDER

Bipolar disorder, formerly called manic-depressive disorder, has similar depressive symptoms in children as adults. However, children's mood swings often occur much faster, and children show more symptoms of anger and irritability than other adult manic symptoms. Bipolar children's most common symptoms include frequent mood swings; extreme irritability; protracted (up to several hours) tantrums or rages; separation anxiety; oppositional behavior; hyperactivity, impulsivity, and distractibility; restlessness and fidgetiness; silly, giddy, or goofy behavior; aggression; racing thoughts; grandiose beliefs or behaviors; risk-taking; depressed moods; lethargy; low self-esteem; social anxiety; hypersensitivity to environmental or emotional triggers; carbohydrate (sugar or starch) cravings; and trouble getting up in the morning. Other common symptoms include bed-wetting (especially in boys), night terrors, pressured or fast speech, obsessive or compulsive behaviors, motor and vocal tics, excessive daydreaming, poor short-term memory, poor organization, learning disabilities, morbid fascinations, hypersexuality, bossiness and manipulative behavior, lying, property destruction, paranoia, hallucinations, delusions, and suicidal ideations. Less common symptoms include migraines, bingeing, self-injurious behaviors, and animal cruelty.

CONDUCT DISORDER IN CHILDREN

Factors contributing to conduct disorders in children include genetic predispositions, neurological damage, child abuse, and other traumatic experiences. Children with conduct disorders display characteristic emotional and behavioral patterns. These include aggression: They bully or intimidate others, often start physical fights, will use dangerous objects as weapons, exhibit physical cruelty to animals or humans, and assault and steal from others. Deliberate property destruction is another characteristic—breaking things or setting fires. Young children are limited in some of these activities by their smaller size, lesser strength, and lack of access; however, they show the same types of behaviors against smaller, younger, weaker, or more vulnerable children and animals, along with oppositional and defiant behaviors against adults. Also, while truancy is impossible or unlikely in preschoolers, and running away from home is less likely, young children with conduct disorders are likely to demonstrate some forms of seriously violating rules, another symptom of this disorder.

SYMPTOMS OF CHILDHOOD-ONSET SCHIZOPHRENIA

The incidence of childhood-onset schizophrenia is rare, but it does exist. One example of differential diagnosis involves distinguishing qualitatively between true auditory hallucinations and young children's "hearing voices" otherwise: in the latter case, a child hears his or her own or a familiar adult's voice in his or her head and does not seem upset by it, while in the former, a child may hear other voices, seemingly in his or her ears, and is frightened and confused by them. Tantrums, defiance, aggression, and other acting-out, externalized behaviors are less frequent in childhood-onset schizophrenia than internalized developmental differences, for example, isolation, shyness, awkwardness, fickleness, strange facial expressions, mistrust, paranoia, anxiety, and depression. Children demonstrate nonpsychotic symptoms earlier than psychotic ones. However, it is difficult to use prepsychotic symptoms as predictors due to variance among developmental peculiarities. While psychiatrists find the course of childhood-onset schizophrenia somewhat more variable than in adults, child symptoms resemble adult symptoms. Childhood-onset schizophrenia is typically chronic and severe, responds less to medication, and has a more guarded prognosis than adolescent- or adult-onset schizophrenia.

DIAGNOSING THE EMOTIONAL DISTURBANCES IN CHILDREN CLASSIFIED AS PSYCHOTIC DISORDERS

Psychosis is a general psychiatric category referring to thought disturbances or disorders. The most common symptoms are delusions (believing things that are not true) and hallucinations (seeing, hearing, feeling, tasting, or smelling things that are not there). While early childhood psychosis is rarer than at later ages, psychiatrists confirm it does occur. Moreover, prognosis is poorer for psychosis with onset in early childhood than in adolescence or adulthood. Causes can be from known metabolic or brain disorders or unknown. Younger children are more vulnerable to environmental stressors. Also, in young children, thoughts distorted by fantasy can be from normal cognitive immaturity, due to lack of experience and a larger range of normal functioning, or pathology; where they lie on this continuum must be determined by clinicians. Believing one is a superhero who can fly can be vivid imagination or delusional; having imaginary friends can be pretend play or hallucinatory. Other developmental disorders can also cloud differential diagnosis.

VISUAL IMPAIRMENTS

DEVELOPMENTAL CHARACTERISTICS OF INFANTS AND YOUNG CHILDREN WITH VISUAL IMPAIRMENTS

Historically, it was thought that visually impaired children developed more slowly than normal; however, it is now known that ages for reaching developmental milestones are equally variable in visually impaired babies as in others and that they acquire milestones within equal age ranges. One developmental difference is in sequence: visually impaired children tend to utter their first words or subject-verb two-word sentences earlier than other children. Some visually impaired children also demonstrate higher levels of language development at younger-than-typical ages. For example, they may sing songs from memory or recall events from the past at earlier ages than other children. This is a logical development in children who must rely more on input to their hearing and other senses than to their vision when the latter is impaired. Totally blind babies reach for objects later, hence explore the environment later; hand use, eye-hand coordination, and gross and fine motor skills are delayed. Blind infants' posture control develops normally (rolling, sitting, all-fours, and standing), but mobility (raising on arms, pulling up, and walking) is delayed.

CAUSES OF VISUAL IMPAIRMENTS IN BABIES AND YOUNG CHILDREN

Syndrome-related and other malformations like cleft iris or lens dislocation causing visual impairment can have prenatal origins. Cataracts clouding the eye's lens can be congenital, traumatic, or due to maternal rubella. Eyes can be normal, but impairment in the brain's visual cortex can cause visual impairment. Infantile glaucoma, like adult glaucoma, causes intraocular fluid buildup pressure and visual impairment. Conjunctivitis and other infections cause visual impairment. Strabismus and nystagmus are ocular-muscle conditions, respectively causing eye misalignments and involuntary eye movements. Trauma damaging the eyeball(s) is another visual impairment cause. The optic nerve can suffer from atrophy (dysfunction) or hypoplasia, that is, developmental regression, usually prenatally due to neurological trauma; acuity cannot be corrected. Refractive errors like nearsightedness, farsightedness, and astigmatism are correctable. Retinoblastoma, or behind-the-eye tumors, can cause blindness and fatality; surgical or chemotherapeutic treatment is usually required before age 2. Premature infants can have retinopathy of prematurity or retrolental fibroplasia. Cryotherapeutic treatment seems to stop disease progression. Its effects range from none to severe visual impairment (approximately 25% of children) to complete blindness.

IMPACTS OF BLINDNESS UPON COGNITIVE DEVELOPMENT

Blind children have more difficulty determining and confirming characteristics of things, hence defining concepts and organizing them into more abstract levels; their problem-solving is active but harder, and they construct different realities than sighted children. Blind babies typically acquire object permanence (the understanding that unseen objects still exist) a year later than normal; they learn to reach for objects only by hearing. Understanding cause-and-effect relationships is difficult without visual evidence. Blind babies and toddlers take longer to understand an object's constancy regardless of their orientation in space, affecting their ability to orient toys and their own hands. Blind children can identify object size differences and similarities, but classifying object differences and similarities in other attributes requires longer times and more exposures to various similar objects. Blind children's development of the abilities to conserve object properties like material or substance, weight, amount and volume, length, and liquid volume is later than normal.

EFFECTS OF BLINDNESS ON EMOTIONAL AND SOCIAL DEVELOPMENT

Blind babies and children are more dependent than others on adults, affecting development. With control of their inner realities but not of their outer environments, blind children may withdraw, seeking and responding less to social interaction. They may not readily develop concepts of the external world or self-concepts as beings separate from the world and the understanding that they can be both agents and recipients of actions relative to the environment. Mother-infant smiling initiates recognition, attachment, and communication in sighted babies; blind infants smile on hearing mother's voice at 2 months. Only tactile stimuli like tickling and nuzzling evoke regular smiling in blind babies. Missing facial expressions and other visual cues, blind children have more complicated social interactions. They often do not understand the basics of playing with others and seem emotionally ambivalent or uninterested and uncommunicative. Peers may reject or avoid them; adults often overprotect them. Self-help skills like chewing, scooping, self-feeding, teeth brushing, grooming, and toilet training are delayed in blind children.

HEARING IMPAIRMENTS
PREVALENCE AND ETIOLOGIES OF HEARING IMPAIRMENTS

Half or more (50% to 60%) of infant hearing losses have genetic origins—Down and other genetically based syndromes or the existence of parental hearing loss. About 25% or more of infant hearing losses are caused by maternal infections during pregnancy, such as cytomegalovirus (CMV), postnatal complications like blood transfusions or infection with meningitis, or traumatic head injuries. Included in this 25% or more are babies having nongenetic neurological disorders or conditions that affect their hearing. Malformations of the ears, head, or face can cause hearing loss in babies. Babies spending five days or longer in neonatal intensive care units (NICUs) or having complications while in the NICU are also more likely to suffer hearing loss. Around 25% of babies are diagnosed with hearing loss whose etiology is unknown.

SIGNS OF HEARING IMPAIRMENTS

If an infant does not display a startle response to loud noises, this is a potential sign of hearing loss. This can also indicate other developmental disabilities, but because hearing loss is the most prevalent disability among newborns, hearing screening is a priority. Between birth and 3 or 4 months old, babies should turn toward the source of a sound; if they do not, it could indicate hearing loss. A child who does not utter first words like *mama* or *dada* by age 1 could have hearing impairment. When babies or young children do not turn their heads when their names are called, adults may mistake this for inattention or ignoring; however, children turning upon seeing adults, but not upon hearing their names, can indicate hearing loss. Babies and children who seem to hear certain sounds but not others may have partial hearing losses. Delayed speech-language development or unclear speech, not following directions, saying "Huh?" often, and wanting higher TV or music volumes can indicate hearing loss in children.

SPEECH AND LANGUAGE IMPAIRMENTS
FACTORS CONTRIBUTING TO SPEECH AND LANGUAGE IMPAIRMENTS

Some speech and language disorders in children have unknown causes. Others have known causes such as hearing loss: speech and language are normally acquired primarily through the auditory sense, so children with impaired hearing have delayed and impaired development of speech and language. Brain injuries, neurological disorders, viral diseases, and some medications can also cause problems with developing language or speech. Children with intellectual disabilities are more likely to have delayed language development, and their speech is also more likely to develop more slowly and to be distorted. Cerebral palsy causes neuromuscular weakness and incoordination of speech. When severe, it can cause the inability to produce recognizable speech sounds; some children without speech can still vocalize, and some cannot. A cleft palate or lip and other physical impairments affect speech. Inadequate speech-language modeling at home inhibits speech-language development. Vocal abuse in children (screaming, coughing, throat clearing, or excessive talking) can cause vocal nodules or polyps, causing voice disorders. Stuttering can be related to maturation, anxiety or stress, auditory feedback defects, or unknown causes.

CHARACTERISTICS

In speech, most phonological disorders are articulatory; that is, children fail to pronounce specific speech sounds or phonemes correctly beyond the normal developmental age for achieving accuracy. Stuttering, disfluency, and rate and rhythm disorders cause children to repeat phonemes, especially initial word sounds; to repeat words; to prolong vowels or consonants; or to block, straining so hard to produce a sound that, pressure builds, but no sound issues. Their speech rates may also increase and decrease irregularly. Children with voice disorders can have voices that sound hoarse, raspy, overly nasal, higher- or lower-pitched than normal, overly weak or strident, and whispery or harsh. Hoarseness is common with vocal nodules and polyps. Cleft palate commonly causes hypernasality. In language, one of the most common impairments is delayed language development due to environmental deprivation, intellectual disabilities, neurological damage or defects, hearing loss, visual impairment, and so on. Children with neurological damage or disorders may exhibit aphasias, language disorders characterized by receptive difficulty with understanding spoken or written language, or expressive difficulty constructing spoken or written language.

PHYSICAL AND HEALTH IMPAIRMENTS

EXAMPLES OF PHYSICAL AND HEALTH IMPAIRMENTS

In the special education field of early childhood education, "other health impairment" is a term referring to health and physical conditions that rob a child of strength, vitality, or alertness or that cause excessive alertness to environmental stimuli, all having the end result of impeding the child's ability to attend or respond to the educational environment. Health problems can be acute(short-term or temporary but serious) or chronic (long-term, persistent, or recurrent). Some examples of such health and physical impairments include cerebral palsy, spina bifida, amputations or missing limbs, muscular dystrophy, cystic fibrosis, asthma, rheumatic fever, sickle-cell anemia, nephritis or kidney disease, leukemia, Tourette syndrome, hemophilia, diabetes, heart disease, AIDS, and lead poisoning. All these conditions and others can interfere with a child's development and ability to attend and learn. In addition to seizure disorders, which often cause neurological damage, seizure-controlling medications also frequently cause drowsiness, interfering with attention and cognition. Attention deficit and attention deficit hyperactivity disorders (ADD and ADHD) limit attention span, focus, and concentration and thus are sometimes classified as health impairments requiring special education services.

CHARACTERISTICS OF BABIES AND CHILDREN WITH PHYSICAL AND HEALTH IMPAIRMENTS

The characteristics of children having various physical or health impairments can range from having no limitations to severe limitations in their activities. Children with cerebral palsy, for example, usually have deficiencies in gross and fine motor development and deficits in speech-language development. Physical and health conditions causing severe debilitation in some children not only seriously limit their daily activities but also cause multiple primary disabilities and impair their intellectual functioning. Other children with physical or health impairments function at average, above-average, or gifted intellectual and academic levels. An important consideration when working with babies and young children having physical or health impairments is handling and positioning them physically. Correctly picking up, holding, carrying, giving assistance, and physically supporting younger children and arranging play materials for them based on their impairment is not only important for preventing injury, pain, and discomfort; it also enables them to receive instruction better and to manipulate materials and perform most efficiently.

Preschoolers with physical impairments also tend to have difficulty with communication skills, so educators should give particular attention to facilitating and developing these.

DEVELOPMENTAL DELAYS
FACTORS LEADING TO DEVELOPMENTAL DELAYS

Developmental delays can come from genetic or environmental causes or both. Infants and young children with intellectual disabilities are most likely to exhibit developmental delays. Their development generally proceeds similarly to that of normal children but at slower rates; milestones are manifested at later-than-typical ages. Sensory impairments such as with hearing and vision can also delay many aspects of children's development. Children with physical and health impairments are likely to exhibit delays in their motor development and performance of physical activities. Another factor is environmental: children deprived of adequate environmental stimulation commonly show delays in cognitive, speech-language, and emotional and social development. Children with autism spectrum disorders often have markedly delayed language and speech development; many are nonverbal. Autistic children also typically have impaired social development, caused by an inability or difficulty with understanding others' emotional and social nonverbal communications. When they cannot interpret these, they do not know how to respond and also cannot imitate them; however, they can often learn these skills with special instruction.

CHARACTERISTICS INDICATING DEVELOPMENTAL DELAYS

Developmental delays mean that a child does not reach developmental milestones at the expected ages. For example, if most babies normally learn to walk between 12 and 15 months of age, a 20-month-old who is not beginning to walk is considered as having a developmental delay. Delays can occur in cognitive, speech-language, social-emotional, gross motor skill, or fine motor skill development. Signs of delayed motor development include stiff or rigid limbs, floppy or limp body posture for the child's age, using one side of the body more than the other, and clumsiness unusual for the child's age. Behavioral signs of children's developmental delays include inattention or shorter-than-normal attention span for the age, avoiding or infrequent eye contact, focusing on unusual objects for long times or preferring objects over social interaction, excessive frustration when attempting tasks normally simple for children their age, unusual stubbornness; aggressive and acting-out behaviors; daily violent behaviors, rocking, excessive talking to oneself, and not soliciting love or approval from parents.

TRAUMATIC BRAIN INJURY (TBI)
IDEA'S LEGAL DEFINITION OF TRAUMATIC BRAIN INJURY

TBI is defined by the IDEA law (the Individuals with Disabilities Education Act) as "an acquired injury to the brain from external physical force, resulting in total or partial functional disability or psychosocial impairment, or both, that adversely affect a child's educational performance." This definition excludes injuries from birth trauma, congenital injuries, and degenerative conditions. TBI is the foremost cause of death and disability in children (and teens) in the USA. The most common causes of TBI in children include falls, motor vehicle accidents, and physical abuse. In spite of the IDEA's definition, aneurysms and strokes are three examples of internal traumas that can also cause TBI in babies and young children. External head injuries that can result in TBI include both open and closed head injuries. Shaken baby syndrome is caused by forcibly shaking an infant. This causes the brain literally to bounce against the insides of the skull, causing rebound injuries, resulting in TBI and even death.

CHARACTERISTICS

TBI can impair a child's cognitive development and processing. It can impede the language development of children, which is dependent upon cognitive development. Children who have sustained TBI often have difficulties with attention, retention, and memory; reasoning, judgment, understanding abstract concepts, and thinking abstractly; and problem-solving abilities. TBIs can also impair a child's motor functions and physical abilities. The sensory and perceptual functions of children with TBI can be abnormal. Their ability to process information is often compromised. Their speech can also be affected. In addition, TBIs can impair a child's psychosocial behaviors. Memory deficits are commonest, tend to be more long-lasting, and are often area-specific; for example, a child may recall personal experiences but not factual information. Other common characteristics of TBI include cognitive inflexibility or rigidity, damaged conceptualization and reasoning, language loss or poor verbal fluency, problems with paying attention and concentrating, inadequate problem solving, and problems with reading and writing.

ETIOLOGIES AND CHARACTERISTICS OF MULTIPLE DISABILITIES

The term *multiple disabilities* refers to any combination of more than one disabling condition. For example, a child may be both blind and deaf due to causes such as having rheumatic fever in infancy or early childhood. Anything causing neurological damage before, during, or shortly after birth can result in multiple disabilities, particularly if it is widespread rather than localized. For example, infants deprived of oxygen or suffering traumatic brain injuries in utero, during labor or delivery, or postnatally can sustain severe brain damage. So can babies having encephalitis or meningitis and those whose mothers abused drugs prenatally. Infants with this type of extensive damage can often present with multiple disabilities, including intellectual disabilities, cerebral palsy, physical paralysis, mobility impairment, visual impairment, hearing impairment, and speech-language disorders. They may have any combination of or all of these disabilities as well as others. In addition to a difficulty or inability with normal physical performance, multiple disabled children often have difficulty acquiring and retaining cognitive skills and transferring or generalizing skills among settings and situations.

PREMATURITY OR PRETERM BIRTH

Babies born before 37 weeks' gestation are classified as premature or preterm. Premature infants can have difficulty with breathing, as their lungs are not fully developed, and with regulating their body temperatures. Premature infants may be born with pneumonia, respiratory distress, extra air or bleeding in the lungs, jaundice, sepsis or infection, hypoglycemia (low blood sugar), severe intestinal inflammation, bleeding into the brain or white-matter brain damage, or anemia. They have lower-than-normal birth weights, body fat, muscle tone, and activity. Additional typical characteristics of premature infants include apnea (interrupted breathing); lanugo (a coating of body hair that full-term infants no longer have); thin, smooth, shiny, translucent skin through which veins are visible; soft, flexible ear cartilage; cryptorchidism (undescended testicles) and small, non-ridged scrotums in males; enlarged clitorises in females; and feeding difficulties caused by weak or defective sucking reflexes or incoordination of swallowing with breathing.

DISABLING CONDITIONS RESULTING FROM PREMATURE BIRTHS

Physicians find it impossible to predict the long-term results of prematurity for any individual baby based on an infant's gestational age and birth weight. However, some related immediate and long-term effects can be identified. Generally, the lower the birth weight and the more prematurely a child is born, the greater the risk is for complications. Infants born at less than 34 weeks of gestation typically cannot coordinate their sucking and swallowing and may temporarily need feeding or breathing tubes or oxygen. They also need special nursery care until able to maintain their body temperatures and weights. Long-term complications of prematurity can include bronchopulmonary dysplasia, a chronic lung condition; delayed physical growth and development; delayed cognitive development; mental or physical delays or disabilities; and blindness, vision loss, or retinopathy of prematurity (formerly called retrolental fibroplasia). While some premature infants sustain long-term disabilities, some severe, other babies born prematurely grow up to show no effects at all; any results within this range can also occur.

Curriculum, Instruction, and Assessment for Young Children

Activities Promoting Development

USING INTEGRATED CURRICULA

Integrating subject/domain content across the curriculum has been used for years at every educational level, from higher education to early childhood education. However, recent demands for accountability, as exemplified and escalated by No Child Left Behind, can distract educators from holistic and overall learning toward preoccupation with developing isolated skills and using test scores to measure achievement. But rather than discarding teaching methods proven effective, early childhood educators need to integrate newer, mandate-related practices into existing plans and methods. Teaching integrated curricula in early childhood classrooms has proven effective for both children and teachers. Integrating learning domains and subject content, in turn, integrates the child's developing skills with the whole child. When teachers use topics children find interesting and exciting, in-depth projects focusing on particular themes, and good children's literature, they give children motivation to learn the important concepts and skills they need for school and life success. Children should bring home from preschool not only further developed skills but also knowledge useful and meaningful in life.

USING MANIPULATIVES FOR PRESCHOOL MATH LEARNING

Young children learn primarily through visually inspecting, touching, holding, and manipulating concrete objects. While they are less likely to understand abstract concepts presented abstractly, such concepts are likelier accessible to preschoolers through the medium of real things they can see, feel, and manipulate. Manipulatives are proven as effective learning devices; some early math curricula (e.g., Horizons) even require them. They are also particularly useful for children with tactile or visual learning styles. Many math manipulatives are available for sale, such as linking cubes; 3-dimensional geometric shapes and "geoboards"; large magnetized numbers for whiteboards; weights, scales, and balances for measurements; math blocks; math games; number boards and color tiles; flashcards; play money and toy cash registers, and activities; objects for sorting and patterning; or tangrams for recognizing shapes, reproducing and designing patterns, and spatial problem-solving. Teachers can create homemade math manipulatives using bottle caps/lids; seashells, pebbles/stones; buttons; keys; variously sized, shaped, and colored balls; coffee stirrers; or cardboard tubes from paper products.

HELPING YOUNG CHILDREN USE INQUIRY AND DISCOVERY IN SCIENCE

Early childhood teachers are advised to "teach what they know," meaning use materials with which they are familiar. For example, teachers who like plants can have young children plant beans, water them, and watch them grow, moreover incorporating this activity with the story "Jack and the Beanstalk." Teachers can bring in plants, leaves, and flowers for children to observe and measure their sizes, shapes, or textures. Experts recommend teachers utilize their everyday environments to procure learning materials, such as pine needles and cones, loose feathers and leaves found outdoors, animal fur from pets or groomers, and/or snakeskins or turtle shells from local pet stores. Experts advise teachers to use their observational skills during inquiry and discovery activities: if children apply nonstandard and/or unusual uses of some materials, teachers should observe what could be a new discovery, wherein students teach adults new learning, too. Teachers should let children play with and explore new materials to understand their purposes, uses, and care before using them in structured activities.

Process Skills Developed by Preschool Science Programs

Experts find three process skills that good early childhood science programs help develop are observation, classification, and communication. Young children are inherently curious about the world and hence enjoy many activities involving inquiry and discovery. Teachers can uncover science in many existing preschool activities. For example, since young children relate to activities focusing on themselves, teachers can have them construct skeletons of dry pasta, using their pictures as heads. Cooking activities involve science, as do art activities. Teachers can have children explore various substances' solubility in water and which colors are produced by mixing which other colors. They can have them compare and contrast different objects. They can create inexpensive science centers using animal puppets; models; thematically-related games, puzzles, books, and writing materials; mirrors, prisms, and magnifiers; scales; magnets; and various observable, measurable objects. Teachers should regularly vary materials to sustain children's interest.

Preschool Activities for Developing Physical Coordination, Fine Motor Skills, and Large Muscle Skills

Preschoolers are more likely to fall because their lower bodies are not yet developed equally to their upper bodies, giving them higher centers of gravity. Therefore, seeing how long they can balance on one foot and hopping exercises help improve balance and coordination. Hopping races let preschoolers participate in groups and observe peer outcomes, which can also enhance self-confidence and supporting others. "Freeze dancing" (like musical chairs without the chair-sitting), without eliminations, provides physical activity and improves coordination. Using writing implements, tying shoes, and playing with small items develop fine motor skills. With preschoolers, it is more effective and developmentally appropriate to incorporate fine motor activities into playtime than to separate quiet activity from play. For example, on nature walks, teachers can have children collect pebbles and twigs and throw them into a stream, developing coordination and various muscles. Running, skipping, and playing tag develop large muscle skills. Kicking, throwing, and catching balls give good unstructured exercise without game rules preschoolers cannot understand. Preschoolers' short attention spans preclude long activity durations.

Benefits of Aesthetic Experiences

To help children learn color names and develop sensory discrimination and classification abilities, some art museums offer preschool lessons, which teachers can also use as models. For example, a teacher can read a children's story or sing a song about color, then present artwork for children to examine, and then a separate display with different shapes of different colors used by the artist, asking children to name these and any other colors they know, and identify any other colors the artist used not represented in the second display. The teacher then demonstrates how mixing produces other colors. After this demonstration with children's discussion, the teacher gives each child a piece of heavy-duty paper and a brush. The teacher pours about an inch-sized puddle of each of the three primary colors—red, blue, and yellow—in the middle of each child's paper. The teacher then tells the children to use their brushes to explore mixing colors and see the variety of other colors they can create.

Benefits of the Line in Visual Arts

Activities focusing on lines in art help young children expand their symbol recognition, develop their comparison-making ability, and facilitate shape recognition. Teachers can begin by singing a song or reading a children's story about lines. Then they can present one painting, drawing, or other artwork and help children point at various kinds of lines that the artist used. The teacher can draw various line types on a separate piece of paper (e.g. wavy, pointy, spiral) and ask children to find similar lines in the artwork. Then the teacher can ask children to try drawing these different lines themselves. Teachers should also inform children of various tools for drawing lines, such as crayons, pencils, markers, chalk, and paint, and let them experiment with these. An early childhood teacher can also supply butcher paper or other roll paper for each child to lie down on in whatever creative body positions they can make. The teacher outlines their body shapes with a marker. Then the teacher has the children explore drawing different kinds of lines, using various kinds of drawing tools, to enhance and personalize their individual body outlines.

AESTHETIC EXPERIENCES INVOLVING SHAPE

Giving young children learning activities that focus on shapes used in art helps them develop their abilities to form concepts and identify discrepancies. Manipulating basic geometric shapes also stimulates their creative thinking skills and imaginations, as well as developing early geometric math skills. For example, an early childhood teacher can first read aloud a children's book about shapes, of which many are available. After reading it through, the teacher can go back through the story, asking children to point to and name shapes they recognize. Then the teacher can show children an artwork. Using line drawings and/or solid geometric shapes, they discuss what shapes the artist used. The teacher can help children arrange solid shapes to form different images (people, flowers, houses). The teacher can then give children paper pulp trays, heavy paper, and/or board; assorted wooden, cardboard, and/or plastic shapes; and instructions to think and arrange shapes they can make with them, and then give them glue to affix the shapes to their trays, paper, and/or board. They can paint their creations after the glue dries.

EXPLORING TEXTURE IN ART

Preschoolers learn much through looking at and touching concrete materials. Activities involving visual and tactile examination and manipulation plus verbal discussion enhance young children's representational/symbolic thinking abilities. Such activities also enable children to explore various ways of representing different textures visually. Teachers can provide "feely bags or boxes"—bags or boxes with variously textured items inside, such as sandpaper, fleece, clay, wool, or tree bark—for children to feel and describe textures before seeing them, and identify objects based on feel. A teacher can then show children a selected artwork, and they can discuss together which textures are included(e.g., smooth, rough, jagged, bumpy, sharp, prickly, soft, or slippery). The teacher can then demonstrate using plaster, thickened paste, or clay how to create various textures using assorted tools (e.g., tongue depressors, plastic tableware, chopsticks, small toys, or child-safe pottery tools) and have children experiment with discovering and producing as many different textures as they can. After children's products dry, they can paint them the next day.

PROVIDING AFFECTIVE LEARNING EXPERIENCES

Providing affective experiences supports young children's emotional development, including understanding and expressing their emotions. These enable development of emotional self-regulation/self-control. Emotional development is also prerequisite to and supportive of social interactions and development. Affective activities also help teachers understand how children feel, which activities they find most fascinating, and/or why they are not participating. "Feelings and Faces" activities are useful. For example, a teacher can have each child draw four different "feeling" faces on paper plates (e.g., happy, sad, angry, confused, excited) and discuss each. A teacher can offer various scenarios, like learning a new song, painting a picture, getting a new pet, or feeling sick, and ask children how they feel about each. Then the teacher can give them new paper plates, having them draw faces showing feelings they often have. Gluing Popsicle sticks to the plates turns them into "masks." The teacher can prompt the children on later days to hold up their masks to illustrate how they feel on a given day and about specific activities/experiences.

MOST IMPORTANT SOCIAL SKILLS

Experts find it crucial for young children's later success in school and life to have experiences that develop understanding of their own and others' emotions, constructive management of their strong feelings, and skills in forming and maintaining relationships. Young children use earlier developed motor skills like pushing/shoving, biting, hitting, or kicking, to get what they want rather than later developing verbal skills. Since physical aggression is antisocial, social development includes learning more acceptable, verbal emotional expressions. "Punch and Judy"–type puppet-shows depicting aggression's failures entertain preschoolers; discussing puppet behavior develops social skills. Teachers have children say which puppets they liked or disliked and considered good or bad, what happened, what might happen next, and how puppets could act differently. Teachers can reinforce children's discussion of meeting needs using words, not violence. Many read-aloud stories explain why people behave certain ways in social contexts; discussion/question-and-answer groups promote empathy, understanding, and listening skills. Assigning collaborative projects, like scrapbooking in small groups, helps young children learn cooperation, turn-taking, listening, and verbally expressing what they want.

PROVIDING AFFECTIVE EXPERIENCES AND PROMOTING EMOTIONAL DEVELOPMENT, PHYSICAL ACTIVITY, AND CREATIVITY

Early childhood teachers can help children understand their feelings and others' feelings, express their emotions, engage in physical exercise, use creative thinking, and have fun by using emotional movement activities. For example, the teacher can begin with prompting the children to demonstrate various types of body movements and postures, like crawling, walking, tiptoeing, skipping, hopping, crouching, slouching, limping, or dancing. Then the teacher can ask the children which feelings they associate with each type of movement and body position. The teacher can play some music for children to move to, and give them instructions such as "Move like you are happy... like you are sad... like you are scared... like you are surprised... like you are angry..." Teachers can also use "freeze"/"statue" dances or games, wherein children move to music and must freeze in position like statues when the music stops; for affective practice, teachers instruct children to depict a certain emotion each time they freeze in place.

Screening, Assessment, Evaluation, and Referral

REQUIRED AND RECOMMENDED INFORMATION IN SCREENING FOR DEVELOPMENTAL DISORDERS

Initial screenings are required, but if a young child has been screened for developmental disorders or delays within the past 6 months and no changes have been observed or reported, repeat screening may be waived. Hearing and vision screenings are mandatory when screening young children. Formal developmental measures are also required, which may include screening tests of motor skills development, cognitive development, social-emotional development, and self-help skills development. Formal screening tests of speech-language development are also required. Additional tests recommended during screening include informal measures. For example, checklists, rating scales, and inventories may be used to screen a child's behavior, mood, and performance of motor skills, cognitive skills, self-help skills, and social and emotional skills. On checklists, parents or caregivers check whether the child does or does not demonstrate listed behaviors, or assessors may complete them via parent or caregiver interviews or interviewing and observing the child. Rating scales ask parents, caregivers, and assessors to rate a child's behaviors, affect, mood, and so on, within a range of numbered and labeled descriptions. Inventories list demonstrated skills and needs. Behavioral observations and existing records and information are also used.

FEATURES OF DEVELOPMENTAL SCREENINGS AND EVALUATIONS

If a child's development is suspected of being delayed—for example, the child is not reaching developmental milestones during expected age ranges—a developmental screening may be administered. Screening tests are quickly performed and yield more general results. The hospital or doctor's office may give a questionnaire to the parent or caregiver to complete for a screening. Alternatively, a health or education professional may administer a screening test to the child. Screening tests are not intended to diagnose specific conditions or give details; they are meant to identify children who may have some problem. Screenings can overidentify or under-identify developmental delays in children. Hence, if the screening identifies a child as having developmental delays, the child is then referred for a developmental evaluation—a much longer, more thorough, comprehensive, in-depth assessment using multiple tests, administered by a psychologist or other highly-trained professional. Evaluation provides a profile of a child's strengths and weaknesses in all developmental domains. Determination of needs for early intervention services or treatment plans is based on evaluation results.

DEVELOPMENTAL EVALUATION DATA TYPES

The child's social history should be obtained, which is typically done by a social worker. Details of the child's developmental progress up until present day; the family's composition, socioeconomic status, and situation; and the child's and family's health and medical histories and status should be emphasized. A physician's or nurse's medical assessment is required, including a physical examination and, if indicated, a specialist's examination. A psychologist typically assesses intellectual and cognitive development; at least one such test is generally required. At least one test of adaptive behavior is also required to assess emotional-social development. Self-help skills are evaluated; this may be included within cognitive, adaptive behavior, or programming assessments. Communication skills are typically evaluated by a speech-language pathologist. Both receptive and expressive language must be tested comprehensively rather than simply by single-word vocabulary tests. As indicated, speech articulation is also tested. At least one test of motor skills, typically administered by a physical or occupational therapist, is required. Programming evaluation requires at least one criterion-referenced or curriculum-based measure, typically administered by an educator.

BEHAVIORAL VARIATIONS AND CHARACTERISTICS OF ADHD

While the chief symptoms associated with ADHD are inattentiveness, impulsive behavior, distractibility, and excessive physical activity, there is considerable variation among individual children having ADHD. For example, the degree of severity of this condition can vary widely from one child to the next. In addition, each child can vary in how much he or she exhibits each of these primary characteristics. Some children might not appear to behave very impulsively but show severe deficits in attention. Some may focus better, but only for short periods, and are very easily distracted. Some display very disruptive behavior, while others do not but may daydream excessively, not attending to programming. In general, children who have ADHD can show deficits in following rules and directions. Also, when their developmental skills are evaluated or observed, they are likely to demonstrate inconsistencies in performance over time. To identify or select specific intervention methods and strategies, professionals should use a comprehensive evaluation to obtain information about the child's specific behaviors in his or her natural environment that need remediation.

CHILD FIND

Child Find is an ongoing process with the aim of locating, identifying, and referring young children with disabilities and their families as early as possible for service programs. This process consists of activities designed to raise public awareness and screenings and evaluations to identify and diagnose disabilities. The federal IDEA law mandates under Part B that disabled children are guaranteed early childhood special education services and under Part C that infants and toddlers at risk for developmental delays are guaranteed early intervention programs. (Eligibility guidelines vary by US state.) The IDEA requires school districts to find, identify, and evaluate children with disabilities in their attendance areas. School districts have facilitated this Child Find process by establishing community-informed referral networks whose members refer children who may have exceptional educational needs (EENs). Network members typically include parents, doctors, birth-to-3 programs, child care programs, Head Start programs, public health agencies, social service agencies, and any other community members with whom the young children come into contact.

CURRENT COLLABORATIVE APPROACHES AND MODELS OF SCREENING

Historically, the tradition was to conduct kindergarten screenings of children entering schools around age 5. However, in recent years, school districts have developed community referral networks to assist in the processes of Child Find, screening, evaluation, and referral for early intervention and early childhood special education and related services. Current models are more informal, proactive, and collaborative. Cooperative educational interagency service efforts give parents information about normal early childhood development and available community resources and offer opportunities for developmental screenings of their young children. Specific procedures are governed by individual US state laws. Generally, district networks implementing current models send developmental review forms to parents to complete in advance, and then they attend a developmental screening at a community site. Parents discuss normal early childhood growth and development with program staff, while, in the same room, trained professionals observe their children as they play. Children's vision and hearing are also screened. Parents can discuss their children's current development with psychologists, early childhood educators, or counselors. Thereafter, they can learn about community resources.

DEFINING DEVELOPMENTAL DELAYS IN INFANTS AND TODDLERS

The IDEA Part C specifies the areas of development that states must include in defining developmental delays. However, individual states must identify the criteria they use to determine eligibility, including pertinent diagnostic instruments, procedures, and functional levels. States currently use quantitative and qualitative measures. Quantitative criteria for developmental delay include the difference between chronological age and performance level, expressed as a percentage of chronological age; performance at a given number of months below chronological age; or number of standard deviations (SDs) below mean of performance on a norm-referenced test. Qualitative criteria include the development considered atypical or delayed for established norms or observed behaviors considered atypical. At least one state differentially defines delay according to a child's age in months, with the rationale that a 25% delay, for example, is very different for a 1-year-old than a 3-year-old. Quantitative criteria for defining delay and determining eligibility vary widely among states. A 25% or 20% delay (2 SDs below mean in 1+ areas or 1.5 SD below mean in 2+ areas) is some common state criteria.

Single and Multiple Risk Factors in Infants and Toddlers for Developmental Delays

Scientists find that developmental outcomes for children are not reliably predicted by any one risk factor or event. Developmental risk increases with increased biological, medical, or environmental risk factors. However, researchers have found some variables that afford resiliency in children to offset risk factors. These can include the child's basic temperament, the child having high self-esteem, the child having a good emotional relationship with at least one parent, and the child having experiences of successful learning. These findings indicate that assessments should include criteria for multiple biological and environmental risk factors, for cumulative biological and environmental risk factors, and for protective or resilience factors, considering all of these in the context of change occurring over time. Under the IDEA, US states have the option to provide early intervention services to children considered at risk for adverse developmental outcomes as well as those already identified with them. Some states apply multiple-risk models, requiring three to five risk factors for service eligibility. Some states also determine eligibility with less DD when biological, medical, or environmental risk factors also exist.

Information Sources on Early Intervention and Preschool Special Education Services

Military families stationed both in the United States and overseas who have young special needs children can seek information and assistance from the federally funded organization Specialized Training of Military Families (STOMP). The staff of STOMP is composed of parents having special needs children themselves, who also have been trained to work with other parents of special needs children. STOMP staff members are spouses of military personnel who thus understand the unique, specialized circumstances and needs of military families. Another government agency, the US Department of Defense, includes the office of the Department of Defense Education Activity (DoDEA) and provides comprehensive guidance to military families with special needs children who are eligible to receive, or are receiving, free appropriate public education (FAPE) as mandated by the IDEA law, whether that education is located in the United States or in other countries.

Providing Special Education Services for Preschoolers

If parents observe that their preschooler is not attaining developmental milestones within the expected age ranges or does not seem to be developing in the same way as most other children, they should seek evaluation for possible developmental delay or disability. Although 3-to-5-year-olds are likely not in elementary school yet, the elementary school in a family's school district is still the best first contact because the IDEA law specifies that school districts must provide special education services at no family cost to eligible children, including preschoolers. Another excellent source of more information about special education is the National Dissemination Center for Children with Disabilities (NICHCY) of the US Department of Education's Office of Special Education Programs. They partner with nonprofit organizations like the Academy for Educational

Development (AED) to produce useful documents for families with special needs children. NICHCY supplies state resource sheets listing main contacts regarding special education services in each US state. Families can obtain these sheets at NICHCY's website or by telephone.

INFORMATION SOURCES FOR EVALUATION TO DETERMINE DEVELOPMENTAL DISABILITY

Under the IDEA (Individuals with Disabilities Education Act), evaluation information sources include: physicians' reports, the child's medical history, developmental test results, current classroom observations and assessments (when applicable), completed developmental and behavioral checklists, feedback and observations from parents and all other members of the evaluation team, and any other significant records, reports, and observations regarding the child. Under the IDEA, the parents are involved in the evaluation, along with at least one regular education teacher and special education teacher, if the child has these, and any special education service provider working with the child—for children receiving early intervention services from birth through age 2 and transitioning to preschool special education, it may be an early intervention service provider; a school administrator knowledgeable about children with disabilities, special education policies, regular education curriculum, and resources available; a psychologist or educator who can interpret evaluation results and discuss indicated instruction; individuals with special expertise or knowledge regarding the child (recruited by school or parents); when appropriate, the child; and other professionals, for example, physical or occupational therapists, speech therapists, medical specialists, and so on.

SPECIAL EDUCATION SERVICES FOR PRESCHOOL CHILDREN

Special education for preschoolers is education specifically designed to meet the individual needs of a child aged 3 to 5 years with a disability or developmental delay. The specialized design of this instruction can include adaptations to the content, the teaching methods, and the way instruction is delivered to meet a disabled child's unique needs. Special education for preschoolers includes various settings, such as in the home, classrooms, hospitals, institutions, and others. It also includes a range of related services, such as speech-language pathology services, specialized physical education instruction, early vocational training, and training in travel skills. The school district's special education system provides evaluation and services to eligible preschoolers free of charge. Evaluation's purposes are to determine whether a child has a disability under the IDEA's definitions and determine that child's present educational needs.

POST-EVALUATION AND THE INDIVIDUALIZED EDUCATION PROGRAM

After a preschool child is evaluated, the parents and involved school personnel meet to discuss the evaluation results. Parents are included in the group that decides whether the child is eligible for special education services based on those results. For eligible children, the parents and school personnel will develop an IEP. Every child who will receive special education services must have an IEP. The main purposes of the IEP are (1) to establish reasonable educational goals for the individual child and (2) to indicate what services the school district will provide to the child. The IEP includes a statement of the child's present levels of functioning and performance. It also includes a list of more general instructional goals for the child to achieve through school and parental support along with more specific learning objectives reflecting those goals and specifying exactly what the child will be able to demonstrate, under what circumstances, how much of the time—for example, a percentage of recorded instances—and within what time period (e.g., 1 year).

INDIVIDUALIZED EDUCATION PROGRAM GOALS AND OBJECTIVES

In an IEP, the goals are more global, describing a skill for the child to acquire or a task to master. The objectives are more specific articulations of achievements that will demonstrate the child's mastery of the goal. For example, if a goal is for the child to increase his or her functional communicative vocabulary, a related objective might be for the child to acquire x number of new words in x length of time; another related objective could be for the child to use the words acquired in 90% of recorded relevant situations. If the goal is for the child to demonstrate knowledge and discrimination of colors, one objective might be for the child to identify correctly a red, yellow, and blue block 95% of the time when asked to point out each color within a group of blocks. Progress toward or achievement of some objectives may be measured via formal tests; with preschoolers, many others are measured via observational data collection.

PROGRESS MONITORING, UPDATING, AND REVISING IEPS

Once a child has been identified with a disability, has been determined eligible for special education and related services under the IDEA, and has had an IEP developed and implemented, the child's progress must be monitored. Monitoring methods may be related to evaluation methods. For example, if a child identified with problem behaviors was initially evaluated using a behavioral checklist, school personnel can use the same checklist periodically, comparing its results to the baseline levels of frequency and severity originally obtained. If an affective disorder or disturbance was identified and instruments like the Beck Depression Inventory or Anxiety Inventory were used, these can be used again periodically; reduced symptoms would indicate progress. If progress with IEP goals and objectives is less or greater than expected, the IEP team meets and may revise the program. This can include specifying shorter or longer times to achieve some goals and objectives; lowering or raising requirements proving too difficult or easy; resetting successive objective criteria in smaller or larger increments; changing teaching methods, content, or materials used; and so on.

INFORMAL ASSESSMENT INSTRUMENTS

Early childhood teachers assess pre-K children's performance in individual, small-group, and whole-class activities throughout the day using informal tools that are teacher-made, school-, program-, or district-furnished, or procured by school systems from commercial educational resources. For classroom observations, teachers might complete a form based on their observations during class story or circle time, organized using three themes per day, each targeting different skills—social-emotional, math, alphabet knowledge, oral language, or emergent writing. They note the names of children demonstrating the specified skill and those who might need follow-up, and provide needed one on one interventions daily. For individual observations, teachers might fill out a chart divided into domains like physical development, oral language development, math, emergent reading, emergent writing, science and health, fine arts, technology and media, social studies, social-emotional development, and approaches to learning, noting one child's strengths and needs in each area per chart. In addition to guided observation records, teachers complete checklists, keep anecdotal and running records, and assemble portfolio assessments of children's work. Tracking children's progress informs responsive instructional planning.

SCREENING VERSUS ASSESSMENT INSTRUMENTS

A variety of screening and assessment instruments exist for early childhood measurement. Some key areas where they differ include which developmental domains are measured by an instrument; for which applications an instrument is meant to be used; to which age ranges an instrument applies; the methods by which a test or tool is administered; the requirements for scoring and interpreting a test, scale, or checklist; whether an instrument is appropriate for use with ethnically diverse populations; and whether a tool is statistically found to have good validity and reliability. Early childhood program administrators should choose instruments that can measure the developmental areas pertinent to their program; support their program's established goals; and include all early childhood ages served in their program. Instruments' administration, scoring, and interpretation methods should be congruent with program personnel's skills. Test/measure administration should involve realistic time durations. Instruments/tools should be appropriate to use with ethnically diverse and non-English-speaking children and families. Tests should also be proven psychometrically accurate and dependable enough.

Typical Applications of Screening and Assessment Instruments

The ways in which screening and assessment instruments applicable to early childhood education are used include a wide range of variations. For example, early childhood education programs typically need to identify children who might have developmental disorders or delays. Screening instruments are used to identify those children showing signs of possible problems who need assessments, not to diagnose problems. Assessment instruments are used to develop and/or confirm diagnoses of developmental disorders or delays. Assessment tools are also used to help educators and therapists plan curricular and treatment programs. Another important function of assessment instruments is to determine a child's eligibility for a given program. In addition, once children are placed in early childhood education programs, assessment tools can be used to monitor their progress and other changes occurring over time. Moreover, program administrators can use assessment instruments to evaluate children's achievement of the learning outcomes that define their program goals, and, by extension, the teachers' effectiveness in furthering children's achievement of those outcomes.

Formal Assessment Instruments

Formal assessment instruments are typically standardized tests, administered to groups. They give norms for age groups/developmental levels for comparison. They are designed to avoid administrator bias and capture children's responses only. Their data can be scaled and be reported in aggregate to school/program administrators and policymakers. The Scholastic Early Childhood Inventory (SECI) is a formal one-on-one instrument to assess children's progress in four domains found to predict kindergarten readiness: phonological awareness, oral language development, alphabet knowledge, and mathematics. Other instruments measuring multiple developmental domains include the Assessment, Evaluation, and Programming System (0–6 years) for planning intervention; the Bayley Scale for Infant Development (1–42 months) for assessing developmental delays; the Brigance Diagnostic Inventory of Early Development (0–7 years) for planning instruction; the Developmental Profile II (0–6 years) to assess special needs and support IEP development; the Early Coping Inventory (4–36 months) and Early Learning Accomplishment Profile (0–36 months), both for planning interventions; and the Infant-Toddler Developmental Assessment (0–42 months) to screen for developmental delays.

Screening and Assessment Instruments Measuring Development

The available screening and assessment instruments for early childhood development cover a wide range in scope and areas of focus. Some measures are comprehensive, assessing young children's progress in many developmental domains, including sensory, motor, physical, cognitive, linguistic, emotional, and social. Some other instruments focus exclusively on only one domain, such as language development or emotional-social development. Some instruments even focus within a domain upon only one of its facets, (e.g., upon attachment or temperament within the domain of emotional-social development). In addition, some tools measure risk and resiliency factors influencing developmental delays and disorders. Programs like Head Start that promote general early childhood development should select comprehensive assessment instruments. Outreach programs targeting better identification of children having untreated and/or undetected mental health problems should choose instruments assessing social-emotional development. Clinics treating children with regulatory disorders might select an instrument measuring temperament. Prevention programs helping multiple-needs families access supports and services could use a measure for risk and resiliency factors. Multifaceted early childhood programs often benefit most from using several instruments in combination.

Age Ranges Included in Various Screening and Assessment Instruments

An important consideration for screening and assessment in early childhood is that early childhood development is very dynamic and occurs rapidly. Hence, screening and assessment instruments must be sensitive to such frequent and pronounced developmental changes. Some instruments target specific age ranges like 0–36 months. Others cover wider ranges, such as children aged 2–16 years. The latter may have internal means of application to smaller age ranges; for example, sections respectively for 3–6-month-old babies, 7–12-month-olds, and 12–18-month-olds. Or they indicate different scoring and interpretation criteria by age; for example, some screening tools specify different numbers of test items depending on the child's age to indicate a need for assessment. Choosing screening and assessment instruments covering the entire age range served in an early childhood education program is advantageous—not only because they can be used with all child ages in the program but also because they can be administered and readministered at the beginning and end of programs and/or in between, to compare and monitor changes, which is difficult with separate, age-specific tests.

Features of Paper-and-Pencil Reports

The most common form of paper-and-pencil report about infants and young children is the questionnaire. Parents, caregivers, and teachers read printed questions or statements and respond by selecting Yes or No to a question or a number/level on a Likert-type scale showing the degree to which they agree with a statement. For self-administration, instruments must contain questions/statements written on reading levels accessible to the respondents and in their native languages. Alternatively, some questionnaires or surveys can be read to the respondent by an interviewer trained in or familiar with administration of the chosen instrument. Such self-reporting instruments usually take fewer than 20 minutes to finish, and early childhood education program personnel need comparatively little training to administer them. However, employees may need further training to score and/or interpret responses, or already-trained specialists may score and interpret them in some cases. Early childhood schools, programs, and agencies can obtain some self-reporting instruments free of charge; other tools' publishers charge for response forms; and others charge only for initially obtaining their materials, allowing purchasers to reproduce them thereafter.

Features of Formal and Informal Observations

Some instruments require early childhood staff to watch a child's behavior and/or interactions with parents/caregivers and/or peers. Formal observations involve watching activities structured for the screening/assessment instrument. Informal observations involve watching a child's activities in natural settings like at home or in preschool during play times. Formal observation tools typically require staff to be trained to administer them. The trained observers' findings can include records of which developmentally normal behaviors a child has attained, incidences of problem behaviors noted, descriptions and evaluations of the quality of a child's social interactions with other people, and other observations of the child's behaviors that can inform screening and assessment. Observational screening and assessment instruments usually take more than 20 minutes for administration. Publishers of observational tests typically charge early childhood programs to order single-use recording forms; some allow them to purchase templates and then reproduce the forms.

SCORING AND INTERPRETATION OF VARIOUS SCREENING AND ASSESSMENT INSTRUMENTS

Some instruments are fairly simple to score and interpret, needing little training of early childhood personnel. For example, paper-and-pencil questionnaires or surveys often only need the points for each item response added up for a total score; or a group of scores is obtained by summing values within sections. Interpreting some screening scores can be as simple as noting whether a child's score surpasses a designated cut-off value that signals assessment is needed. Such screenings can be scored and interpreted right after administration and readily shared with parents and other stakeholders. Assessment instruments using more complicated scoring and interpretation include such procedures as weighting item values, reversing point values for certain items, converting raw scores into standardized scores or percentages, and referring to tables giving national norms for comparison. Standardized tests, including preschool IQ scales, commonly involve such methods. Assessors often need considerable training, advanced psychometric education and experience, thorough knowledge of early childhood development, and additional time to score and interpret these tests. Results may be discussed in separately scheduled meetings.

INTERVIEW FEATURES

In early childhood programs conducting assessments, personnel usually conduct interviews with a child's parents, teachers, and/or caregivers. Interviews can be made in structured formats, wherein the administrator reads prescribed questions as written to the interviewee, or semi-structured formats, wherein the administrator uses his or her judgment to add more questions to the written ones until he or she determines that the information provided is complete enough. Interview questions vary, covering subjects of parental concern, the child's identified areas of strengths and accomplishments, the child's identified areas of deficits or needs, the interactions between parents and child, and the child's behavior. Interviews can be brief, but usually, they are longer than paper-and-pencil self-reporting questionnaires, surveys, or checklists. Early childhood personnel frequently need to be trained to administer published interview-based instruments. Publishers typically charge schools, programs, and agencies for ordering multiple, single-use response forms, or they may require a one-time order and allow them to reproduce the forms from their initial purchase to use for multiple administrations.

FEATURES OF SCREENING AND ASSESSMENT TOOLS USING STRUCTURED TASKS

Screening and assessment instruments that use structured tasks involve a list of behaviors and/or skills that a child is expected to attain by a certain age range or developmental level. The administrators must present various activities or tasks to a child and then record the details of the child's performance of each activity or task. Instruments using structured tasks require early childhood staff training for administration. They take over 20 minutes to complete. Early childhood programs, schools, and agencies must buy testing equipment and materials as well as single-use recording forms. Because paper-and-pencil questionnaires and surveys are easy to administer, apply across various settings (e.g., preschools, pediatricians' waiting rooms, homes, etc.), cost comparatively little, require minimal administrator training, and are frequently short, they are appropriate for screening use. While formal and informal observational tools, structured and semi-structured interview tools, and structured-task tools take more training, time, and expense, they also provide more detailed information, making them useful for determining diagnoses and/or developing individualized care or instruction plans. Instruments using multiple methods, such as collecting data from various settings and respondents, yield the most comprehensive information.

TEST-RETEST RELIABILITY

Test-retest reliability is a measure of how consistent an instrument's results are across test administrations. An instrument with good test-retest reliability yields the same results when administered twice or more to the same child within a short time. For example, the same assessor gives a child the same test twice within a few days or weeks, comparing the results. The more similar the results between and among administrations, the higher the test-retest reliability. This implies the instrument measures an attribute or construct that is stable over a short time. Due to the inherent rapidity and dynamism of early childhood development, significant developmental changes are expected over years and months, but over only weeks or days, we expect little or no substantial change. Therefore, instruments whose results are not stable over a short time are less utile for early childhood screening or assessment. For example, a child's scoring with "typical development" on one administration but "possible delay/disorder" a week later means the instrument does not define the child's developmental needs and thus is not reliable.

INTER-RATER RELIABILITY OF SCREENING AND ASSESSMENT INSTRUMENTS

Inter-rater reliability is a measure of how stable an instrument's results are across different individual administrators (raters). Good inter-rater reliability means the instrument will give the same or similar results for the same child, at the same time, in the same setting, when administered by different people. This shows that the instrument measures a quality or construct that remains stable regardless of who administers the test. Significant differences among different raters' results present problems, especially with instruments using unstructured interviews, observations, or structured tasks. For example, if one rater scores a child as possibly having a developmental delay or disorder while another rater using the same test scores the same child as within the range of normal development, the instrument does not identify the child's true developmental needs and is unreliable. When different assessors (like parent vs. teacher) observe a child in different settings, though, like home vs. preschool, and/or at different times, varying results are expected and not necessarily indicative of inter-rater unreliability because children's behaviors can vary by setting.

INTERNAL CONSISTENCY REGARDING TEST INSTRUMENTS

A testing instrument is said to have internal consistency when its individual items correlate strongly with each other and with the total test score. This means that all of the individual items (questions, stimuli, tasks, etc.) measure parts of the same construct that the test is intended to measure. A test with low internal consistency could be measuring additional attributes that the authors did not define or mean for the test to measure. Children with disparate developmental needs could thus receive similar scores, based on different test items. With comprehensive screening and assessment instruments that cover multiple domains of development, early childhood educators should look for internal consistency within each subscale of the test or within each domain tested. However, they should not necessarily expect internal consistency among the different domains or at the level of the test's overall score. For example, they should not expect a high correlation between a test's subscale measuring a child's language skills development and its subscale measuring a child's gross motor skills development.

INTERNAL CONSISTENCY AND SCREENING AND ASSESSMENT INSTRUMENTS

Whether a test's individual items contribute to measuring the construct the test is supposed to measure is internal consistency. It is determined by how much the test's individual items correlate with one another and with the overall score. A test with high internal consistency more accurately measures the specific content area, developmental domain, or construct it means to measure. A test with low internal consistency poses problems when children who might have very different needs get the same score. For example, if a test meant to measure aggression has low internal consistency, its individual items are not correlated with one another or the overall score, implying it tests more than one construct. Two children given this test could score beyond the cutoff level, indicating diagnosis or assessment need, but their scores could be due to completely different individual test items. Since individual test items do not correlate, the two children might have markedly different needs. Furthermore, those needs may not be related to aggression, since the test probably unintentionally measures additional constructs.

CONCURRENT VALIDITY REGARDING SCREENING AND ASSESSMENT INSTRUMENTS

When a screening or assessment instrument yields results comparable to those of another instrument whose validity has been previously established, it has good concurrent validity. Since the test used for comparison was already found valid, users have confidence in its results. Therefore, their confidence is warranted in another test showing high concurrent validity with the established test. For example, the Stanford-Binet Intelligence Scales and the Wechsler Preschool and Primary Scales of Intelligence (WPPSI) are both well-established IQ tests with demonstrated statistical validity and reliability. So if early childhood educators have found or been given a new instrument for measuring intelligence, they are likely to find that its authors have compared the test's results to the results obtained by the Stanford-Binet and/or WPPSI. Educators who have confidence in the Stanford-Binet and/or the WPPSI are then justified in having comparable confidence in the new test if its results were found similar to those of the established tests, indicating its high concurrent validity.

CONTENT VALIDITY REGARDING SCREENING AND ASSESSMENT INSTRUMENTS

Whether a test instrument measures the entire content area it purports to measure is known as content validity. It determines whether a test can yield accurate and fair measures of the totality of the construct that the assessor wants to test. For example, if a screening instrument is intended to measure social-emotional development in a young child, it should include individual test items covering the range of this domain's important components. A screening test that covers a child's interactions with caregivers but not with peers; screens attention but not initiation of play; or screens for social skills but not communication skills would not address all elements of social-emotional development and thus not have good content validity. Early childhood educators can use instruments with high content validity to generalize with more confidence about how a child's test performance predicts his or her levels of functioning in real life. By contrast, if a test has low content validity, generalizations about the tested child's development can exceed the test's scope and be inaccurate and/or unrealistic.

PREDICTIVE VALIDITY IN SCREENING AND ASSESSMENT INSTRUMENTS

A screening/assessment instrument's prediction of a child's behavior in real life is predictive validity. For example, an instrument screening for social-emotional disorders in preschool children might predict tantrums and/or oppositional behaviors in kindergarten. In another example, you would expect a screening instrument for social-emotional disorders to differentiate between children with typical social-emotional development and those with mental health disorders. If a screening tool identifies a child with a potential mental health disorder and has high predictive validity, a complete clinical diagnostic evaluation of the screened child would diagnose a mental health disorder. Sensitivity is the instrument's accuracy—here, in identifying developmental disorders/delays, if it correctly identifies 9 of 10 children really having disorders/delays, it has 90 percent sensitivity. Specificity conversely would be accuracy in identifying children without disorders/delays. Despite high sensitivity and specificity, screeners yield some errors. False-positives over-identify delays/disorders where none exist; false-negatives under-identify existing delays/disorders. Unnecessary concern is a consequence of false positives; lack of prevention, early intervention, and/or treatment are more serious consequences of false negatives.

NORM-REFERENCED VERSUS CRITERION-REFERENCED TESTS

Norm-referenced tests compare a child's test results to those of a comparison group of other children in the same age group, grade, or developmental level. This comparison group is called a normative or standardization sample. Norm-referenced tests show how an individual child's performance compares to that of the general population of children. Criterion-referenced tests compare a child's test results to a predetermined standard of performance for the child's age group/grade/level. They show how an individual child's performance compares to standards established by educational experts. Norm-referenced tests are useful for determining whether a child is similar to the "average" child and identifying children performing significantly above or below average. Criterion-referenced tests are good for measuring the extent to which an individual child has mastered areas or domains of development and for monitoring changes over time in the child's levels of mastery.

APPLYING ASSESSMENT RESULTS TO PLANNING INSTRUCTION FOR INDIVIDUALS AND GROUPS

Early childhood education settings should provide organized outlines of developmentally appropriate guidelines for their children, including when and how to introduce and reinforce guidelines at each learning stage. These outlines are foundations for anecdotal observations and authentic assessments tracking developmental progress. Early childhood education programs supply opportunities and activities to develop each discrete skill, including copious review and practice young children require for retention. Teachers should plan learning experiences meaningfully promoting developing identified guidelines and addressing children's interests. Early childhood education settings should have organized progress-tracking systems following developmental sequences. These help teachers determine whether a child can move to the next level or prior skills that need additional reinforcement. Tracking systems should be easy to maintain and immediately give teachers basic information regarding each child's level of functioning for planning activities and discussions. Teachers should then create "ready reference" charts/graphs of assessment and monitoring results, giving an idea of the class/group's general functioning level, to inform activity and lesson planning and additional support needed for individual children—one on one for those below class/group level, enriched for those above it.

ESTABLISHING AND MAINTAINING GOOD COMMUNICATION WITH PARENTS

When teachers send home a letter to parents explaining classroom practices and giving contact information at the beginning of the school year, parents perceive them as approachable and available. When a teacher calls each parent/guardian during school's first two weeks, parents appreciate and enjoy conversations. Calls also make it easier for teachers to contact parents later in the year regarding child issues if needed. Experts find it effective to mail postcards home, addressed to children or parents. Establishing simple class websites including teacher contact information facilitates parental access. Teachers' printing business cards and attaching them to their first parent letters conveys professionalism. Teachers using the internet or print to publish regular class newsletters informally keep parents apprised of children's instruction and teach parents to expect communication. Teachers can send parents invitations to visit prior to school or program open houses; teachers are perceived as more approachable when more parents are comfortable in classrooms. Having children write appreciation letters to parents for open houses encourages children to invite parents; parents also perceive teacher appreciation by association.

Play and Learning Environment for Young Children

Developmentally Appropriate Learning Environment

LEV VYGOTSKY AND THE ZONE OF PROXIMAL DEVELOPMENT

Vygotsky identified an area or range of skills wherein a learner can complete a task he or she could not yet complete independently, given some help. He termed this area the zone of proximal development (ZPD). Vygotsky found if a child is given assistance, guidance, or support from someone who knows more—especially another child just slightly more advanced in knowledge and/or skills—the first child can not only succeed at a task he or she is still unable to do alone, but that child also learns best through accomplishing something just slightly beyond his or her limits of expertise to do alone. Jerome Bruner coined the term *scaffolding* to describe temporary support that others give learners for achieving tasks. Scaffolding is closely related to the ZPD in that only the amount of support needed is given, and it allows the learner to accomplish things he or she could not complete autonomously. Scaffolding is gradually withdrawn as the child's skills develop, until the child reaches the level of expertise needed to complete the task on his or her own.

MONTESSORI METHOD

SECTIONS OF THE MONTESSORI METHOD OF EARLY CHILDHOOD INSTRUCTION

The Practical Life area of Montessori classes helps children develop care for self, others, and the environment. Children learn many daily skills, including buttoning, pouring liquids, preparing meals, and cleaning up after meals and activities. The Sensorial area gives young children experience with learning through all five senses. They participate in activities like ordering colors from lightest to darkest, sorting objects from roughest to smoothest texture, and sorting items from biggest to smallest/longest to shortest. They learn to match similar tastes, textures, and sounds. The Language Arts area encourages young children to express themselves in words, and they learn to identify letters, match them with corresponding phonemes (speech sounds), and manually trace their shapes as preparation for learning reading, spelling, grammar, and writing. In the Mathematics and Geometry area, children learn to recognize numbers, count, add, subtract, multiply, divide, and use the decimal system via hands-on learning with concrete materials. In the Cultural Subjects area, children learn science, art, music, movement, time, history, geography, and zoology.

ASPECTS OF THE PHILOSOPHY OF THE MONTESSORI METHOD AS A CURRICULUM APPROACH

Maria Montessori's method emphasizes children's engagement in self-directed activities, with teachers using clinical observations to act as children's guides. In introducing and teaching concepts, the Montessori Method also employs self-correcting ("autodidactic") equipment. This method focuses on the significance and interrelatedness of all life forms and the need for every individual to find his or her place in the world and to find meaningful work. Children in Montessori schools learn complex math skills and gain knowledge about diverse cultures and languages. Montessori philosophy puts emphasis on adapting learning environments to individual children's developmental levels. The Montessori Method also believes in teaching both practical skills and abstract concepts through the medium of physical activities. Montessori teachers observe and identify children's movements into sensitive periods when they are best prepared to receive individual lessons in subjects of interest to them that they can grasp readily. Children's senses of

81

autonomy and self-esteem are encouraged in Montessori programs. Montessori instructors also strive to engage parents in their children's education.

GENERAL PRACTICES IN THE MONTESSORI METHOD

What Montessori calls "work" refers to developmentally appropriate learning materials. These are set out so each student can see the choices available. Children can select items from each of Montessori's five sections: Practical Life, Sensorial, Language Arts, Mathematics and Geometry, and Cultural Subjects. When a child is done with a work, he or she replaces it for another child to use and selects another work. Teachers work one-on-one with children and in groups; however, the majority of interactions are among children, as Montessori stresses self-directed activity. Not only teachers but also older children help younger ones in learning new skills, so Montessori classes usually incorporate 2- or 3-year age ranges. Depending on students' ages and the individual school, Montessori school days are generally half-days, 9 a.m.–noon or 12:30 p.m. Most Montessori schools also offer afternoon and/or early evening options. Children wanting to "do it myself" benefit from Montessori, as do special-needs children. Individualized attention, independence, and hands-on learning are emphasized. Montessori schools prefer culturally diverse students and teach about diverse cultures.

SCHEDULES OF REINFORCEMENT IN BEHAVIORISM

Continuous schedules of presenting rewards or punishments are fixed. Fixed ratio schedules involve introducing reinforcement after a set number of instances of the targeted behavior. For example, when asking a preschooler to put away materials, a teacher might present punishment for noncompliance only after making three consecutive requests. The disadvantage is that even young children know they can get away with ignoring the first two requests, only complying just before the third. Fixed interval schedules introduce reinforcement after set time periods. Again, there is a disadvantage: even multiply disabled infants quickly learn when to expect reinforcement, rather than associating it with how long they have engaged in a desired behavior; young children only change their behavior immediately before the teacher will observe and reward it. Variable ratio and variable interval schedules apply reinforcement following irregular numbers of responses or irregular time periods, respectively. The advantage of variable schedules is that, since children cannot predict when they will receive reinforcements, they are more likely to repeat/continue desired behaviors more and for longer times.

BANK STREET CURRICULUM APPROACH TO EARLY CHILDHOOD EDUCATION

Lucy Sprague Mitchell founded the Bank Street curriculum, applying theoretical concepts from Jean Piaget, Erik Erikson, John Dewey, and others. Bank Street is called a developmental-interaction approach. It emphasizes children's rich, direct interactions with a wide variety of ideas, materials, and people in their environments. The Bank Street method gives young children opportunities for physical, cognitive, emotional, and social development through engagement in various types of child care programs. Typically, multiple subjects are included and taught to groups. Children can learn through a variety of methods and at different developmental levels. By interacting directly with their geographical, social, and political environments, children are prepared for lifelong learning through this curriculum. Using blocks, solving puzzles, going on field trips, and doing practical lab work are among the numerous learning experiences Bank Street offers. Its philosophy is that school can simultaneously be stimulating, satisfying, and sensible. School is a significant part of children's lives, where they inquire about and experiment with the environment and share ideas with other children as they mature.

CLASSROOM CHARACTERISTICS FOR 5- TO 6-YEAR-OLDS

The Bank Street approach to teaching recommends that children 5–6 years old should have classrooms that are efficient, organized, conducive to working, and designed to afford them sensory and motor learning experiences. Classrooms should include rich varieties of appealing colors, which tend to energize children's imaginations and activity and encourage them to interact with the surroundings and participate in the environment. "Interest corners" in classrooms are advocated by the Bank Street approach. These are places where children can display their artworks, use language, and depict social life experiences. This approach also recommends having multipurpose tables in the classroom that children can use for writing, drawing, and other classroom activities. The Bank Street approach also points out the importance of libraries in schools, not just for supporting classroom content but for providing materials for children's extracurricular reading.

REQUIREMENTS AND ROLES OF CLASSROOMS AND TEACHERS

The Bank Street approach requires educators to create well-designed classrooms: this curriculum approach finds children are enabled to develop discipline by growing up in such controlled environments. Teachers are considered to be extremely significant figures in their young students' lives. The Bank Street approach requires that teachers always treat children with respect, to enable children to develop strong senses of self-respect. Teachers' having faith in their students and believing in their ability to succeed are found to have great impacts on young children's performance and their motivation to excel in school and in life. The Bank Street Curriculum emphasizes the importance of providing transitions from one type of activity to another. It also stresses changing the learning subjects at regular time intervals. This facilitates children's gaining a sense of direction and taking responsibility for what they do. Bank Street views these practices as helping children develop internal self-control, affording them discipline for dealing with the external world.

FROEBEL'S EDUCATIONAL THEORY REGARDING LEARNING AND TEACHING

Friedrich Froebel (1782–1852) originated the concept and practice of kindergarten (German for "child's garden"). He found that observation, discovery, play, and free, self directed activity facilitated children's learning. He observed that drawing/art activities develop higher-level cognitive skills and that virtues are taught through children's games. He also found nature, songs, fables, stories, poems, and crafts to be effective learning media. He attributed reading and writing development to children's self-expression needs. Froebel recommended activities to develop children's motor skills and stimulate their imaginations. He believed in equal rather than authoritarian teacher-student relationships, and advocated family involvement/collaboration. He pointed out the critical nature of sensory experiences, and the value of life experiences for self-expression. He believed teachers should support students' discovery learning rather than prescribing what to learn. Like Piaget, Dewey, and Montessori, Froebel embraced constructivist learning, i.e. children construct meaning and reality through their interactions with the environment. He stressed the role of parents, particularly mothers, in children's educational processes.

FROEBEL'S FAMOUS ACHIEVEMENT

Froebel's theory of education had widespread influences, including using play-based instruction with young children. Froebel's educational theory emphasized the unity of humanity, nature, and God. Froebel believed the success of the individual dictates the success of the race, and that school's role is to direct students' will. He believed nature is the heart of all learning. He felt unity, individuality, and diversity were important values achieved through education. Froebel said education's goals include developing self-control and spirituality. He recommended curricula include math, language, design, art, health, hygiene, and physical education. He noted school's role in social development. According to Froebel, schools should impart meaning to life experiences; show students relationships among external, previously unrelated knowledge; and associate facts with principles. Froebel felt human potential is defined through individual accomplishments. He believed humans generally are productive and creative, attaining completeness and harmony via maturation.

SIEGFRIED ENGELMANN'S CONTRIBUTIONS TO EARLY CHILDHOOD EDUCATION

Siegfried Engelmann (b. 1931) cofounded the Bereiter-Engelmann Program with Carl Bereiter with funding from the US Office of Education. This project demonstrated the ability of intensive instruction to enhance cognitive skills in disadvantaged preschool-aged children, establishing the Bereiter-Engelmann Preschool Program. Bereiter and Engelmann also conducted experiments reexamining Piaget's theory of cognitive development, specifically concerning the ability to conserve liquid volume. They showed it could be taught, contrary to Piaget's contention that this ability depended solely on a child's cognitive-developmental stage. Engelmann researched curriculum and instruction, including preschoolers with Down syndrome and children from impoverished backgrounds, establishing the philosophy and methodology of Direct Instruction. He designed numerous reading, math, spelling, language, and writing instruction programs, as well as achievement tests, videos, and games. Engelmann worked with Project Head Start and Project Follow Through. The former included his and Wesley Becker's comparison of their Engelmann-Becker model of early childhood instruction with other models in teaching disadvantaged children. The latter is often considered the biggest controlled study ever comparing teaching models and methods.

ENGELMANN'S METHODS AND FEATURES OF HIS CURRICULA

In the 1960s, Engelmann noted a lack of research into how young children learn. Wanting to find out what kinds of teaching affected retention and what the extent was of individual differences among young learners, Engelmann conducted research, as Piaget had done, using his own children and those of colleagues and neighbors. With a previous advertising background, Engelmann formed focus groups of preschool children to test-market teaching methods. Main features of the curricula Engelmann developed included emphasizing phonics and computation early in young children's instruction; using a precise logical sequence to teach new skills; teaching new skills in small, separate, "child-sized" pieces; correcting learners' errors immediately; adhering strictly to designated teaching schedules; constantly reviewing to integrate new learning with previously attained knowledge; and scrupulous measurement techniques for assessing skills mastery. To demonstrate the results of his methods for teaching math, Engelmann sent movies he made of these to educational institutions. They showed that with his methods, toddlers could master upper-elementary-grade-level computations and even simple linear equations.

DIRECT INSTRUCTION METHOD OF TEACHING CHILDREN

Direct Instruction (DI) is a behavioral method of teaching. Therefore, learner errors receive immediate corrective feedback, and correct responses receive immediate, obvious positive reinforcement. DI has a fast pace—10–14 learner responses per minute overall—affording more attention and less boredom, reciprocal teacher-student feedback, immediate indications of learner problems to teachers, and natural reinforcement of teacher activities. DI thus promotes more mutual student and teacher learning than traditional "one-way" methods. Children are instructed in small groups according to ability levels. Their attention is teacher-focused. Teacher presentations follow scripts designed to give instruction the proper sequence, including prewritten prompts and questions developed through field-testing with real students. These optimized prepared lessons allow teachers to attend to extra instructional and motivational aspects of learning. Cued by teachers, who control the pace and give all learners with varying response rates chances for practice, children respond actively in groups and individually. Small groups are typically seated in semicircles close to teachers, who use visual aids like blackboards and overhead projectors.

PROJECT FOLLOW THROUGH

In 1967, President Lyndon B. Johnson declared his War on Poverty. This initiative included Project Follow Through, funded by the US Office of Education and Office of Economic Opportunity. Research had previously found that Project Head Start, which offered early educational interventions to disadvantaged preschoolers, had definite positive impacts, but these were often short-lived. Project Follow Through was intended to discover how to maintain Head Start's benefits. Siegfried Engelmann and Wesley Becker, who had developed the Engelmann-Becker instructional model, invited others to propose various other teaching models in communities selected to participate in Project Follow Through. The researchers asked parents in each community to choose from among the models provided. The proponents of each model were given funds to train teachers and furnish curriculum. Models found to enhance disadvantaged children's school achievement were to be promoted nationally. Engelmann's Direct Instruction model showed positive results surpassing all other models. However, the US Office of Education did not adopt this or other models found best.

APPROACHES TO REMEDIAL OR COMPENSATORY EDUCATION

A huge comparative study of curriculum and instruction methods, Project Follow Through incorporated three main approaches: Affective, Basic Skills, and Cognitive. Affective approaches used in Project Follow Through included the Bank Street, Responsive Education, and Open Education models. These teaching models aim to enhance school achievement by emphasizing experiences that raise children's self-esteem, which is believed to facilitate their acquisition of basic skills and higher-order problem-solving skills. Basic Skills approaches included the Southwest Labs, Behavior Analysis, and Direct Instruction models. These models find that mastering basic skills facilitates higher-order cognitive and problem-solving skills, and higher self-esteem. Cognitive approaches included the Parent Education, TEEM, and Cognitively Oriented Curriculum models. These models focus on teaching higher-order problem-solving and thinking skills as the optimal avenue to enhancing school achievement and to improving lower-order basic skills and self-esteem. Affective and Cognitive models have become popular in most schools of education. Basic Skills approaches are less popular but are congruent with other, very effective methods of specialized instruction.

CONTRIBUTIONS OF CONSTANCE KAMII TO EARLY CHILDHOOD EDUCATION

Professor of early childhood education Constance Kamii, of Japanese ancestry, was born in Geneva, Switzerland. She attended elementary school in both Switzerland and Japan, completing secondary school and higher education degrees in the United States. She studied extensively with Jean Piaget, also of Geneva. She worked with the Perry Preschool Project in the 1960s, fueling her subsequent interest in theoretically grounded instruction. Kamii believes in basing early childhood educational goals and objectives upon scientific theory of children's cognitive, social, and moral development, and moreover that Piaget's theory of cognitive development is the sole explanation for child development from birth to adolescence. She has done much curriculum research in the US and published a number of books on how to apply Piaget's theory practically in early childhood classrooms. Kamii agrees with Piaget that education's overall, long-term goal is developing children's intellectual, social, and moral autonomy. Kamii has said, "A classroom cannot foster the development of autonomy in the intellectual realm while suppressing it in the social and moral realms."

THEORETICAL ORIENTATION, PHILOSOPHY, AND APPROACH OF THE KAMII-DEVRIES APPROACH

Constance Kamii and Rheta DeVries formulated the Kamii-DeVries Constructivist Perspective model of preschool education. It is closely based upon Piaget's theory of child cognitive development and on the constructivist theory to which Piaget and others subscribed, which dictates that children construct their own realities through their interactions with the environment. Piaget's particular constructivism included the principle that through their interacting with the world within a logical-mathematical structure, children's intelligence, knowledge, personalities, and morality develop. The Kamii-DeVries approach finds that children learn via performing mental actions, which Piaget called operations, through the vehicle of physical activities. This model favors using teachers experienced in traditional preschool education, who employ a child-centered approach and establish active learning settings, are in touch with children's thoughts, respond to children from children's perspectives, and facilitate children's extension of their ideas. The Kamii-DeVries model has recently been applied to learning assessments using technology (2003) and to using constructivism in teaching physics to preschoolers (2011).

HIGHSCOPE CURRICULUM

David Weikart and colleagues developed the HighScope Curriculum in the 1960s and 1970s, testing it in the Perry Preschool and Head Start Projects, among others. The HighScope philosophy is based on Piaget's constructivist principles that active learning is optimal for young children; that they need to become involved actively with materials, ideas, people, and events; and that children and teachers learn together in the instructional environment. Weikart and colleagues' early research focused on economically disadvantaged children, but the HighScope approach has since been extended to all young children and all kinds of preschool settings. This model recommends dividing classrooms into well-furnished, separate "interest areas" and regular daily class routines, affording children time to plan, implement, and reflect upon what they learn and to participate in large and small group activities. Teachers establish socially supportive atmospheres; plan group learning activities; organize settings and set daily routines; encourage purposeful child activities, problem-solving, and verbal reflection; and interpret child behaviors according to HighScope's key child development experiences.

HIGHSCOPE CURRICULUM'S KEY EXPERIENCES FOR PRESCHOOLERS

The HighScope Curriculum model identified a total of 58 "key experiences" it found critical for preschool child development and learning. These key experiences are subdivided into ten main categories:

- Creative representation, which includes recognizing symbolic use, imitating, and playing roles
- Language and literacy, which include speaking, describing, scribbling, and narrating/dictating stories
- Initiative and social relations, including solving problems, making decisions and choices, and building relationships
- Movement, including activities like running, bending, stretching, and dancing
- Music, which includes singing, listening to music, and playing musical instruments
- Classification, which includes sorting objects, matching objects or pictures, and describing object shapes
- Seriation, or arranging things in prescribed orders (e.g., by size or number)
- Numbers, which for preschoolers focuses on counting

- Space, which involves activities like filling and emptying containers
- Time, including concepts of starting, sequencing, and stopping actions.

TECHNOLOGY USE, SCHOOL DAY DURATIONS AND SETTINGS, AND TARGETS FOR ITS APPLICATION

The HighScope Curriculum frequently incorporates computers as regular program components, including developmentally appropriate software, for children to access when they choose. School days may be full-day or part-day, determined by each individual program. Flexible hours accommodate individual family needs and situations. HighScope programs work in both child care and preschool settings. HighScope was originally designed to enhance educational outcomes for young children considered at-risk due to socioeconomically disadvantaged, urban backgrounds and was compatible with Project Head Start. This model of early childhood curriculum and instruction advocates individualizing teaching to each child's developmental level and pace of learning. As such, the HighScope approach is found to be effective for children who have learning disabilities and also for children with developmental delays. It works well with all children needing individual attention. HighScope is less amenable to highly structured settings that use more adult-directed instruction.

HEAD START PROGRAM

Head Start was begun in 1964, extended by the Head Start Act of 1981, and revised in its 2007 reauthorization. It is a program of the US Department of Health and Human Services designed to give low-income families and their young children comprehensive services of health, nutrition, education, and parental involvement. While Head Start was initially intended to "catch up" low-income children over the summer to reach kindergarten readiness, it soon became obvious that a six-week preschool program was inadequate to compensate for having lived in poverty for one's first five years. Hence, the Head Start Program was expanded and modified over the years with the aim of remediating the effects of system-wide poverty upon child educational outcomes. Currently, Head Start gives local public, private, nonprofit, and for-profit agencies grants for delivering comprehensive child development services to promote disadvantaged children's school readiness by improving their cognitive and social development. It particularly emphasizes developing early reading and math abilities preschoolers will need for school success.

GENESIS AND RATIONALE OF THE HEAD START PROGRAM

After research had accumulated considerable evidence of how important children's earliest years are to their ensuing growth and development, the US Department of Health and Human Services Administration for Children and Families' Office of Head Start established the Early Head Start Program in 1995. Early Head Start works to improve prenatal health, improve infant and toddler development, and enhance healthy family functioning. It serves children from 0–3 years. Like the original program, Early Head Start stresses parental engagement in children's growth, development, and learning.

EMERGENT LITERACY THEORY
EMERGENT LITERACY VERSUS READING READINESS

Historically, early childhood educators viewed "reading readiness" as a time during young children's literacy development when they were ready to start learning to read and write, and taught literacy accordingly. However, in the late 20th and early 20th centuries, research has found that children have innate learning capacities and that skills emerge under the proper conditions. Educational researchers came to view language as developing gradually within a child rather than a child's being ready to read at a certain time. Thus, the term *emergent* came to replace *readiness*, while *literacy* replaced *reading* as referring to all of language's interrelated aspects of listening, speaking, writing, and viewing, as well as reading. Traditional views of literacy were based only on children's reading and writing in ways similar to those of adults. However, more recently, the theory of emergent literacy has evolved through the findings of research into the early preschool reading of young children and the associated characteristics of them and their families.

EMERGENT LITERACY THEORY'S PRINCIPLES ABOUT HOW YOUNG CHILDREN LEARN TO READ AND WRITE

Through extensive research, emergent literacy theorists have found the following:

- Young children develop literacy through being actively involved in reading and rereading their favorite storybooks. When preschoolers "reread" storybooks, they have not memorized them; rather, theorists find this activity to exemplify young children's reconstruction of a book's meaning. Similarly, young children's invented spellings are examples of their efforts to reconstruct what they know of written language; they can inform us about a child's familiarity with specific phonetic components.
- Adults' reading to children, no matter how young, is crucial to literacy development. It helps children gain a "feel" for the character, flow, and patterns of written/printed language, and an overall sense of what reading feels like and entails. It fosters positive attitudes toward reading in children, strongly motivating them to read when they begin school. Being read to also helps children develop print awareness and formulate concepts of books and reading.
- Influenced by Piaget and Vygotsky, emergent literacy theory views reading and writing as developmental processes having successive stages.

PERSPECTIVE REGARDING INSTRUCTIONAL MODELS

The emergent literacy theoretical perspective yields an instructional model for the learning and teaching of reading and writing in young children that is founded on building instruction from the child's knowledge. Emergent literacy theory's assumption is that young children already know a lot about language and literacy by the time they enter school. This theory furthermore regards even 2- and 3-year-olds as having information about how the reading and writing processes function, and as having already formed particular ideas about what written/printed language is. From this perspective, emergent literacy theory then dictates that teaching should build upon what a child already knows and should support the child's further literacy development. Researchers conclude that teachers should furnish open-ended activities allowing children to show what they already know about literacy, to apply that knowledge, and to build upon it. From the emergent literacy perspective, teachers take the role of creating a learning environment with conditions that are conducive to children's learning in ways that are ideally self-motivated, self-generated, and self-regulated.

HOW BABIES AND YOUNG CHILDREN LEARN TO READ AND WRITE

According to the theory of emergent literacy, even infants encounter written language. Two- and three-year-olds commonly can identify logos, labels, and signs in their homes and communities. Also, young children's scribbles show features/appearances of their language's specific writing system even before they can write. For example, Egyptian children's scribbles look more like Egyptian writing; American children's scribbles look more like English writing. Young children learn to read and write concurrently, not sequentially; the two abilities are closely interrelated. Moreover, though with speech, receptive language comprehension seems to develop easier/sooner than expressive language production, this does not apply to reading and writing: first learning activities involving writing are found easier for preschoolers than those involving reading. Research finds that form follows function, not the opposite: young children's literacy learning is mostly through meaningful, functional, purposeful/goal-directed real-life activities. Literacy comprises not isolated, abstract skills learned for their own sake but rather authentic skills applied to accomplish real-life purposes, the way children observe adults using literacy.

Developmentally Inappropriate Kindergarten and Preschool Literacy Practices

Research finds some preschools are like play centers but are not optimal for literacy because their curricula exclude natural reading and writing activities. Researchers have also identified a trend in many kindergartens to ensure children's "reading readiness" by providing highly academic programs, influencing preschool curricula to get children "ready" for such kindergartens. Influenced and even pressured by kindergarten programs' academic expectations, parents have also come to expect preschools to prepare their children for kindergarten. However, experts find applying elementary-school programs to kindergartens and preschools developmentally inappropriate. Formal instruction in reading and writing and worksheets are not suitable for younger children. Instead, research finds print-rich preschool environments both developmentally appropriate and more effective. For example, when researchers changed classrooms from having a "book corner" to having a centrally located table with books plus paper, pencils, envelopes, and stamps, children spent 3 to 10 times more time on direct reading and writing activities. Children are found to take naturally to these activities without prior formal reading and writing lessons.

Planning a Play-Based Curriculum

To plan a curriculum based on children's natural play with building blocks (Hoisington, 2008), a teacher can first arrange the environment to stimulate further such play. Then he or she can furnish materials for children to make plans/blueprints for and records and models of buildings they construct. The teacher can make time during the day for children to reflect upon and discuss their individual and group-building efforts. Teachers can also utilize teaching strategies that encourage children to reflect on and consider in more depth the scientific principles related to their results. A teacher can provide building materials of varied sizes, shapes, textures, and weights, and can provide props to add realism, triggering more complex structures and creative, dramatic, emotional, and social development. Teachers can take photos of children's structures as documents for discussions, stimulating language and vocabulary development. Supplying additional materials to support and stick together blocks extends play-based learning. Active teacher participation by offering observations and asking open-ended questions promotes children's standards-based learning of scientific, mathematical, and linguistic concepts, processes, and patterns.

Supporting and Integrating Standards-Based Learning in Scientific, Mathematical, and Linguistic Domains

When children play at building with blocks, for example, they investigate material properties such as various block shapes, sizes, and weights and the stability of carpet vs. hard floor as bases. They explore cause-and-effect relationships, make conclusions regarding the results of their trial-and-error experiments, draw generalizations about observed patterns, and form theories about what does and does not work to build high towers. Ultimately, they construct their knowledge of how reality functions. Teachers support this by introducing relevant learning standards in the play context meaningful to children. For example, math standards, including spatial awareness, geometry, number, operations, patterns, and measurement, can be supported through planning play. By encouraging and guiding children's discussion and documentation of their play constructions, and supplying nonfictional and fictional books about building, a teacher also integrates learning goals and objectives for language and literacy development. Teachers can plan activities specifically to extend learning in these domains, like counting blocks, comparison/contrast, matching, sorting, sequencing, phonological awareness, alphabetic awareness, print awareness, book appreciation, listening, comprehension, speech, and communication.

Using Thematic Teaching Units

To develop a thematic teaching unit, a teacher designs a collection of related activities around certain themes or topics that crosses several curriculum areas or domains. Thematic units create learning environments for young children that promote all children's active engagement, as well as their process learning. By studying topics children find relevant to their own lives, thematic units build upon children's preexisting knowledge and current interests and also help them relate information to their own life experiences. Varied curriculum content can be more easily integrated through thematic units in ways that young children can understand and apply meaningfully. Children's diverse individual learning styles are also accommodated through thematic units. Such units involve children physically in learning; teach them factual information in greater depth; teach them learning process-related skills, such as "learning how to learn"; holistically integrate learning; encourage cohesion in groups; meet children's individual needs; and provide motivation to both children and their teachers.

Project Approach

The Project Approach (Katz and Chard, 1989) entails having young children choose a topic interesting to them, studying this topic, researching it, and solving problems and questions as they emerge. This gives children greater practice with creative thinking and problem-solving skills, which supports greater success in all academic and social areas. For example, if a class of preschoolers shows interest in the field of medicine, their teacher can plan a field trip to a local hospital to introduce a project studying medicine in depth. During the trip, the teacher can record children's considerations and questions, and then use these as guidelines to plan and conduct relevant activities that will further stimulate the children's curiosity and imagination. Throughout this or any other in-depth project, the teacher can integrate specific skills for reading, writing, math, science, social studies, and creative thinking. This affords dual benefits: enabling both children's skills advancement and their gaining knowledge they recognize is required and applies in their own lives. Children become life-long learners with this recognition.

Integrated Curriculum and Early Childhood Education

An integrated curriculum organizes early childhood education to transcend the boundaries between the various domains and subject content areas. It unites different curriculum elements through meaningful connections to allow study of wider areas of knowledge. It treats learning holistically and mirrors the interactive nature of reality. The principle that learning consists of series of interconnections is the foundation for teaching through use of an integrated curriculum. Benefits of integrated curricula include an organized planning mechanism, greater flexibility, and the ability to teach many skills and concepts effectively, include more varied content, and enable children to learn most naturally. By identifying themes children find most interesting, teachers can construct webs of assorted themes, which can provide the majority of their curriculum. Research has proven the effectiveness of integrated teaching units for both children and their teachers. Teachers can also integrate new content into existing teaching units they have identified as effective. Integrated units enable teachers to ensure children are learning pertinent knowledge and applying it to real-life situations.

Skills, Topics, Strategies, and Benefits Related to Creating Thematically-Based Teaching Units

EC teachers can incorporate many skills into units organized by theme. This includes state governments' educational standards/benchmarks for various skills. Teachers can base units on topics of interest to young children, such as building construction, space travel, movie-making, dinosaurs, vacations, nursery rhymes, fairy tales, pets, wildlife, camping, the ocean, and studies of particular authors and book themes. Beginning with a topic that motivates the children is best; related activities and skills will naturally follow. In planning units, teachers should establish connections among content areas like literacy, physical activity, dramatic play, art, music, math, science, and social studies. Making these connections permits children's learning through their strongest/favored modalities and supports learning through meaningful experiences, which is how they learn best. Theme-based approaches effectively address individual differences and modality-related strengths, as represented in Gardner's theory of multiple intelligences. Thematic approaches facilitate creating motivational learning centers and hands-on learning activities and are also compatible with creating portfolio assessments and performance-based assessments. Teachers can encompass skill and conceptual benchmarks for specific age/developmental levels within engaging themes.

GUIDELINES FOR INDOOR AND OUTDOOR SPACE USE

Indoor and outdoor early childhood learning environments should be safe, clean, and attractive. They should include at least 35 square feet indoors and 75 square feet outdoors of usable play space per child. Staff must have access to prepare spaces before children's arrival. Gyms or other larger indoor spaces can substitute if outdoor spaces are smaller. The youngest children should be given separate outdoor times/places. Outdoor scheduling should ensure enough room and prevent altercations/competition among different age groups. Teachers can assess if enough space exists by observing children's interactions and engagement in activities. Children's products and other visuals should be displayed at child's-eye level. Spaces should be arranged to allow individual, small-group, and large-group activity. Space organization should create clear pathways enabling children to move easily among activities without overly disturbing others, and should promote positive social interactions and behaviors; activities in each area should not distract children in other areas.

ARRANGEMENT OF LEARNING ENVIRONMENTS

ARRANGING INDOOR LEARNING ENVIRONMENTS ACCORDING TO CURRICULAR ACTIVITIES

EC experts indicate that rooms should be organized to enable various activities, but not necessarily to limit activities to certain areas. For example, mathematical and scientific preschool activities may occur in multiple parts of a classroom, though the room should still be laid out to facilitate their occurrence. Sufficient space for infants to crawl and toddlers to toddle is necessary, as are both hard and carpeted floors. Bolted-down/heavy, sturdy furniture is needed for infants and toddlers to use for pulling up, balancing, and cruising. Art and cooking activities should be positioned near sinks/water sources for cleanup. Designating separate areas for activities like block-building, book-reading, musical activities, and dramatic play facilitates engaging in each of these. To allow ongoing project work and other age-appropriate activities, school-aged children should have separate areas. Materials should be appropriate for each age group and varied. Books, recordings, art supplies, and equipment and materials for sensory stimulation, manipulation, construction, active play, and dramatic play, all arranged for easy, independent child access and rotated for variety, are needed.

ARRANGING LEARNING ENVIRONMENTS TO CHILDREN'S PERSONAL, PRIVACY, AND SENSORY NEEDS

In any early childhood learning environment, the indoor space should include easily identifiable places where children and adults can store their personal belongings. Since early childhood involves children in groups for long time periods, they should be given indoor and outdoor areas allowing solitude and privacy while still easily permitting adult supervision. Playhouses and tunnels can be used outdoors, while small interior rooms and partitions can be used indoors. Environments should include softness in various forms like grass outdoors; carpet, pillows, and soft chairs indoors; adult laps to sit in and be cuddled; and soft play materials like clay, Play-Doh, finger paints, water, and sand. While noise is predictable, even desirable in early childhood environments, undue noise causing fatigue and stress should be controlled by noise-absorbing elements like rugs, carpets, drapes, acoustic ceilings, and other building materials. Outdoor play areas supplied by a school or community should be separated from roadways and other hazards by fencing and/or natural barriers. Awnings can substitute for shade, and inclines/ramps for hills, when these are not naturally available. Surfaces and equipment should be varied.

PRINCIPLES RELATED TO EARLY CHILDHOOD BEHAVIOR MANAGEMENT

Repetition and consistency are two major elements for managing young children's behavior. Adults must always follow and enforce whichever rules they designate. They must also remember that they will need to repeat their rules over and over to make them effective. Behaviorism has shown it is more powerful to reward good behaviors than punish bad behaviors. Consistently rewarding desired behaviors enables young children to make the association between behavior and reward. Functional behavior analysis can inform adults: knowing the function of a behavior is necessary to changing it. For example, if a toddler throws a tantrum out of frustration, providing support/scaffolding for a difficult task, breaking it down to more manageable increments via task analysis, and giving encouragement would be appropriate strategies. If the tantrum was a bid for attention, adults would only reinforce/strengthen tantrum recurrence by paying attention. Feeling valued and loved within a positive relationship greatly supports young children's compliance with rules. The "10:1 Rule" prescribes at least 10 positive comments per 1 negative comment/correction.

INCLUDING FAMILIES IN CHILDREN'S EDUCATION

First, early childhood education personnel can make sure that communication between the school/program and family is reciprocal and regular. early childhood educators should promote and support the enhancement and application of parenting skills. They should also acknowledge that parents have an integral part in supporting children's learning. All school personnel should make parents feel welcome in school, and moreover should seek parents' help and support. When school administrators, teachers, and other staff make educational decisions that affect the children and their families, they should always be sure that the children's parents are involved in these decisions. In addition, educational personnel should not just work on children's educational goals, learning objectives, and curricular and instructional planning and design on their own, keeping the school or program isolated; they should make use of all available community resources. Instead of trying to educate young children within a school bubble, educators who collaborate with their communities realize the benefits of stronger families, schools, and child learning.

MANAGING THE NORMAL BEHAVIOR OF YOUNG CHILDREN

Before reacting to young children's behaviors, adults should make sure children understand the situation. They should state rules simply and clearly, repeat them frequently for a long time for young children to remember and follow them, and state and enforce rules very consistently to avoid confusion. Adults should tell children clearly what they expect of them. They should never assume they need do nothing when children follow rules; they should consistently give rewards for compliance. Adults should also explain to young children why they are or are not receiving rewards by citing the rule they did or did not follow. Adults can arrange the environment to promote success. For example, if a child throws things that break windows, adults can remove such objects and substitute softer/more lightweight items. Organization is also important. Adults should begin with a simple, easy-to-implement plan and adhere to it. They should record children's progress; analyzing the records shows what does and does not work and why, enabling new/revised plans.

> **Review Video: Promoting Appropriate Behavior**
> Visit mometrix.com/academy and enter code: 321015

Behavior Management

AGGRESSION

Preschoolers typically demonstrate some aggressive behavior, which tends to peak around age 4. Instrumental aggression is one basic type: younger preschoolers frequently shout, hit, or kick others to get concrete objects they want. Middle preschoolers are more likely to exhibit hostile aggression, including getting even for wrongs or injuries they feel others have done to them. Hostile aggression occurs in two subtypes: overt and relational. Overt aggression involves physically harming others or threatening to do so, while relational aggression involves emotional/social harm, such as rejecting or excluding another from a group of friends or spreading malicious rumors about another. Young boys are more likely to engage in overt aggression, while young girls are more likely to engage in relational aggression. These gender preferences in aggressive behaviors tend to remain the same at all ages if aggression exists. While most young children eventually phase out aggression as they learn other ways of resolving social conflicts, some persist in verbally and/or physically aggressive behavior, causing problems.

MINIMIZING AGGRESSIVE BEHAVIOR

While it is normal for preschoolers to exhibit some physical and verbal aggression until they have learned more mature ways of expressing feelings, getting what they want, and settling disputes, there are things adults can do to influence them such that aggressive behavior does not develop into a predominant method of social interaction. Adults set examples for children, and children learn by observing and imitating those examples. Therefore, parents, caregivers, and teachers should not model verbally and/or physically aggressive behaviors such as calling others names, yelling at others, or punishing others' undesirable behaviors using physical force. Not only should adults avoid disciplining children physically, but they should also avoid physically and/or verbally violent interactions with other adults. Social learning theorist Albert Bandura proved that children who viewed violent videos imitated what they observed and engaged in more aggressive behavior, so adults should also prevent young children's exposure to violent TV programming and video games.

PREJUDICE AND DISCRIMINATION

Prejudice literally means prejudging, which is judging someone or something negatively before or without knowing anything about who or what one is judging. Prejudice gives rise to discrimination in that prejudiced ideas motivate unfair and discriminatory behaviors toward others. Psychologist Albert Bandura, who developed social learning theory, identified the process whereby children acquire attitudes and behaviors they observe in others, which he named vicarious learning. Children commonly pick up beliefs, attitudes, and behaviors from adults around them, without applying any critical thinking to these. They are often not even aware of the attitudes and beliefs they assume in this way. Thus, they will engage in prejudicial attitudes and discriminatory behaviors without thinking through what they are doing. Though such behavior is not justified, children simply assume it is because of adults' examples. Thus, adults must carefully inspect their own beliefs and attitudes, as well as what they do and say, because these are what children will imitate.

PREJUDICIAL THINKING

Prejudicial thinking about certain groups of people is uninformed and/or misinformed thinking. It is typically based on fear of the unknown due to lack of knowledge and/or fear due to erroneous beliefs about people. Thus, the best way to dispel prejudice is to provide information where there was none and/or to correct wrong information. When unfamiliar groups become more familiar, and when wrong assumptions are corrected, people's misconceptions are replaced by reality and they become less afraid. For example, children having no experience with people from other racial, ethnic, or socioeconomic groups are likely to fear these people (as are many adults). Adults can help young children by furnishing them with many opportunities—not just isolated ones—to interact with people from diverse cultural and socioeconomic milieus. For children to experience true learning, which will supersede negative, uninformed first impressions, they must have multiple such social opportunities. School, outside classes, sports, and camp are activities affording such opportunities.

BULLYING

Children who are bullied by others are victims of prejudicial thinking and discriminatory actions. Common negative effects of bullying include rage, feelings of hopelessness, anxiety, and depression. Left untreated, children with these feelings can develop suicidal ideations and actions as they grow older if bullying persists. When young, children have the additional problem of not yet knowing how to manage their negative feelings caused by others' aggression or even how to express them. Adults can give them much-needed help by assisting them in articulating their emotions openly but nonviolently. Adults must realize that young children, especially those who have experienced others' violent treatment, may not recognize that anger can be expressed in any ways other than violent ones. Based on their experience, children may internalize assumptions that they can only act out their anger through self-destructive behaviors. When adults consistently model positive, proactive ways of discussing negative emotions, children observe that more constructive behaviors are possible and learn to adopt these as more effective coping strategies.

SEX/GENDER-ROLE DEVELOPMENT

Various theories of development, such as psychoanalytic, behaviorist, cognitive, and social learning, have differing views of why and how children develop sexual/gender identities. To address these differences, psychologists have endeavored to produce some general conclusions about young children's self-concepts of gender. They find that during preschool ages, children gradually develop concepts of what being a girl or a boy in their culture means. These concepts become clearly articulated and shape their behaviors. Between the ages of 2 and 6, children are in the process of putting together the pieces of these gender concepts. Developing sex-appropriate behaviors and developing categories of gender roles both appear to be influenced by a combination and interaction of biological and sociological variables. Psychologists additionally conclude that children perform some mental matching process enabling them to isolate features they share in common with others, and that young children's abilities to observe, imitate, and categorize influence their later concepts of sex-appropriate behaviors. By ages 5–6, most children clearly identify with one sex or the other.

COMBATING CULTURAL STEREOTYPES AND DISCRIMINATION

When children experience stereotyping of and discrimination against their cultural group, adults can counter these negative reflections on the group by correcting erroneous opinions they have heard. By giving children plenty of examples of positive accomplishments by members of their group, they convey cultural pride, affording children a sense of empowerment. Adults should consistently model positive, constructive, and non-violent methods of addressing prejudice for children. If prejudice proves ongoing, caregivers and teachers must assertively advocate on behalf of children and their cultures to shut down prejudicial sources. If they hear young children furthering cultural stereotypes they have absorbed, adults should immediately correct their statements and behaviors, explaining why certain words and actions harm others and are unacceptable. Extended discussions with young children are important for putting prejudice into perspective and context to help them understand it. Adults can also apply behavioral methods, such as associating prejudicial behaviors with consequences (e.g., losing a privilege or gaining work) and providing related learning activities to prevent repeated instances.

Using Historical Contexts and Real-Life Examples to Address Prejudicial Attitudes

Because many prejudicial attitudes exist in our society on both individualized and institutionalized levels, it is all too easy for children to absorb and emulate them. When children who have been victims of prejudice learn they were attacked not as individuals but members of a group, this does not eliminate negative effects but can help them see it from a different perspective. Adults can place prejudice and discrimination in their historical contexts so children realize they are not lone victims but part of a larger group. Correcting false beliefs, as in Albert Ellis's Rational-Emotive Behavior Therapy and other forms of cognitive-behavioral therapy, can be applied by adults' pointing out the irrational, flawed thinking involved and supplying examples contradicting that thinking. For example, if children have been influenced to think certain groups are less intelligent or lazier than others, adults can show them examples of many members of those groups with outstanding achievements in society. They can do this through biographies, personal anecdotes, and introductions to living people.

Genetic and Environmental Influences on Behavior

Research into factors influencing early childhood behavior identifies both genetic variables and environmental ones, like corporal punishment, affecting young children's propensities toward antisocial behavior. Children experiencing more corporal punishment and children who are at greater genetic risk display greater behavior problems. However, boys at higher genetic risk for behavior problems who also experience more corporal punishment exhibit the most antisocial behavior. Therefore, both genetic risk factors and corporal punishment significantly predict preschoolers' antisocial behavior. Additionally, the nature-nurture interaction of genetic risk factors and environmental punishment is statistically significant for young boys but not young girls. Such evidence shows that environmental learning is not wholly responsible for antisocial behavior: genetic variables predispose some young children to antisocial behaviors more than others.

Behaviorist Learning Theories

Ivan Pavlov's experiments with dogs proved that when a stimulus evoking a reflexive response—drooling at the taste of meat—was repeatedly paired with an unrelated or "neutral" stimulus—a bell ringing—dogs came to associate the unrelated stimulus with the original response and drooled on hearing the bell without tasting meat. This proved generalizable to humans. Edward L. Thorndike's experiments with cats also applied to humans. Thorndike introduced the Law of Effect: we are more likely to repeat behaviors receiving desirable consequences. This set the stage for B. F. Skinner's later work. John B. Watson maintained that because inner states cannot be observed or measured, only observable outer behaviors should be used in psychology and learning. Skinner experimented with operant conditioning, wherein behaviors are trained and shaped through manipulating their antecedents/preceding stimuli and consequences/following stimuli. He expanded behaviorism into a comprehensive theory, including detailed rules for teaching new behaviors and modifying established behaviors.

Positive and Negative Reinforcement and Positive and Negative Punishment

In behaviorism, reinforcement means strengthening the probability a behavior will be repeated. Skinner used the terms *positive* vs. *negative* to mean *introducing* vs. *removing*, not *good* vs. *bad*. Therefore, **positive reinforcement** is introducing something rewarding immediately after a behavior. When a child's behavior is rewarded, he or she will repeat it to obtain repeated rewards: If Johnny gets a treat or praise for putting away his toys, he will do it again. **Negative**

reinforcement is rewarding by removing something unwanted. Say Johnny dislikes noisy crowds at preschool. One day he wakes up earlier, is taken to preschool earlier, and finds it quieter and less crowded; he will want to get up and arrive earlier again. **Positive punishment** is introducing an aversive consequence for a behavior: When Johnny refuses to put toys away, his parents then make him clean up the entire room, making him less likely to repeat the refusal. **Negative punishment** is removing a desirable stimulus: When Johnny refuses to put away toys, his parents prohibit watching TV, making him less likely to keep refusing.

Research has found positive reinforcement to be the most powerful of all these. One reason is that people are highly motivated by rewards. Another is that all behaviors meet needs; punishment suppresses certain behaviors, but then other behaviors must emerge to fill the same need. If a child misbehaves to get attention, even scolding can constitute attention. But if rewarded for more appropriate behavior to get attention, like asking an available adult or peer for interaction, the child meets the attention need while replacing a maladaptive behavior with an adaptive one. Another reason is punishment's limitations: preschoolers may stop misbehaving after one teacher's punishment, but not with another teacher; punishment not applied consistently loses its effect. Also, punishment can cause resentment, anger, defiance, or fearfulness in young children.

Collaboration with Families and Colleagues

GENETIC AND BIOLOGICAL INFLUENCES ON CHILDREN RELATIVE TO ADDICTIVE BEHAVIORS

Adopted children with one or both biological parents having histories of alcohol abuse, criminal records, and/or major psychiatric illness are at double the risk for drug abuse as those having biological parents without such histories. While this risk is genetic, differential environmental influences can exacerbate or mitigate children's biological risk for engaging in addictive behaviors. For example, adopted children who experience difficulties in their adopted families, such as deaths or divorce, are at higher risk of developing drug abuse problems. Conversely, children whose biological parents' histories put them at higher genetic risk for abusing drugs—but who were adopted into loving, stable families—are less at risk for developing addictions. Researchers conclude that children with higher genetic risks for addiction are more vulnerable to adverse environmental influences in their adopted families than children with lower genetic risks. Also, genetic risks become less powerful in adoptive families having lower environmental risk factors.

ALFRED ADLER'S THEORETICAL CONCEPTS OF THE EFFECTS OF BIRTH ORDER

ONLY CHILD AND OLDEST CHILD

Neo-Freudian psychologist Alfred Adler proposed that a child's birth order relative to other children in a family is associated with corresponding influences on the child's personality and behaviors. For example, Adler found that the only child is regarded as a miracle of birth by parents with no prior experience of having a baby. This child receives the undivided attention of both parents, who may be overprotective of the child and/or spoil him or her. Some general characteristics of only children include preferring adults' company, using adult language, enjoying being the center of attention from adults, and finding it difficult to share with other children. Adler said the oldest/older child has been "dethroned"/displaced by a younger sibling and must learn to share. Parents often have very high expectations of the oldest/older child, give him or her much responsibility, and expect him or her to set an example for younger siblings. Older/oldest children may turn to fathers once a sibling is born. They may feel entitled to power, developing strict/authoritarian attitudes and behaviors. Given encouragement, they can develop helpful attitudes and behaviors.

SECOND CHILD AND MIDDLE CHILD

The second-born child was described by Adler as having a "pacemaker" in that there is always an older sibling ahead of this child. Adler found that the results of this position include the child's becoming more competitive out of attempts to overtake the elder sibling. He noted that competition could devolve into sibling rivalry. A second child might develop into a rebellious sort or might develop a habit of always trying to "top" or exceed everybody else's accomplishments. Adler described the middle child in a family as being "sandwiched" between older and younger siblings so that he or she can feel "squeezed out" of any privileged or significant position. While some middle children may grow up to fight against injustice or unfairness, others may encounter difficulty establishing places for themselves. Some middle children develop even-tempered dispositions, with no extreme opinions and "take-it-or-leave-it" attitudes.

YOUNGEST CHILD AND TWIN CHILDREN

Adler found that the youngest child in a family, like an only child, is never "dethroned" or displaced by a new sibling. However, unlike an only child, the youngest sibling has many "parents" in the form of older siblings who help to raise, instruct, and influence him or her. Youngest siblings are often spoiled by the combined attentions of parents and older siblings. Some youngest children continue to feel and behave like the "baby" of the family indefinitely. Many youngest children, always being littlest, wish to be bigger than siblings. As they grow, youngest siblings may make grandiose plans that never succeed. Adler found with twins, one is usually more active or stronger and is often perceived by the parents as older—he or she may have been born a minute earlier and/or they perceive him or her as more mature. The stronger twin may develop as the leader; the other may develop problems with identity.

MALE AND FEMALE SIBLING CHARACTERISTICS

Adler stated the only male with female siblings, surrounded by females when the father is not there, can develop either of opposite extremes: he may engage excessively in behaviors to prove he is the "man of the family" or develop effeminate behaviors through identifying with surrounding females. Adler found when a child is the only female among male siblings, her older brothers can behave protectively toward her. An only female among males may make efforts to please the father and develop either of two opposing extremes: becoming a tomboy to compete with brothers or developing very feminine behaviors to differentiate from them. In families with all-male or all-female children, Adler noted parents who wanted a child of the other sex might dress one child as the opposite sex. The child may either exploit this role reassignment or strongly object to it.

"GHOST CHILD" AND THE ADOPTED CHILD

Adlerian psychoanalytic theory describes a child who is born after an older child has died as having a "ghost" ahead of him or her. Such a child, called a "ghost child," is likely to be subject to overprotection by the mother, who fears losing him or her after losing a child previously. The child may respond to parental overprotectiveness by taking advantage of the parent to get what he or she wants. Alternatively, some ghost children resent feeling parental comparisons to the deceased child, whose memory parents have idealized; in this case, the child may rebel. Adler noted that adoptive parents can be so grateful to have a child and so anxious to make up for the child's loss of biological parents, that they may spoil him or her; thus, the adopted child is more liable to develop very demanding, spoiled behaviors. The adopted child may ultimately either resent his or her biological parents for rejecting and/or leaving him or her or idealize them, negatively comparing the adoptive parents.

MURRAY BOWEN'S FAMILY SYSTEMS THEORY

Dr. Bowen identified four basic family relationship patterns within what he called the nuclear family emotional system. These patterns dictate where problems develop when the family system is under tension. Bowen labeled these patterns as marital conflict, dysfunction in one spouse, impairment of one or more children, and emotional distance, the latter of which is associated with the first three. Regarding the impairment of one or more children, the parents focus their anxieties on one or more of their children. Their perception of the child(ren) is either negative or idealized. The more the parents focus on one child, the more that child reciprocally focuses on them, becoming more reactive to parental expectations, needs, and attitudes than siblings are. This process undermines the child's differentiation of self, a key factor in healthy individual development, according to Bowen. The child becomes more susceptible to internalizing or externalizing family tensions, affecting his/her social relationships, school performance, and physical and mental health.

FAMILY PROJECTION PROCESS

In the family projection process, Dr. Murray Bowen found that parents can project their anxieties onto their children. When parents worry overly that something is wrong with one child, they may see everything the child does as proof of that worry. Their excessive efforts to remedy the child's "problem" can actually cause the child to develop the problem in reality, as the child's self-image becomes aligned with parental perceptions. While parents with such worries usually feel guilty of not giving the "problem" child enough attention, they have in fact directed more attention to this child than his or her siblings. Bowen found that children less engaged in this process have more realistic, mature relationships with parents and develop into more goal-oriented, less reactive, and less emotionally needy individuals. Both parents participate equally in the process in different ways; both are insecure relative to the child, but Bowen said that, typically, one parent pretends to feel secure with the other's complicity.

In his theory, Bowen referred to the way parents transmit their emotional issues to children as the family rejection process, which involves three steps:

1. A parent focuses on a child, fearing something is wrong with that child.
2. The parent perceives the child's behavior as confirmation of this fear.
3. The parent then treats the child as though something really is wrong.

When parents try to "fix" what they perceive is a problem in the child, their perception can become a self-fulfilling prophecy as the child eventually embodies that perception. For example, if parents perceive a child as helpless and are always helping her excessively, the child's self-image comes to mirror the parents' perception; the child becomes de facto helpless and dependent even though she may not have been so initially. The more intense this process is, the greater relationship sensitivities children develop, beyond those of their parents.

Professionalism and Growth Through Professional Development

IDEA Law

Public Law 94-142, the Education for All Handicapped Children Act/Education for the Handicapped Act (EHA), passed in 1975; and Public Law 99-457, the EHA Amendments, passed in 1986, provided foundations that were expanded by new 1990 legislation. As a result, EHA was renamed the Individuals with Disabilities Education Act (IDEA). The IDEA's six main principles follow:

1. Publicly funded education cannot exclude any student because of the student's disability.
2. The rights of students with disabilities and of their parents are assured by the protection of due process procedures.
3. The parents of students with disabilities are encouraged to participate in their children's educations.
4. The assessment of all students must be fair and unbiased.
5. All students must be given a free, appropriate public education (FAPE), and it must be provided in the least restrictive environment (LRE) where the student and other students can learn and succeed.
6. Information related to students with disabilities and their families must be kept confidential.

Section 504, EHA, EHA Amendments, and ADA

In 1973, Section 504 of the Rehabilitation Act, also called Public Law 93-112, was enacted to ensure individuals with disabilities equal access to federally financed programs and to promote their participation in them. A child must have a physical or mental impairment that substantially limits a major life activity to be eligible for a free, appropriate public education (FAPE) under Section 504. This law stimulated motivation to educate students with disabilities, contributing to the passage of the Education for All Handicapped Children Act, also called Public Law 94-142, in 1975. This law provides that all children with disabilities must receive a FAPE provided in the least restrictive environment possible and individualized. Its procedural safeguards mandate due process. The EHA amendments of 1986, or Public Law 99-457, extended special education to disabled preschoolers aged 3 to 5 years; services to infants and toddlers are at each US state's discretion. The Americans with Disabilities Act (ADA), made effective in 1990, requires access for disabled people to public buildings and facilities, transportation, and communication but does not cover educational services.

> **Review Video: 504 Plans and IEPs**
> Visit mometrix.com/academy and enter code: 881103

US Federal Legislation Passed in 1997, 2001, and 2004

The 1990 Individuals with Disabilities Education Act (IDEA) was reauthorized in 1997 and numbered Public Law 108-446. It provided more access for children with disabilities to the general education curriculum and extended collaborative opportunities for teachers, other professionals, and families of children with disabilities. The No Child Left Behind Act of 2001 (NCLB, replaced by the Every Student Succeeds Act, ESSA, in 2015), the reauthorization of the Elementary and Secondary Education Act (ESEA), stressed accountability for outcomes by identifying schools and districts needing improvement and assuring teacher quality. It required school performance data to include disabled students' standardized test scores. NCLB emphasized giving teachers and administrators better research information and schools more resources, parents more information about their children's progress and the school's performance, and more local flexibility and control in utilizing federal education funds and in improving teacher qualifications, for example, through alternative certifications. IDEA's reauthorization in 2004, the Individuals with Disabilities Education Improvement Act (IDEIA), covers better alignment of NCLB with IDEA, appropriately identifying students needing special education, ensuring reasonable discipline while protecting special needs students defining highly qualified teachers, reducing paperwork, and increasing cooperation to decrease litigation.

RECENT LEGAL CHANGES TO THE AMERICANS WITH DISABILITIES ACT

The ADA Amendments Act (ADAAA, 2009) overrules prior Supreme Court decisions narrowly interpreting the ADA. This qualifies many more conditions as disabilities.

- Physical or mental impairments substantially limiting one or more life activities now include immune system functioning; normal cell growth; and brain, neurological, respiratory, circulatory, endocrine, reproductive, digestive, bowel, and bladder functions. These have been added to the existing activities of eating, sleeping, thinking, communicating, concentrating, lifting, and bending.
- Impairments include physical (e.g., deafness, blindness, or paralysis), medical (e.g., AIDS, diabetes, or epilepsy), mental or psychological (e.g., ADHD, Asperger's, or bipolar). Coverage of the definition also includes record of impairment, cancer in remission, for example.
- Reasonable accommodations mean adaptations or modifications enabling persons with disabilities to have equal opportunities. The ADA describes this regarding equal employment opportunities, but it could also be interpreted relative to equal educational opportunities.
- Reasonable accommodations that would cause undue hardship (e.g., financial hardship) are not required.

LEGAL RESPONSIBILITIES OF EARLY CHILDHOOD PROFESSIONALS

Historically, special education was introduced with the purpose of separating special-needs children from their normally developing peers. However, since 1991, the IDEA legislation has established the necessity of inclusion in normal care and educational environments, including early childhood (EC) settings, for children with disabilities. EC professionals know excluding any child is illegal. Another example of legal responsibilities is the "mandated reporter" status of caregivers, teachers, and other adults working with children and families. They are legally required to report suspected child abuse and neglect; the law penalizes them for not reporting. For example, say an EC teacher sees injuries to a child. The child knows the mother has a new boyfriend, displays a fearful attitude, and responds evasively to teacher questions. Later, the child tells the teacher that he or she has been hurt by the boyfriend. The teacher pities the mother, realizing she needs the boyfriend financially and emotionally, and reporting suspected abuse could make the mother lose her children or their home. Regardless, the teacher must report suspicions by law, which was enacted to stop violence against children.

REGULATIONS REGARDING THE CONFIDENTIALITY OF RECORDS

In early childhood settings, records kept about children and their families must be treated with strict confidentiality. Early childhood centers/programs/preschools/agencies should limit access to student records to children's immediate family members, only those employees authorized, and agencies having legal authority to access records. Confidentiality of records and restricted access to them in all centers/programs/preschools/agencies that receive federal funding are mandated by the Family Educational Rights and Privacy Act (FERPA). Moreover, with the ongoing trend toward educational inclusion, many EC settings serve children with disabilities, whose student records are additionally subject to regulations under the federal Individuals with Disabilities Education Act (IDEA) and also to the special education laws of their respective US states. An exception to the laws regarding records confidentiality is mandated reporting by EC personnel of suspected child abuse and neglect. Laws applying to child abuse and neglect supersede FERPA regulations. Legally, EC employees are required to report the suspected abuse and neglect of children, and they are immune from liability for releasing child records information relevant to their reporting.

QUALITY CARE AND ECONOMIC CONSIDERATIONS

To furnish and sustain quality care in early childhood settings is always challenging to care providers. It is even more so during difficult economic times. Many early childhood centers must face whether to downsize the services they offer or to go out of business. When administrators choose to remain in operation, they encounter equally difficult decisions regarding how to reduce services, but not at the expense of quality. A legal issue related to such economic considerations is that EC personnel are often placed at legal risk when service quality is compromised. While EC employers, employees, young children's parents, and educational researchers are all interested in and pursue a definition of quality care, no single operational definition has been attained. However, early childhood professionals with ample work experience in EC centers have contributed various definitions. The consensus of their contributions includes the following common elements: a nurturing environment; employees trained in EC development and methods; age-appropriate curricula; sufficient space, equipment, and materials; safety and good maintenance of physical environments; and good parent-teacher communication.

MEDICAL CARE AND TREATMENT EMPHASIZED IN LEGAL REGULATIONS

The child care licensing regulations of each US state government mostly govern children's medical care and treatment in early childhood settings. Overall, state regulations emphasize four areas of medical care and treatment:

- Health requirements for all employees, such as having no communicable diseases, passing a TB test, having no health conditions preventing active child care, and maintaining accurate employee and child health records
- Administration by staff of medication to children being served in EC settings
- Management by EC staff of emergencies due to illness, injury, and accidents
- Treatment of nonemergency minor illnesses, injuries, and accidents occurring to children in EC settings

To protect children's health and safety, EC programs/schools/centers must maintain written policies and procedures for emergency and nonemergency care. To protect personnel from litigation, they must adhere scrupulously to written policies and procedures. Litigation for damages or injury is likely when not following procedures. Not reporting suspected or observed child abuse/neglect and not completing accident reports also invite lawsuits.

ADMINISTRATION OF MEDICATION GUIDELINES

The administration of medication to children in early childhood settings has been subject to much controversy due to obvious issues of dangers and liability. EC centers and programs must write their policies and procedures to include their state government's licensing requirements for medical care and treatment, which they must follow closely. Experts recommend that parent and doctor permission be required for administering any prescription and nonprescription medications to children. EC settings should keep on file written parental consent for each medication and review these records regularly for changes. They should also post separate charts, easily accessible to staff, with each child's name, medication, dosage, administration time, and teacher initials. These provide documentation of teachers following parent directions and can prevent mistakes. Staff should label all medications with the drug name, child's name, doctor's name and contact information, and administration instructions. EC centers seasonally and frequently contain many children simultaneously recovering from a variety of illnesses; labeling prevents giving children the wrong medication. Empty drug containers should be returned to parents.

TRANSPORTATION FROM EARLY CHILDHOOD LOCATIONS AND EMERGENCY MEDICAL TREATMENT

For a child's non-life-threatening medical emergencies, early childhood personnel should request transportation by the child's parents. However, if parents cannot transport the child, or in a more severe emergency, EC administrators should call an ambulance. In life-threatening emergencies that preclude waiting for an ambulance, EC administrators must designate the vehicle and responsible employee for transporting the child to the hospital; this information should be posted in the facility's emergency procedures. Administrators should keep the number of staff involved in emergency medical treatment to a minimum. Those employees they designate for involvement should be willing to take on the responsibility and should have current first aid training. The administrators can include a clause in these employees' job descriptions providing for their transporting children in the event of an emergency. The EC facility may also pay for additional or separate liability insurance coverage of the employees they designate as responsible for providing necessary emergency medical treatment.

CHILD CUSTODY ISSUES INVOLVING EARLY CHILDHOOD FACILITIES

EC facilities are affected by two types of issues involving child custody:

- Parents are pursuing legal and/or physical custody of the child, but they are not living together.
- State authorities have removed a child from the parents' legal and physical custody.

Parents frequently demand the right to visit with and/or take the child home on occasion. Two types of custody are legal custody, defined as an individual's or agency's right to make decisions on a child's behalf regarding the child's place of residence, medical treatment, and education; and physical custody, defined as an individual's or agency's right and responsibility to provide a child with immediate care, and a household or care facility for the present and immediate future. Physical custody does not include all of the rights of full legal custody. It is serious for a child to be in the middle of a custody battle between divorcing parents or between parents and foster parents; therefore, early childhood facilities need the most concise, clear-cut guidelines possible.

EMERGENCY MEDICAL TREATMENT AND FIRST AID RECOMMENDATIONS

EC programs and preschools must write specific, detailed procedures regarding emergency treatment and keep these on file. Children's parents as well as early childhood administrators and staff need to be informed regarding what will occur in the event of a child's serious illness or injury. EC settings must also keep written, signed parental consent forms on file, as well as parent contact information, parental physician and hospital preferences, and health insurance information. EC staff should have current, regularly updated first aid training. First aid equipment should be stored in locations accessible to personnel, who should be frequently reminded of these locations. Lists of each staff member's first aid responsibilities and training should be posted, also accessibly. Licensing regulations require early childhood facilities to notify parents of emergencies; not doing so is subject to legal action. In non-life-threatening emergencies, staff should ask parents to furnish transportation and medical treatment. For grave emergencies, parental consent forms should be filed and updated semiannually, including physician and hospital names, ambulance service, and other transportation procedures.

Non-Emergency Medical Illnesses

EC programs must keep procedures for, and reports on, nonemergency medical treatment of children on file just as they do for emergency procedures and reporting. Staff must contact and notify a sick child's parents, who decide if the child should leave the center/preschool. If so, parents should transport their child. Parental consent forms should authorize a doctor or nurse to provide routine medical treatment. early childhood centers/preschools should have sick children wait to be picked up in a location that is separate from other children and activities but closely supervised by staff. For children with allergies, diabetes, and other chronic medical conditions, early childhood centers/preschools should not only keep this information on file in records but also post it accessibly at all times for staff reference. Instructions for any special treatment should be included. For any health impairments a child has that could potentially involve emergency treatment, directions for staff should be visibly posted, including specific employees designated to administer treatment. This protects children from harm and caregivers and educators from legal liability.

Custody Status

It is recommended that during a child's enrollment, early childhood programs procure a signed, dated document clarifying the child's custody status, including names, contact information, and relationships of all individuals authorized to pick up the child. Copies of any separation agreement or court decree should also be filed. Any time EC staff do not recognize an individual coming to pick up a child, they should ask the person to produce photo identification, which they should closely inspect. EC program administrators cannot make decisions regarding who has legal or physical custody of a child they serve. When a parent or other adult enrolls a child in an early childhood program, that adult is asked to list other persons to be contacted in the event of an emergency. EC administrators are advised to present all parents/guardians with a statement that the early childhood center will only release their child to someone the enrolling parent/adult listed on the emergency form as authorized to pick up the child.

Picking Up Children

Non-Custodial or Non-Authorized Adults Attempting to Pick Up Children

EC centers should always have up-to-date documentation on file of a child's custodial arrangements, signed and dated by the enrolling adult. If an adult not authorized to pick up the child attempts to do so, an early childhood administrator should inform that adult of the center's policies and procedures regarding custody. They may even show the unauthorized adult their copy of the custodial court order if needed. If the unauthorized adult then departs, the administrator must notify the enrolling adult of the incident; file a written report of it; meet with the custodial adult to clarify custody arrangements anew; document this meeting, including its date and signatures; and file the document in the child's record. If the unauthorized adult refuses to leave and makes a scene or threatens/displays violence, the EC administrator should call the police if needed. The EC center's having a procedure in place for protecting children against emotionally upsetting scenes and/or violent adult behavior is crucial to the children's safety and well-being.

Legal Responsibilities When Children Are Not Picked Up Timely

If a child is not picked up on time from an early childhood center at the end of its defined day, the EC center has the legal responsibility for the child's welfare as long as the child is on the premises. In the event that a child is left at the EC center for a long time and the parent/authorized adult has not notified the center why and/or when the child will be picked up, EC personnel are advised that keeping the child at the center is less likely to incur legal liability than for the child to stay at an EC staff member's home, for example. If the child has to be removed, it is important for EC staff to inform the police of this and where they are taking the child. If parents are chronically tardy picking up children, EC staff should review the child's information and/or inquire further of parents to ascertain reasons and possible solutions because they are legally responsible for reporting suspected child neglect.

ATTRIBUTES INDICATING EARLY CHILDHOOD EDUCATORS' PROFESSIONALISM AND PROFESSIONAL RESPONSIBILITY

While care and instruction of young children are delivered through a variety of program types, early childhood educators share common general goals. They appreciate early childhood as a unique period in life. They work to educate holistically, considering the mind, feelings, and body of the whole child. The educational goals they develop are designed to support each child's fulfilling his or her individual potential within relationship contexts. EC professionals realize children are inseparable from their social milieus of family, society, and culture; they work to relate to and understand children in these contexts while also appreciating and supporting family ties. They apply their knowledge of child development, teaching according to how children learn and what they need, and apply research in the field to differentiate common assumptions and myths from valid scientific findings. They have appropriate behavioral expectations for children at each developmental stage. EC professionals realize the significance of confidentiality; they never gossip or tell families personal information about other families. Lifelong learners, they set their own professional goals, pursuing ongoing professional development.

INTERACTIONS WITH ADULTS IN THE LEARNING ENVIRONMENT

Regarding teachers' roles, much of the focus is on observing children and their behaviors, helping children manage peer interactions, and giving children opportunities for developing peer-group social skills. Too often, a similar emphasis is not accorded to teachers' reflecting on their interactions and behaviors with other adults, learning to collaborate with other adults, and developing skills for conflict resolution and managing disagreements with other adults. Some experts say teachers should work diligently and deliberately to make adult interactions integral parts of daily classroom activity. For group early childhood education settings to attain their goals, adults must make and implement plans collaboratively. However, mandatory staff meetings are commonly occupied with curricular and administrative requirements; beyond these, little or no attention or time is applied to nurturing adult-adult relationships. Adults interact during in-service trainings and professional development experiences but rarely outside of daily classroom settings. Nevertheless, these experiences can be used as foundations for better adult-adult communication within early childhood education contexts. Conscious efforts to develop adult-adult relationships benefiting children's growth, development, and learning are necessary.

POSITIVE INTERACTIONS AMONG ADULTS WITHIN THE EARLY CHILDHOOD EDUCATION SETTING

Adults engage in positive interactions with each other within early childhood education programs when they make time to share their anecdotal records and observations of their young students and collaboratively plan instruction based on their collective contributions. When adults share information and communicate with one another about the children and their families with whom they work, they interact positively together. When EC educators engage in problem-solving activities and dialogues, these help them identify which learning goals and experiences they can make more effective for the children and how they can do this. Adults within early childhood education settings should engage in reciprocal exchanging of ideas about the EC learning environment and about how to share responsibilities for performing instructional tasks, rearranging classrooms as needed, setting up class projects, taking care of class pets and plants, and other such daily duties.

ADULT-ADULT INTERACTIONS

Early childhood education research contains little work addressing adults' cooperation and collaborative expertise with each other and the influences of these on children. However, the HighScope curriculum model, The Creative Curriculum, and similar curriculum models and approaches do address adult-adult interactions by stressing how important teamwork is in planning lessons and sharing responsibilities and information. In addition, some educational experts have written about power struggles and other interactional dynamics in adult-adult relationships that can impede employee performance in a variety of settings. Professional development and training programs rarely include adult conflict-resolution techniques, instruction in working collaboratively, or adult learning principles. Hence, educators must consider how their adult-adult interactions can support children's development of competence, capability, and confidence. Sharing instructional goals, planning learning experiences that support goals, and sharing responsibilities as a team for implementing projects establishes climates of safety and trust for children.

APPLYING QUALITY TIME TO EARLY CHILDHOOD EDUCATORS' INTERACTIONS WITH ADULTS

Educators have noted that attitudes and things we commonly say to children, such as, "Your actions speak louder than your words," would equally benefit us in addressing our own behaviors as adults. Applying the same principles we teach children to interactions among adults in the learning community can positively influence those interactions, which in turn affects adult-child/teacher-student interactions and overall classroom atmospheres. Without such atmospheres conducive to trust and honesty in adult relationships, educators can fall prey to misunderstandings and internalizing negative attitudes, which influence not only coworker interactions but moreover classroom climates. One solution is for adults in early childhood education to establish occasions affording "quality adult time." Psychotherapist and psychological theorist Virginia Satir, pioneer of family therapy, found interpersonal dynamics influenced by positive adult-adult communication. Trust-building, mutual colleague support, and sharing experiences/feelings—related or unrelated to classrooms—promote adult relationships that benefit teacher-learner relationships and thus enhance young children's development and learning.

Praxis Practice Test

1. Which of these is NOT one of the major personality structures proposed by Sigmund Freud in his psychoanalytic theory of development?

    a. Id
    b. Ego
    c. Libido
    d. Superego

2. To support EC language development, experts advise which of the following teacher practices?

    a. Asking children linear or one-way questions
    b. Doing most of the talking in their classrooms
    c. Focusing on durations of verbal interactions
    d. Asking children more open-ended questions

3. According to Piaget's theory of cognitive development, _____ and _____ are processes included in the overall process of _____.

    a. Assimilation; accommodation; adaptation
    b. Adaptation; assimilation; accommodation
    c. Accommodation; adaptation; assimilation
    d. Adaptation; accommodation; equilibrium

4. Piaget coined the term "schema" to describe:

    a. Mental constructs for individual objects.
    b. Mental concepts of categories or classes.
    c. Mental programs only for motor actions.
    d. Mental ideas governing inborn reflexes.

5. The concept of object permanence is best characterized as:

    a. "Out of sight, out of mind."
    b. "Out of mind, out of sight."
    c. "Out of sight, still exists."
    d. "Out of sight, out of time."

6. According to Piaget's theory, in what age range do children begin representing things with symbols?

    a. Between birth and 6 months
    b. Between 6 and 12 months
    c. Between 12 and 18 months
    d. Between 18 and 24 months

7. A toddler sees a large brown dog and says, "Moo!" This is an example of:

    a. Egocentrism.
    b. Equilibrium.
    c. Accommodation.
    d. Assimilation.

8. According to Piaget's theory, the term *conservation* means which of these?

    a. The idea that our natural resources are finite and hence, we must conserve them
    b. The idea that amounts/numbers can be retained or conserved in one's memories
    c. The idea that even when we cannot see an object, its existence is still conserved
    d. The idea that amounts/numbers are the same regardless of shape or appearance

9. When a young child believes his/her thoughts caused something external to happen, which is the *most specific* Piagetian term to describe this phenomenon?

    a. Animism
    b. Centration
    c. Egocentrism
    d. Magical thinking

10. Which of the following processes occurs earliest in children?

    a. Inductive logic
    b. Conservation
    c. Centration
    d. Decentration

11. In which of the six stages of art growth and development do children begin to develop a visual schema?

    a. Scribble
    b. Preschematic
    c. Schematic
    d. Dawning Realism

12. Which of the following is most effective for teaching pre-math and manipulative skills to preschool children?

    a. Giving them solid objects to manipulate physically
    b. Giving them information for mental manipulation
    c. Giving them math processes to memorize by rote
    d. Giving them lessons to listen to while they sit still

13. At what age do children typically undergo the second of three periods of language/communication development?

    a. From 0 - 6 months
    b. From 6 - 18 months
    c. From 8 - 12 months
    d. From 18-24 months

14. Which of the following is most typical of the language development of a two-year-old?
   a.   Using three-word sentences with ease
   b.   Knowing and naming major body parts
   c.   Using at least two pronouns correctly
   d.   Using about three pronouns correctly

15. Which of these is more typical of the language development of a two to three year old than of a preschooler?
   a.   Describing unseen objects
   b.   Telling "make-believe" stories
   c.   Speaking in complete sentences
   d.   Expressing opinions/preferences

16. Which of these is correct about one-on-one vs. group conversations between adults and young children?
   a.   Adults should discuss one on one during whole-group preschool activities.
   b.   Adults can better reinforce what children say in group discussions.
   c.   Adults have less chance to extend what children say in one on one context.
   d.   Adults can better elicit children's abstract idea comprehension one on one.

17. Which of the following teacher actions is most effective for fostering greater depth of preschoolers' comprehension of word meanings?
   a.   Focusing on one definition for a new vocabulary word
   b.   Introducing new concepts separately from new words
   c.   Limiting added information to simplify comprehension
   d.   Giving multiple definitions and examples of new words

18. What is correct about how teachers can support young children's language development when the children tell stories?
   a.   Teachers should not supply a vocabulary word if the child does not know it.
   b.   When listening to children's storytelling, teachers should not ask questions.
   c.   Storytelling permits young children to exercise their powers of imagination.
   d.   Teachers should let children express their ideas without building onto them.

19. What is the most typical age for children to understand common opposites like big/little, hot/cold, etc.?
   a.   Three years old
   b.   Five years old
   c.   Two years old
   d.   Four years old

20. According to Roger Brown's (1973) Stage I sentence types, which of these is classified under "Operations of Reference"?
   a.   A negation
   b.   An action
   c.   An agent
   d.   An entity

21. In Brown's (1973) Stages of Syntactical and Morphological Development, which of these age ranges is associated with what he designated as Stage I?

    a. 12-26 months
    b. 15-30 months
    c. 24-36 months
    d. 27-30 months

22. A child who correctly uses irregular past tenses of verbs, e.g. *went, fell, froze*, etc., would be in which of Roger Brown's Stages of Syntactic and Morphological Development?

    a. Stage I
    b. Stage II
    c. Stage III
    d. Stage IV

23. According to Roger Brown, a child who indicates the regular plural by saying "My toys" is in which of his Stages of Syntactical and Morphological Development?

    a. Stage V
    b. Stage IV
    c. Stage III
    d. Stage II

24. When characterizing young children, what did Vygotsky mean by the term "private speech" that he coined?

    a. Speaking in private dialogue with another child
    b. Speaking in private conversations with an adult
    c. Speaking silently to themselves in their minds
    d. Speaking aloud to themselves during activities

25. Among the following auditory disabilities, which one does not involve any part of the hearing mechanism?

    a. Only sensorineural-type hearing loss
    b. The conductive form of hearing loss
    c. Central auditory processing disorder
    d. The condition of complete deafness

26. To promote young children's developing abstract thinking, which teacher technique(s) to use during and after shared readings is/are best suited for use with children in the younger, rather than older, ages of early childhood?

    a. Asking children to predict what they think will happen next in the story
    b. Asking children to imagine beyond the story: "What would you do if...?"
    c. Asking children to identify vocabulary words and describe story details
    d. Asking them to make conclusions about why characters do/feel things

27. When a student considers whether an information source is reputable, has been proven objectively, and is accepted by experts in its discipline, which element of critical thinking does the student demonstrate?
   a. Evaluating supporting evidence
   b. Judging the quality of material
   c. Distinguishing fact from opinion
   d. Finding evidence/no evidence

28. What is true about the sequence that teachers should use for phonics instruction with young children?
   a. Teachers should introduce letters with similar sounds in separate lessons.
   b. Teachers should introduce stop consonants before continuous consonants.
   c. Teachers should introduce letters that look similar during the same lesson.
   d. Teachers should introduce low-utility before high-utility letters and sounds.

29. Which of these is correct regarding teacher assessment of early childhood print awareness using a storybook?
   a. Teachers can ask children to point out uppercase/lowercase letters and punctuation marks.
   b. It is not possible to conduct any accurate assessment of print awareness using a storybook.
   c. It is unnecessary to ask children to identify the front, back, spine, and title of the storybook.
   d. It does not inform assessment to have children show the first and last words in a sentence.

30. From birth to the age of 2 years, children typically grow to ___ times their newborn weights.
   a. Three
   b. Four
   c. Two
   d. Five

31. By the time they are two years old, children's brains typically have grown to __ of their adult sizes.
   a. 90%
   b. 75%
   c. 55%
   d. 40%

32. What is true regarding children's motor development from infancy to preschool ages?
   a. Proprioception is established at birth and does not progress any further.
   b. The voluntary behaviors of newborns eventually progress into reflexes.
   c. Motor skills development involves learning of new physical movements over the course of time.
   d. Motor skills are largely known at infancy, but infants lack the strength to execute complex movements.

33. Which of these accurately reflects research findings on gender differences in early childhood motor development?

a. Preschool girls are found to be equally muscular as, but more physically mature than, boys are in preschool.
b. Preschool boys exhibit both more strength and coordination in large-muscle gross-motor skills than girls do.
c. Preschool girls exhibit more fine-motor skills, but less gross-motor coordination, than boys do in preschool.
d. Despite certain differences, preschool motor development between genders is more similar than different.

34. Regarding the three basic temperament types identified by psychologists in infants, which of these is true?

a. There is no clear majority among infants having one of the types.
b. The majority of babies are found to be of Difficult temperament.
c. The majority of infants are found to be Slow to Warm Up types.
d. The majority of infants are found to have the Easy temperament.

35. When a child gives reasons for succeeding at something, which of the following reflects an internal locus of control?

a. "I did well because the teacher helped me."
b. "I got a good mark because I was just lucky."
c. "I did well because Danny showed me how."
d. "I did a good job because I worked so hard."

36. For children with a primarily visual learning style, which material would be most effective to give them to help them understand abstract concepts and relationships?

a. Soft clay to sculpt
b. Dance movements
c. Multicolor graphics
d. Sporting activities

37. Which of Erikson's psychosocial stages of development corresponds to ages 2-3 years in early childhood?

a. Basic Trust vs. Mistrust
b. Autonomy vs. Shame
c. Initiative vs. Guilt
d. Industry vs. Inferiority

38. Which of the following reflects an adult expectation of a child that is developmentally appropriate?

a. Expecting a six-year-old to stay in-seat and attend to a first-grade lesson
b. Expecting a five-year-old to sit still and be quiet during long-term activity
c. Expecting a toddler to balance upon one foot and/or to hop on one foot
d. Expecting a four-month-old baby to sit up without any external support

39. According to Alfred Adler's theory about birth order, which of these applies to only or oldest children?

    a.   Only children tend to prefer the company of children to the company of adults.
    b.   Only children tend to prefer the company of adults to the company of children.
    c.   Only children tend to share things with other children more easily than others.
    d.   Older/oldest children never develop strict or authoritarian attitudes/behaviors.

40. Which of the following correctly reflects Adler's theory of birth order's influences on personality development?

    a.   The youngest children in families have no features in common with only children.
    b.   Twins are identical in activity and/or strength and parents perceive them as equal.
    c.   Some "babies" of the family grow to make grandiose plans, which never succeed.
    d.   Adler never noted any differences between twins as to personality development.

41. In Adler's psychoanalytic theory, which of these did he believe about male/female siblings in family birth orders?

    a.   An only boy with girl siblings will more likely behave effeminately than as overly masculine in the father's absence.
    b.   An only girl with boy siblings will more likely become a tomboy than become very feminine to differentiate herself.
    c.   Adler stated parents of all males/females wanting a child of the other sex never dress one child as the opposite sex.
    d.   Boy siblings of an only girl can behave protectively toward her; and she may make extra effort to please the father.

42. According to Murray Bowen's Family Systems Theory, which of the following accurately reflects what he called the Family Projection Process?

    a.   A parent's fear about something being wrong with a child is based on a real problem in the child.
    b.   The child's behavior confirms the parent's fears because something really is wrong with the child.
    c.   In focusing on the child, parents' perceptions come to mirror the child's self-image and behaviors.
    d.   Parental perception of child problems can become self-fulfilling prophecy in the child's self-image.

43. Typically, young children eat most of the same foods as adults by the age of ___.

    a.   Five years old.
    b.   Four years old.
    c.   Three years old.
    d.   Two years old.

44. Which of the following is most accurate about the sleep needs and behaviors of young children?

    a.   Children typically need 9-11 hours of sleep from ages 2-5 years.
    b.   Children typically need 7-9 hours of sleep at the ages 2-5 years.
    c.   Children typically need 10-12 hours of sleep at ages of 2-5 years.
    d.   Children typically need long daytime naps at the ages 2-5 years.

45. What is most true about hand-washing hygiene during early childhood?
   a.   Parents continue to wash children's hands during the early childhood years.
   b.   Young children are unlikely to wash their hands long or thoroughly enough.
   c.   Toddlers are not exposed to more germs during the toilet-training process.
   d.   Germ exposure in daycare/preschool is not a significant cause for concern.

46. Which of these most accurately reflects findings about mass media and other cultural influences on young children?
   a.   Viewing video violence has been proven to increase young children's aggressive behaviors.
   b.   Young children get more cognitive stimulation from watching TV than interactive activities.
   c.   In larger families, children do not need 1:1 time with parents; group activities are as good.
   d.   Parents should discourage playing "house" and other make-believe play as it is unrealistic.

47. Which of the following have research studies found regarding the relative individualism or collectivism of different world cultures?
   a.   American culture has been found to be the most interdependent.
   b.   Asian and Latin American cultures are both more interdependent.
   c.   European cultures are found more individualistic than in the USA.
   d.   European cultures are found more collectivistic than those in Asia.

48. What is true regarding survey findings about family differences among American socioeconomic and racial groups?
   a.   Cultural and demographic factors influence disagreement styles more than parental stress does.
   b.   Low-socioeconomic young children have no more development/behavior problems than others.
   c.   Data have shown more violence in African-American families, followed by Latino and then White families.
   d.   Socioeconomically disadvantaged children have more problems and receive more help for these.

49. Which of these have researchers found about cultural and familial influences on school readiness and achievement?
   a.   A national survey has not found significant differences in parenting practices among racial/ethnic groups.
   b.   Varying degrees of early childhood development are unrelated to home routines, safety, and parenting.
   c.   Researchers do not think racial and ethnic disparities in school achievement contribute to discrimination.
   d.   American children in minority groups show lower average school readiness than American white children.

50. Which of the following reflects an early childhood application of Freud's psychoanalytic theory of development?
   a.   Providing opportunities for children to "make believe"
   b.   Providing models of behaviors children see and imitate
   c.   Providing timely, consistent nursing/feeding to a baby
   d.   Providing safe and sanitary objects for babies to mouth

51. Which of the following is an early childhood practice that best applies knowledge of Piaget's first stage of cognitive development?

    a. Introducing topics to children seen from others' perspectives
    b. Encouraging make-believe and pretend play that use symbols
    c. Introducing simple, basic arithmetic ideas as early as possible
    d. Providing many manipulable toys that move and make noises

52. The animation of letters and numbers in Sesame Street, or of objects in Spongebob Squarepants, appeals to children in Piaget's Preoperational stage of cognitive development because of their:

    a. Logical thinking.
    b. Magical thinking.
    c. Animistic thinking.
    d. Egocentric thinking.

53. Which of the following is NOT one of Bandura's conditions required for learning?

    a. Attention
    b. Cognition
    c. Retention
    d. Motivation

54. When a toddler begins to shout, "NO!" often, Erikson would characterize this behavior as:

    a. Developing autonomy
    b. Developing initiative
    c. Developing industry
    d. Developing mistrust

55. In Maslow's theory, which needs are at the base of the pyramid?

    a. Self-actualizing
    b. Physiological
    c. Security
    d. Esteem

56. According to Carl Rogers, a child who relies primarily on external locus of control demonstrates:

    a. Incongruence
    b. Conditions of worth
    c. Conditional positive self-regard
    d. Unconditional positive regard

57. A young child wakes up early one day and enjoys not being rushed by his mother in getting ready for preschool. This child then makes a point of waking up early again on subsequent days. According to behaviorist theory, this illustrates which principle?

    a. Positive reinforcement
    b. Positive punishment
    c. Negative punishment
    d. Negative reinforcement

58. Which statement is most accurate about the Montessori Method of education?
   a.   Practical skills and abstract concepts are taught via mental tasks.
   b.   Teachers observe and guide children but parents are uninvolved.
   c.   Learning environments are keyed to group developmental levels.
   d.   The self-direction and self-correction of children are emphasized.

59. Which of these correctly represents an element of the Bank Street Curriculum approach to early childhood education?
   a.   Children learn separate subjects, one at a time.
   b.   Children learn as individuals via 1:1 instruction.
   c.   Children learn in one type of childcare program.
   d.   Children learn at various developmental levels.

60. Which statement accurately reflects Friedrich Froebel's philosophy of early childhood education?
   a.   Froebel believed schools should not direct student will.
   b.   Froebel believed in group, not individual, attainments.
   c.   Froebel believed that nature is the heart of all learning.
   d.   Froebel believed instruction should not be play-based.

61. Of the following, which is true of Siegfried Engelmann's contributions to early childhood education?
   a.   The Bereiter-Engelmann Preschool Program tested teaching methods with affluent college faculty's children.
   b.   Engelmann demonstrated that Piaget's conservation of liquid volume did not depend only on a child's stage.
   c.   The philosophy and methodology of Direct Instruction were developed by somebody other than Engelmann.
   d.   Engelmann's research into curriculum and instruction excluded the study of children who had any disabilities.

62. The HighScope Curriculum for preschoolers (Weikart et al) identifies 58 key developmental experiences for active learning, dividing them into 10 main categories. Which of the following does NOT correctly represent one of the first five of these 10 categories?
   a.   Music, including being able to write musical notation and compositions
   b.   Language/literacy including speaking, scribbling, describing, storytelling
   c.   Creative representation; symbol recognition, imitation; and playing roles
   d.   Initiative, social relations; problem-solving, decisions, and relationships

63. Which of these statements accurately reflects principles of emergent literacy theory?
   a.   Children's first encounters with written language occur during early childhood.
   b.   Young children learn reading and writing concurrently rather than sequentially.
   c.   All young children's scribbles look similar regardless of native written language.
   d.   Comprehension develops receptively before expressively with speech and print.

64. Which of the following is true about the whole language approach to early childhood literacy instruction?

    a.   The whole language approach to literacy is very similar to phonics in their analytical nature.
    b.   The whole language approach to literacy is quite similar in character to alphabetic learning.
    c.   The whole language approach is based on the philosophy and psychology of constructivism.
    d.   The whole language approach emphasizes the similarity of each child's learning experience.

65. What statement correctly represents how the whole language instructional approach addresses young children's mechanical errors in early literacy learning?

    a.   Using printed language with technical correctness early is the priority in this method.
    b.   Whole language teachers ignore young children's mechanical errors when they occur.
    c.   Whole language teachers use only summative assessments of young children's errors.
    d.   Children's overall engagement, comprehension, and appreciation precede correction.

66. When children construct meaning, they may address new information that does not fit into their existing concepts or schemes by either forming a new scheme or changing an existing one. What is this process called?

    a.   Adaptation
    b.   Assimilation
    c.   Equilibration
    d.   Accommodation

67. Which statement correctly describes some benefits to young children of the Language Experience Approach (LEA)?

    a.   The LEA teaches beginning reading by using printed language apart from students' lives.
    b.   With the LEA young students learn to use different words/language than they usually do.
    c.   Instruction using the LEA enables the students to interact with text at one level at a time.
    d.   Children realize they acquire knowledge and understanding from their own experiences.

68. Which of the following is correct regarding early childhood reading instruction using basal readers?

    a.   Texts used for basal readers include children's literature rather than other genres.
    b.   Basal reader texts graded by reading level use narrative instead of expository work.
    c.   Instruction from smaller to larger skills helps student transitions from part to whole.
    d.   Progressing in skills following a rigid, systematic sequence is less helpful to students.

69. Which of these helps young children to decode text in the basal reader approach to reading instruction?

    a.   Precise control of word analysis skills
    b.   All of these help for decoding of text
    c.   Exactly controlling vocabulary items
    d.   Included use of enlarged "big books"

70. What statement is accurate regarding the Directed Reading Activity (DRA) instructional practice using basal readers?

    a. Teachers first prepare students to read by introducing new concepts, words, and stimulating motivation.

    b. Before teachers give students motivation, vocabulary, and concepts, students silently do guided reading.

    c. When students are reading silently, teachers do not interfere by presenting any questions or statements.

    d. Student reading comprehension is developed by teacher actions rather than through student discussion.

71. Which best expresses what the Directed Reading-Thinking Activity (DR-TA) is intended to accomplish?

    a. To develop critical thinking through using individual 1:1 instruction

    b. To develop critical reading through teaching group comprehension

    c. To engage children in processing information without any feedback

    d. To engage children only by their asking questions about the reading

72. Which accurately reflects a contrast between the Directed Reading Activity (DRA) and the Directed Reading-Thinking Activity (DR-TA) as methods of reading instruction using basal readers?

    a. DR-TA only works with basal readers but DRA can work for other curriculum plans.

    b. The pre-teaching of new vocabulary is featured in DR-TAs but is absent from DRAs.

    c. DRA requires convergent thinking whereas DR-TA also requires divergent thinking.

    d. DR-TA approaches specify when to teach which skills, but DRA approaches do not.

73. What statement is most accurate about using manipulatives in preschool math instruction?

    a. Young children cannot understand abstract concepts at all.

    b. Young children can only understand solid, concrete objects.

    c. There are no early math curricula to require manipulatives.

    d. Manipulatives are proven to be effective learning devices.

74. Which of the following foundational science skills is best illustrated by an activity comparing non-standard measures, such as using scales to find the weight ratio when comparing apples and grapes.

    a. Observation

    b. Inference

    c. Communication

    d. Classifying

75. Which of the following is true about preschool activities to teach scientific inquiry and discovery?

    a. Exploring the solubility in water of various substances is not a scientific activity.

    b. Seeing what colors result from mixing other colors is strictly an art class activity.

    c. Comparing similarities and contrasting differences in objects are good activities.

    d. For a preschool teacher to create a science center is typically always expensive.

76. What statement is most appropriate regarding how teachers can help preschoolers learn to use scientific inquiry and discovery?

    a. Children learn best from age-appropriate science textbooks.
    b. Teachers can find materials in their everyday environments.
    c. Found objects from the natural world are not good materials.
    d. Teachers should not obtain materials from local businesses.

77. Which of these is accurate regarding physical and motor development in preschoolers?

    a. Preschool children's bodies have higher centers of gravity.
    b. Preschoolers are no more likely to fall than older children.
    c. Preschool teachers should not encourage children to hop.
    d. Balance/coordination exercises have no emotional benefit.

78. Of the following, which is true of teaching preschool children about the visual art element of color?

    a. Teachers cannot use stories or songs to teach children about colors.
    b. Children can learn color names, discrimination, and classification.
    c. There are no art museums that offer lessons for preschool ages.
    d. Preschool children cannot appreciate viewing works of fine art.

79. What can preschool children learn from lessons about the visual art element of line?

    a. This will not help them make better comparisons.
    b. Children's symbol recognition will not be affected.
    c. Children's ability to recognize shapes will develop.
    d. Preschoolers cannot distinguish among line types.

80. What is included in benefits of instructional activities teaching preschoolers about the visual art element of shape?

    a. These are unrelated to concept formation.
    b. Other elements help identify discrepancies.
    c. Creative thinking skills will not be affected.
    d. Early geometric math skills are developed.

81. What is the correct meaning of cognitive dissonance?

    a. A cognitive processing disorder affecting understanding
    b. A disruption of cognition caused by a sensory overload
    c. A feeling of discomfort due to contradictory information
    d. A lack of compatibility between instruction and learning

82. Of the following, which is true about providing affective learning experiences for preschoolers?

    a. Affective learning activities help children express, but not understand, emotions.
    b. Learning to understand their feelings will not help children with self-regulation.
    c. Affective activities cannot inform teachers of children's feelings or preferences.
    d. Children's social development and interactions require emotional development.

83. Giving preschool children an activity using different body postures and movements to portray different emotions can accomplish which of these?
    a. Children understand their own emotions but not others'.
    b. Children understand emotions, but do not express them.
    c. Children participate in physical exercise while having fun.
    d. Children use creative thinking without emotional benefit.

84. Which of the following most accurately describes aspects of early childhood social development?
    a. Young children tend to use speech more than physical aggression.
    b. Young children develop and apply motor skills before verbal skills.
    c. Young children know constructive management of strong emotion.
    d. Young children learn social skills directly rather than with puppets.

85. How much usable play space at a minimum do experts recommend for indoor and outdoor early childhood learning environments?
    a. At least 35 sq. ft. indoors and 75 sq. ft. outdoors
    b. At least 25 sq. ft. indoors and 50 sq. ft. outdoors
    c. At least 50 sq. ft. indoors and 100 sq. ft. outside
    d. At least 45 sq. ft. indoors and 85 sq. ft. outdoors

86. Which of these is correct regarding expert guidelines for indoor and outdoor spaces in EC learning environments?
    a. Children's products and other visual elements should be put at adult eye level.
    b. Spaces should be arranged for individual, small-group, and large-group activity.
    c. Spaces should be organized to prohibit children from moving among activities.
    d. Spaces should be arranged so children are not distracted by social interactions.

87. Of the following, which is correct about considerations in arranging indoor learning environments to fit with curriculum planning for toddlers and preschoolers?
    a. Rooms should be arranged to limit activities to certain areas.
    b. The floors in all the rooms should be covered with carpeting.
    c. The rooms should be organized to enable different activities.
    d. Math and science activities should be in one classroom area.

88. A teacher tells a class that anybody who gets 100 percent on the next quiz will be excused from doing homework for that day. According to behaviorist terminology relative to motivation theory, this incentive is an example of what technique?
    a. Positive reinforcement
    b. Primary reinforcement
    c. Negative reinforcement
    d. Secondary reinforcement

89. In indoor EC learning environments, which of the following is most related to providing for children's privacy needs?
    a. Adult laps for cuddling
    b. Pillows and soft upholstery
    c. Areas of floor with thick carpets
    d. Small inner rooms and partitions

90. Which statement is true regarding principles of early childhood behavior management?

a. Punishing bad behaviors is more powerful.
b. Punishments and rewards work equally well.
c. Rewarding good behaviors is more powerful.
d. Rewarding good behaviors should be occasional.

91. When considering behavior management with young children, which of these is most accurate?

a. Behaviors can be replaced regardless of their function.
b. To change a behavior, one must first know its function.
c. Behaviors need no change if one knows their functions.
d. The same consequences are applied for every function.

92. According to the provisions of FERPA, when can schools furnish student records without consent?

a. To some doing studies, if on behalf of the school.
b. Court orders and legal subpoenas are insufficient.
c. Safety or health emergencies still require consent.
d. To juvenile justice system authorities in all states.

93. How are teachers required to ensure educational equity?

a. By delivering uniform instruction to all students
b. By offering different opportunities to students
c. By treating students less fairly if they deserve it
d. By using materials reflecting multicultural views

94. What is the meaning of the "10:1 Rule" relative to early childhood behavior management?

a. For every 10 negative comments/corrections, give 1 positive comment.
b. For every 1 positive comment, give 10 negative comments/corrections.
c. For every 1 new behavior to be learned, 10 repetitions are necessary.
d. For every 1 negative comment/correction, give 10 positive comments.

95. Which statement is correct about managing young children's typical behaviors in care and educational settings?

a. Adults do not need to do anything if children follow the rules.
b. Withholding rewards for noncompliance needs no explanation.
c. Once adults have stated rules, they need not constantly repeat.
d. Children should be consistently rewarded for following the rules.

96. What applies for EC educators to include children's families in their educations?

a. The family use of parenting skills is none of the educators' business.
b. One-way educator communication to families periodically is enough.
c. Educators should acknowledge parents' integral role in child learning.
d. School staff should make parents feel welcome but not ask their help.

97. Which of these is most appropriate to EC educators for involving diverse families in children's educations?

    a. When educators design IFSPs for preschoolers, it is unnecessary to involve the family.
    b. Educators should ask families to develop their own goals for educational participation.
    c. Educators should create volunteer calendars and assign parents times for participating.
    d. It is not the educators' problem if families have difficulty with printed/written English.

98. Which of these should EC educators communicate to diverse families of the children they instruct?

    a. Information about their child instead of developmental milestones
    b. Information about developmental milestones rather than methods
    c. Information about development and methods for nurturing growth
    d. Information about class content but not developmental milestones

99. For teachers to make informal assessments of pre-K classes, which of these would apply?

    a. Teachers assess during small-group rather than whole-class activities.
    b. Teachers only make assessments during activities for the whole class.
    c. Teachers can organize assessments by using around ten themes a day.
    d. Teachers make classroom observations each targeting different skills.

100. Which of these is accurate concerning formal assessment instruments used in early childhood education?

    a. Formal assessment instruments cannot prevent administrator bias.
    b. Formal assessment instruments record more than child responses.
    c. Formal assessment data should not be compared by ages or levels.
    d. Formal assessments are typically standardized tests given to groups.

101. In his social learning theory, what does Bandura mean by reciprocal determinism?

    a. Learning mutually involves both the learner and the instructor.
    b. Learning mutually involves both the behavior and environment.
    c. Learning mutually involves both the individual and environment.
    d. Learning mutually involves individual, behavior, and environment.

102. What is accurate about different screening and assessment instruments used in EC education programs?

    a. All these instruments measure the same developmental domains.
    b. These instruments are all meant for use with the same applications.
    c. Not all of these are appropriate with ethnically diverse populations.
    d. The same methods of administration are used with all instruments.

103. Which statement is true about different screening and assessment instruments that can be used by educational programs for testing young children?

    a. These instruments are all comprehensive in assessing multiple domains.
    b. There are some instruments focusing on only one facet within a domain.
    c. Some instruments focus on a single domain but not on parts of domains.
    d. Tests measure developmental domains but not risk or resiliency factors.

104. Of the following, what is most accurate regarding ECE applications of screening and assessment instruments?

    a. Assessment instruments are used in planning curriculum and treatment programs.
    b. Screening instruments are routinely used for diagnosing developmental problems.
    c. It is inappropriate to use assessment instruments to develop or confirm diagnoses.
    d. ECE programs never use assessment instruments in determining a child's eligibility.

105. What is an accurate statement about selecting screening and assessment instruments according to the age ranges they cover for use in ECE programs?

    a. Tests covering the entire age range served in a program are less useful because they are not age-specific.
    b. Tests covering the entire age range served in a program can be used in mid-program to monitor progress.
    c. Tests that are separate and specific to different ages make it easier to compare before and after programs.
    d. Tests that cover the whole range of ages served in the program are not as accurate for all of the child ages.

106. Regarding paper-and-pencil reports for adults to provide screening and assessment of young children, which of these best reflects their characteristics?

    a. Such reports must be self-administered at respondents' reading levels in their native languages.
    b. These surveys or questionnaires must not be read to respondents even by trained interviewers.
    c. Self-reporting instruments have the advantage that they usually take shorter times to complete.
    d. ECE program personnel need relatively little training to administer, score, and interpret reports.

107. Adult interviews used to gather screening/assessment information about infants and young children:

    a. Are conducted in structured formats with assigned questions.
    b. Are in semi-structured formats using administrator judgment.
    c. Cover only the child's identified areas of strengths and needs.
    d. Are brief but usually still longer than self-reporting measures.

108. Which of the following screening and assessment methods yield the most comprehensive information for determining EC diagnoses and/or developing individualized plans for EC care or instruction?

    a. Self-reporting questionnaires/surveys
    b. Formal or informal observational tools
    c. Structured/semi-structured interviews
    d. Instruments that use multiple methods

109. Which of these is a correct definition of test-retest reliability?

    a. An instrument gives the same results for the same child at the same time and setting, by different persons.

    b. An instrument's individual items correlate highly with one another and with the overall instrument's score.

    c. An instrument includes individual items that cover the entire range of the content area that it claims to test.

    d. An instrument gets the same results when given twice or more to the same child within a short time period.

110. Of the following, which defines internal consistency in EC screening and assessment instruments?

    a. Two children score beyond a test's cutoff for assessment need, via different test items.

    b. A test's individual items are found to have low correlations with the test's overall score.

    c. Two children score past a test's cutoff for assessment need on most of the same items.

    d. The individual questions on a test are found to have low correlations with one another.

111. Which of these would apply to a test of EC social-emotional development with high content validity?

    a. A screening test screens for a child's interactions with caregivers and not those with the child's peers.

    b. A child's performance on the test can be used to generalize about how it predicts real-life functioning.

    c. A screening test screens for a child's social skills and does not screen for his/her communication skills.

    d. A screening test screens for a child's levels of attention and does not screen for his/her initiating play.

112. What is correct regarding predictive validity, sensitivity, specificity, and false-positive and false-negative errors in screening and assessment instruments used with preschool children?

    a. A screening tool identifies a potential mental health disorder which a complete evaluation then diagnoses.

    b. An instrument correctly identifying 6 of 10 children with disorders/delays is said to have a specificity of 60%.

    c. An instrument correctly identifying 8 of 10 children as not having disorders/delays shows sensitivity of 80%.

    d. A screening tool identifying delays or disorders in children where none exists contains false-negative errors.

113. How can assessment results be applied to instructional planning for ECE groups and individual children?

    a. If EC educators record careful anecdotal observations and authentic assessments, outlines are not necessary.

    b. Making organized outlines of developmental guidelines gives bases for anecdotal and authentic assessments.

    c. The extensive practice and review needed for young children to retain skills are outside of ECE program scope.

    d. Developmental sequences are irrelevant to systems that ECE programs utilize for tracking children's progress.

114. In a hypothetical scenario, an EC teacher sees injuries to a child in her class. She also has observed that this child's mother has a new boyfriend; behaves fearfully; and is evasive with the teacher's questions. Then the child tells this teacher that this new boyfriend hurt the child. Which description of the teacher's response would best meet legal responsibilities for a professional in the ECE setting?

    a. The teacher feels sorry for the mother and her situation and does not report suspicions she cannot prove.

    b. The teacher knows the mother depends on the boyfriend financially and emotionally and does not report.

    c. The teacher reports her suspicions because the law requiring it was made to stop violence against children.

    d. The teacher reports her suspicions regardless because the law requires it and penalizes her for not doing it.

115. Which of the following best reflects actions that enable and support positive interactions among adults within ECE settings?

    a. EC educators should respect student privacy by not sharing anecdotal records and observations with colleagues.

    b. Communicating to other adults about children and families is not positive interaction because of confidentiality.

    c. EC educators should share their observations and records on students, but should not plan instruction together.

    d. EC educators use problem-solving activities and dialogues to discern how to enhance child learning experiences.

116. Among the following, which is correct regarding legal regulations of records confidentiality in ECE settings?

    a. The FERPA mandates student records confidentiality for every ECE program/facility/agency existing in the USA.

    b. The special education laws of each U.S. state supersede the IDEA for confidentiality of disabled student records.

    c. Laws penalize ECE employees for releasing records but require them to report suspected child abuse or neglect.

    d. Laws require ECE employees to report suspected abuse/neglect and prevent liability for related records release.

117. What is true about guidelines for ECE personnel regarding medications administered to children in EC care and education settings?

a. ECE centers/programs should write their own policies and procedures, regardless of state licensing requirements.
b. ECE experts find it unnecessary for centers to require doctor and parent permission for giving medication to children.
c. If written parent consent to give medication is kept on file, separate charts for staff are redundant and enable errors.
d. Staff should label all medications by drug name, child name, doctor name and contact information, and instructions.

118. What is recommended for ECE settings regarding emergency first aid and medical treatment?

a. Written parental consent is unnecessary in real emergencies.
b. Centers need not file parental doctor or hospital preferences.
c. Information on family health insurance should be kept on file.
d. Notifying parents of emergencies is desired but not required.

119. Which of these accurately represents child custody issues affecting ECE facilities and types of custody?

a. Legal custody is an individual/agency's right and responsibility to give a child immediate care and housing.
b. One issue that affects ECE facilities is when state authorities have removed a child from parental custody.
c. Two parents' pursuing custody of a child but not living together will not have any impact on ECE facilities.
d. Physical custody is an individual/agency's right to decide for a child on housing, education, and medicine.

120. Of the following, which reflects recommend procedures for ECE facilities if non-custodial or non-authorized adults try to pick up children served at a facility?

a. ECE administrators should inform unauthorized adults of policies and procedures, including custodial court orders.
b. If an unauthorized adult refuses to leave, threatens/shows violence, or makes a scene, police should not be called.
c. After an unauthorized adult leaves, the administrator must notify enrolling adults but need not file written reports.
d. After an unauthorized adult leaves, the administrator must meet with the custodial adult without filing documents.

Answer Key and Explanations

1. C: The libido is part of the id according to Freud. It represents psychic energy as well as sex drive. Freud's three major personality structures are the id (A), which generates unconscious impulses; the ego (B), which realistically regulates acting on id impulses; and the superego (C), which pursues morality and perfection.

2. D: Researchers advise EC teachers to ask children more open-ended questions, the kind that allow the children and the teacher to give two- and three-way responses in conversations, rather than the more common but less desirable practice of asking linear questions that demand one-way responses (A). They also criticize teachers' tendency to do most of the talking (B) in classrooms rather than encouraging children to use conversational language, which is preferable. Experts advise teachers not to focus only on the quantity of conversations (C), but equally on their quality.

3. A: Assimilation is fitting a new experience into an existing schema. Accommodation is altering an existing schema or forming a new schema to accommodate a new experience. These two processes are part of the overall process of adaptation, i.e. adjusting one's thinking to the environment via interacting with it. This adaptation process helps the individual to maintain equilibrium, or balance.

4. B: Schemata (plural of schema) are mental constructs or concepts of categories or classes of things, e.g. things I can suck on; things I can throw; furry four-legged animals, etc. They are not concepts of individual objects (A). They are not programs only for motor actions (C), but ideas for categorizing different components of the environment. Inborn reflexes are not governed by ideas (D) but are automatic reactions.

5. C: Object permanence, which babies develop during Piaget's first, Sensorimotor stage of cognitive development, is the realization that objects still exist even when they are out of sight. (A) is the opposite of this. The other choices are not related to the concept of object permanence.

6. D: Piaget theorized that children begin to use symbols to represent other things around the ages of 18-24 months. This is evident in their pretend play, when they might use a broom to represent a horse or a guitar, or a block to represent a phone; and pretend to be adults when playing "House," etc. Children are not observed to use symbols this way during the age ranges of (A), (B), or (C); and not doing so until later than 24 months would represent a cognitive developmental delay.

7. D: This is an example of assimilation. The toddler has a schema (concept) of large, brown, four-legged, furry animals as being cows. Seeing a large, brown, four-legged, furry dog, s/he fits it into the cow schema. When the child forms a new schema for dogs to include the different animal s/he saw, this would be an example of accommodation (C). Egocentrism (A) is Piaget's term for young children's inability to see things from another person's perspective, including from their physical position in space. Equilibrium (B) is the balance Piaget said children maintain through adaptation, the process of adjusting to the environment via assimilation and accommodation.

8. D: Piaget used the term *conservation* to mean the ability children develop in the stage of Concrete Operations to conserve the concept of the same quantity regardless of changes in appearance, shape, or arrangement. He did not use this term to refer to conserving natural resources (A) or retaining memories of quantities (B). (C) describes what Piaget termed object permanence.

9. D: The most specific description of this in Piaget's terms is magical thinking. Animism (A) is his term for ascribing human qualities to inanimate objects. Centration (B) is his term for focusing or

127

centering on one quality of something, e.g. the height but not the width of a container. Egocentrism (C) is the inability to see others' perspectives. Egocentrism also applies to viewing everything as revolving around oneself, of which magical thinking and animism are more specific phenomena.

10. C: Preoperational children centrate, or focus, on one attribute of an object to the exclusion of others. Thus they think, for example, that a tall, thin beaker contains more fluid than a short, wide one when both contain the same amount. Later, children achieve decentration (D), allowing them to include more than one attribute. Hence they are capable of conservation (B), the knowledge that the amount is the same despite different appearances or shapes. Children develop inductive logic (A), i.e. generalizing from specific events, in Piaget's stage of Concrete Operations, along with decentration and conservation.

11. B: During the Preschematic stage, around the ages of 4-6 years, children begin to develop a visual schema. In the Scribble (A) stage, which precedes the Preschematic, children first make uncontrolled scribbles; then controlled scribbles; and then name what their scribbles represent. In the Schematic (C) stage, around 7-9 years of age, following the Preschematic, children draw pictures more accurately reflective of real physical proportions, body parts, features, and colors. In the stage of Dawning Realism (D), around the ages of 9-11 years, children make increasingly representational drawings.

12. A: Young children must have concrete things they can see, touch, and manipulate. They are not yet cognitively capable of manipulating information mentally (B). They are not yet able to memorize math processes by rote (C), as older elementary-age children can memorize times tables, etc. They are too young to benefit from "sit still and listen" types of lessons (D).

13. B: Children to three developmental periods in language and communication. The first is using crying and eye contact for expressive behaviors from birth to six months. The second period, from 6-18 months, involves intentional communication. The third period is typically from the age of 18 months on, involving the use of language as the primary method of communicating.

14. C: Typically, a two-year-old's language development includes correctly using at least two pronouns (e.g. *me* and *you*). Using three-word sentences with ease (A), knowing and naming the major body parts (B), and using three pronouns correctly (D) in speech are characteristics typical of a three-year-old's language development.

15. D: The toddler years are typically when children begin to express their opinions, likes and dislikes as well as their feelings and ideas; and to ask questions. The early preschool years are typically when children are able to describe unseen objects (A), tell "make-believe" stories (B), and speak in complete sentences (C).

16. D: It is easier for adults to find out what young children understand about abstract concepts during one to one conversations than in group conversations. At preschools, adults should engage each child in one on one conversations at times like when children arrive and leave; during center time; and during shared reading activities with 1-2 children rather than during whole-group activities (A). 1:1 conversations enable adults to reinforce what children say by repeating it better in one on one than in group discussions (B). Adults also have *more* chance to extend what children say by adding to it in 1:1 conversations (C); and to restate what children say so they hear their own ideas reflected back to them one on one than in group conversations.

17. D: To deepen young children's comprehension of word meanings, teachers should provide them with multiple definitions and examples for each word rather than only one (A). They should introduce new concepts together with new vocabulary words (B) associated with the concepts.

They should provide additional information to give children's comprehension of meanings more depth (C).

18. C: It is true that one benefit of children's storytelling is that it allows them to engage and exercise their imaginations. When young children tell stories and need a vocabulary word they do not know, their teachers *should* supply them with the word (A). Teachers *should* also ask children questions (B) about their storytelling to model correct sentence structure and get children to elaborate on what they say. Teachers should not only let children express their ideas through storytelling; they should also build further upon these ideas (D) by asking them guiding questions to elicit more information.

19. B: Most children typically understand common antonyms around the age of five years. At three years (A), they understand simple questions and can answer what to do when they are hot or cold, hungry or thirsty, etc., but will not necessarily understand opposites. At two years (C), children typically can respond to some questions or directions, like "Where are your ears?" or "Show me your eyes," but cannot yet contrast opposing qualities. At four years (D), children can understand simple comparatives like "bigger" and "smaller" when given things of contrasting sizes, but do not necessarily have a consistent understanding of various common antonyms. By six years, children should have already achieved this understanding and been applying it in their speech for about a year.

20. A: Brown's "operations of reference" in Stage I sentence types include nomination (e.g. "this truck"), recurrence (e.g. "more juice"), and negation, which includes denial (e.g. "no drink"), rejection (e.g. "no more"), and nonexistence (e.g. "doggie go"). Actions (B), agents (C), entities (D), and objects are all classified under "semantic relations" and used in pairs, e.g. action + agent, action + object, agent + object, action + locative, entity + locative, possessor + object/possession, and demonstrative + entity.

21. A: Brown designated Stage I as typical of children 12 to 26 months old. 15-30 months (B) and 24-36 months (C) are not age ranges used by Brown for the developmental stages he defined. 27-30 months (D) is the age range Brown designated as associated with his Stage II of language development. 31-34 months is the age range Brown associated with his Stage III of language development.

22. C: Brown (1973) categorized correct use of irregular past tenses of verbs in his Stage III, associated with the age range of 36-42 months. Stage I (A) is associated with Stage I Sentence Types (Operations of Reference subtypes and Semantic Relations subtypes). Stage II (B) is associated with using the present progressive verb tense, regular –s plural endings, and the prepositions *in* and *on*. Stage IV (D) is associated with using articles, regular past tenses, and regular present tenses in the third person. Stage V is associated with using third-person irregular verbs, the uncontactable auxiliary form of "to be", the contractible copula form of "to be", and the contractible auxiliary form of "to be".

23. D: Brown classified use of the regular plural –s ending in his Stage II of Syntactical and Morphological Development. He defined his Stage V (A) with more advanced usages, like third-person irregular verbs and the uncontactable and contractible auxiliary and contractible copula forms of "to be". He identified his Stage IV (B) as using regular past tense, regular third-person present tense, and articles. He defined his Stage III (C) as using irregular past tense, possessive ('s) endings, and the uncontactable copula form of "to be". He associated his Stage I with use of the Stage I Sentence Types characterized by short utterances, usually 1 to 2 morphemes total and lacking usage of possessives and structured morphology.

24. D: By "private speech", Vygotsky meant the way that young children typically verbalize aloud to themselves while engaging in solitary activities. This helps them to think through their actions; make decisions; solve problems; and strengthen their knowledge of the correct sequences in activities with multiple steps. In using the term "private speech," Vygotsky was not referring to a private conversation with another child (A) or an adult (B); or silent mental speech (C)—which Vygotsky termed "inner speech." He said that children eventually internalized their external private speech: it progressed from overtly speaking aloud to oneself, to mentally speaking silently to oneself. Both private and inner speech serve the same functions at different ages.

25. C: Central auditory processing disorder is categorized as an auditory disability because it impairs the ability to understand spoken language received through the auditory sense (hearing). But it does not involve the outer, middle, or inner ear or auditory nerves. It involves a deficit in the brain's ability to interpret the meanings and structures of speech sounds. Sensorineural hearing loss (A) involves the cochlea in the inner ear and/or auditory nerves leading to the brain. Conductive hearing loss (B) involves the outer and/or middle ear, where something obstructs conduction of sound, e.g., a deformed pinna/auricle, wax buildup, a closed or malformed or ear canal, fluid/pus buildup in the middle ear due to otitis media (middle ear infection), otosclerosis immobilizing the ossicles in the middle ear, etc. Complete deafness (D) most typically involves total sensorineural hearing loss.

26. C: Teachers can ask children at younger ages of early childhood to identify vocabulary words used in shared readings, e.g. "What was this called?"; and describe story details, e.g. "How did they do that?" Asking children to predict coming events in a story (A), to imagine applications of story situations beyond the story (B), and to conclude why story characters act/feel as they do (D) are all appropriate techniques to use during and after shared readings with children at older ages of early childhood. These elements of literature may be too abstract with the younger ages of early childhood.

27. A: Each of the answer choices describes an element of critical thinking. The student's described actions correspond to evaluating evidence used to support arguments or statements (a), since the student should consider whether a source is reputable, proven, and accepted by authorities in the field before using evidence from that source. Judging the quality of material (b) or information can be done by comparing it to other material/information, consulting one's own previous experience, and listening to one's own intuition. Distinguishing fact from opinion (c) in text or speech is done by looking for objectivity, facts, and proof vs. subjectivity, non-factual information, and absence of proof. Identifying whether a source contains evidence or no evidence (d) to support the writer's or speaker's arguments can be done by examining the ideas and information in the text or speech. The quality of a source, the source's use of fact and opinion, and whether the source contains evidence that supports an argument are all factors that should be considered when evaluating evidence. Since the student's described actions are also used to evaluate supporting evidence, Choice A is the correct answer.

28. A: Teachers should keep from confusing young children by introducing letters to them that have similar sounds in separate lessons. They should introduce continuous consonant sounds (f, r, s, m, n), which are easier to produce in isolation with less distortion, before they teach consonant sounds that are stops (p, b, t, d, k, g), which are more difficult for young children to produce, not vice versa (B). Letters with similar appearances should be presented during separate lessons, not the same one (C), also to prevent confusion. Teachers should introduce high-utility letters/sounds first, not low-utility (D), as the high-utility ones are those they will hear, see, and use most often.

29. A: Teachers can obtain a good assessment of the level of print awareness a young child has developed by using a storybook; hence (B) is incorrect. The teacher should first ask a young child to identify the front, back, spine, and title of the book; this is not unnecessary (C) because some children with undeveloped/less developed print awareness may not know these things, as well as where to start reading a book. Teachers should also ask children to point out a letter and a word in the book, and the first and last words in a sentence in the book, which does inform the assessment (D) by indicating whether they know how letters are combined to form words and words are arranged into sentences in books, and how they are separated by punctuation and spaces. They should also ask children to identify punctuation marks, uppercase letters, and lowercase letters. Teachers should not only praise children's correct responses; they should also correct wrong responses and review the corrections.

30. B: Typically, between birth and the age of two years, children grow to four times their newborn weights. This is the most rapid period of physical growth. After this, children's growth slows incrementally, decreasing between two and three years and decreasing even more between four and six years.

31. C: By the age of two years, children's brains have typically grown to 55% of their adult size. Their brains do not reach 90% (A) of adult size until they are around six years old. Their brains grow to 75% (B) of their adult sizes between the ages of approximately four and five years. Children's brains are 33% (E) and 40% (D) of their adult sizes before the age of two years.

32. C: The development of children's motor skills involves both learning new physical movements (C), and integrating previously learned motor movements into continuous, smooth patterns of combined motions, as with learning to throw a ball with skill. Proprioception, i.e. knowing the size, shape, and position of their body parts and of their bodies in space and relative to other objects, progresses from infancy to become more accurate by preschool ages (A). Newborn motor movements are largely reflexive and progress to become voluntary movements by preschool years rather than vice versa (B). (D) is incorrect because there are several limiting factors in motor development, including coordination, muscular strength, and bone strength. As young children develop motor skills, each of these three categories are strengthened.

33. D: Researchers have observed consistent gender differences in preschool physical and motor development; however, they also observe that in spite of these differences, overall the physical and motor development of preschoolers is more similar than different between genders. In general, the differences are not significant enough to place any emphasis on motor development differences between preschool boys and girls. Some known differences, however, include that preschool boys are more muscular than preschool girls, but preschool girls are more physically mature than preschool boys (A). While preschool boys exhibit more strength in large-muscle, gross-motor skills, preschool girls exhibit more coordination in large-muscle, gross-motor skills (B and C). Additionally, preschool girls are superior to preschool boys in fine-motor skills as well as gross-motor coordination (C).

34. D: Psychologists studying infant behaviors have classified their basic temperaments into Easy, Difficult, and Slow to Warm Up. They find that the majority of babies have the Easy temperament. Thus (A) is incorrect, and babies with Difficult temperaments are not in the majority (B); neither are Slow to Warm Up types (C).

35. D: When a person attributes his/her success to internal attributes, like hard work or intelligence, psychologist Julian Rotter named this internal locus of control. He described external locus of control as attributing one's success to external factors outside of one's control, like getting help from the teacher (A) or a classmate/friend (C); or luck (B); or other factors, such as other peoples' efforts. Internal and external loci of control apply to people's attribution of causes for failures as well as successes.

36. C: Children with primarily visual learning styles focus on appearances and what they can see. They can understand and learn abstract concepts and relationships best when they are given visual stimuli like multicolor graphics, pictures, colorful objects, and other visual illustrations. Sculpting soft clay (A) would help a child who has a primarily haptic or tactile learning style, focusing on textures and movements. Dance movements (B) and sporting activities (D) are also stimuli that would help children with haptic learning styles to understand and learn abstract concepts and relationships. A primarily auditory learning style could be targeted with musical recordings, which can help a child to understand and learn abstract relationships and concepts.

37. B: Erikson saw infancy revolving around the nuclear conflict of Basic Trust vs. Mistrust. If a baby's needs are met, e.g. being fed timely, adequately, and consistently, s/he develops basic trust; if not, s/he develops basic mistrust. Autonomy vs. Shame (B) and Self-Doubt is Erikson's second stage, around the ages of 2-3 years. Children learn to walk and are toilet-trained, developing physical control. They feel autonomy/ independence through succeeding, and shame and self-doubt through failing. Initiative vs. Guilt (C) is Erikson's third stage, associated with the preschool years, around 3-5 years old. Children explore their environments, exercising power over them. Success results in a sense of purpose, disapproval for wielding excessive power in guilt. Industry vs. Inferiority (D) is Erikson's fourth stage during elementary school ages, around 6-11 years. Children adjust to new academic and social requirements. Success results in a sense of competence, failure in a sense of inferiority. Intimacy vs. Isolation is Erikson's sixth stage during young adulthood (the fifth is Identify vs. Role Confusion during adolescence).

38. A: The fact that most children are around six years old when they enter first grade is not a coincidence. This is the age when they are first able to stay in their seats, be quiet, and attend to a lesson without getting up and running around, shouting out on impulse, and/or having their attention wander. Thus the expectations of first-graders are normally appropriate for most six-year-olds. However, kindergarten classes feature activities with shorter time spans and more physical activity to suit five-year-old developmental levels, so (B) is inappropriate. Similarly, toddlers have not yet developed steady gaits and cannot be expected to balance or hop on one foot (C). Babies younger than about five months cannot be expected to sit up unsupported (D) as they have not developed the strength to do so.

39. B: Adler observed that only children are likely to prefer the company of adults over that of children as their early experiences are with parents rather than siblings. Therefore, (A) is incorrect. Adler also found that only children have more difficulty sharing things with other children rather than finding it easier (C) because they have not had to share with siblings. He stated that older/oldest children may develop strict or authoritarian attitudes and behaviors (D) through feeling power over younger siblings; and that with encouragement, older/oldest children can develop helpful attitudes and behaviors.

40. C: One of the characteristics Adler described about the youngest siblings in families is that being the smallest, they often wish to be bigger than their older siblings; so as they grow, they may make grandiose plans which never succeed. Adler found that while youngest children, unlike only children, have multiple older siblings who "parent" them, they also have in common with only children (A) the fact that they are never displaced ("dethroned") by younger siblings. Adler observed that one twin is usually more active or stronger than the other and perceived by parents as older; and that the twin born a minute or more earlier may be perceived by the parents as more mature (B). Adler noted that one twin may develop a leadership role while the other may develop identity issues (D). Adler also commented that while some "babies" of the family may grow out of this role, others continue to feel and behave as the baby of the family indefinitely.

41. D: Adler observed that the boy siblings of the only girl in a family can behave overprotectively toward her, and that the only girl may go to more effort to please the father. He believed that an only boy among girl siblings was equally likely to behave effeminately to fit in with them, or to exhibit overly masculine behaviors to differentiate himself as the "man of the family" (A). Similarly, Adler believed that an only girl among boy siblings was equally likely to identify with her brothers by becoming a tomboy, or to adopt extremely feminine behaviors to differentiate herself from them (B). Adler believed parents of all boys or girls who wanted a child of the other sex might dress one child as the opposite sex (C); and that this child was equally likely either to object strongly to such a role reassignment, or to take advantage of it.

42. D: Bowen described how the parents' perception of a child can become self-fulfilling prophecies by influencing the child's self-image. For example, a child may not initially be helpless or dependent, but if the parents perceive and thus treat the child that way by helping her/him too much, the child can actually become helpless and dependent. Thus the child's self-image and behaviors come to mirror the parents' perceptions rather than vice versa (C). This process reflects parental fears that something is wrong with a child, not that there really is (A). The parents find the child's behavior to confirm their fears because they perceive the behavior through the distorting lens of their own anxiety, not because something is really wrong with the child's behavior (B). Bowen stated that the more intense this process is, the more the child develops relationship sensitivities beyond those of the parents.

43. D: Most children with typical development receive nourishment from mother's milk or infant formula during infancy, and then from baby foods until their teeth erupt. By the age of two years, young children eat most of the same foods that adults eat. Their nutritional needs at this age are similar to those of adults, though they eat smaller quantities of food. To begin eating the same foods as adults only by the age of three (C), four (B), or five (A) years is not developmentally typical.

44. C: At the ages of 2-5 years, young children typically need about 10-12 hours of sleep per 24 hours. They typically need 9-11 hours of sleep (A) at the ages of 5-7 years. Sleeping 7-9 hours (B) is generally inadequate during early childhood. While some young children sleep fewer nighttime hours and need long daytime naps (D) at the ages of 2-5 years, other children these ages need long, uninterrupted sleep at night but rarely take naps. This varies among individual children rather than one or the other being the rule for all young children.

45. B: Young children have short attention spans and tend to be impatient, so they are unlikely to wash their hands long enough or thoroughly enough. Parents and teachers must encourage them to do so by, for example, teaching them to sing "Happy Birthday" or songs/verses of similar duration while washing their hands, which makes it more fun while assuring they wash them for long enough times. A major transition of early childhood is that while parents washed their infants' hands for them, children learn to wash their own hands during toddlerhood and preschool years rather than parents continuing to do it for them (A). During the toilet-training process, toddlers get many more germs on their hands (C). Young children are also exposed to more unfamiliar germs in daycare and preschool (D).

46. A: Social psychologist Albert Bandura has proven that when children viewed videos with violent content, their aggressive behaviors increased. Hence adults must monitor and control what young children view. Intense and/or violent video content can frighten young children who cognitively cannot yet distinguish fantasy from reality In leisure activities, numerous studies show that children get more cognitive stimulation from interactive games, arts and crafts, music, puzzles, storytelling, and other activities than from watching TV for long time periods (B). In larger families, researchers find it is important for each individual child to have some 1:1 time with each parent, even during unstructured activities, rather than only interacting groups (C). Parents should encourage, not discourage children in playing "house", "dress-up", "auto shop", etc. as make-believe play is a significant developmental hallmark wherein children understand and use symbols (D), enabling them to learn to read and write the print language that symbolizes spoken language.

47. B: Research studies find that both Asian and Latin American cultures are more collectivist and interdependent than American and European cultures. American culture is found to be the most independent and individualistic, hence the *least* interdependent (A). European cultures are in the middle between the two extremes: they are *less* individualistic than in America (C), but also *less* collectivistic than Asian cultures (D).

48. C: Data collected from 2003 show that more than 15% of African-American families had violent conflicts; over 11% of Latino families did; and fewer than 9% of White families did. While researchers concede that cultural and demographic variables can influence styles of disagreement in families, they find parental stress the strongest influence on whether family conflicts become violent (A). The National Survey of Child and Adolescent Well-Being found that children of socioeconomically disadvantaged families have more developmental and behavioral problems than in other groups (B). However, these children were also less likely to receive help with their problems (D). For example, more than 40% of toddlers and more than 68% of preschoolers in contact with the child welfare system had high levels of developmental and behavioral needs; yet fewer than 23% of these children were receiving services to address those needs.

49. D: The National Survey on Early Childhood Health recently did find significant differences in parenting practices, as well as in home routines and home safety measures, of Latino and African-American families (A). The researchers associate these differences with different degrees of positive early childhood development (B). Researchers also believe that disparities among racial and ethnic groups in children's school readiness and ensuing school achievement may contribute to discrimination by teachers and other educational personnel against minority racial and ethnic groups (C). This survey found American minority children to have lower average school readiness than American white children. Moreover, most of these differences in school readiness are also associated with family income differences.

50. D: Freud's theory was that babies are in the first, Oral stage of development: because nursing is a primary need and activity, their attention is orally focused; they put everything in their mouths to explore and learn about the environment. In applying this theory, adults accept object-mouthing by babies; they prevent access to dangerous/unsanitary objects, providing safe and sanitary things they can mouth. Providing opportunities to "make believe" (A) reflects application of Piaget's theory of cognitive development, wherein children in his second, Preoperational stage develop symbolic representation. Modeling behaviors children can observe and imitate (B) reflects application of Bandura's Social Learning Theory, wherein children learn by seeing and imitating others' behaviors. Providing timely, consistent nursing/feeding to a baby (C) reflects application of Erikson's psychosocial theory: in his first, Basic Trust vs. Mistrust stage, babies develop trust when fed regularly, enough, and in time; or mistrust when feeding is late/irregular/inadequate.

51. D: Piaget's first stage is Sensorimotor, when infants learn about the world by receiving sensory input and engaging in motor activities to interact with the environment. Adults can apply knowledge of this stage by giving them a variety of toys babies can manipulate, and which spin, twirl, roll, bounce, fly, make noises, etc. and engage all of the sensory modalities. Introducing topics from others' perspectives (A) will not appeal to children this age, who are cognitively unable to understand others' points of view. Encouraging make-believe/pretend play (B) is inappropriate to this stage as children have not yet developed the ability to understand or use symbols. They are also not unable to understand logical operations like arithmetic (C). Adults understanding this stage should also not punish repeated throwing of objects out of the crib, a normal part of the learning process wherein babies observe what reactions their actions elicit, making cause-and-effect connections.

52. C: Piaget defined one characteristic of preschoolers' Preoperational thinking as animism, i.e. assigning human qualities to inanimate objects. Preoperational children do not yet think logically (A). Magical thinking (B), another characteristic Piaget defined of Preoperational children, means believing that one's thoughts or words cause external events to occur. Egocentric thinking (D), another Preoperational characteristic, means seeing things only from one's own viewpoint but not others'.

53. B: Cognition was not one of the conditions Albert Bandura has specified as requisite for learning in his theory. Bandura specified that first one must pay Attention (A) to another person's behavior in order to observe it, and also to observe reinforcement the other person may receive for performing it. One must then remember the behavior (and reinforcement when applicable), which is Retention (C). Bandura theorized that one must have the Motivation (D) to imitate the behavior, as well as the ability to imitate the observed behavior.

54. A: Toddlers are typically in Erikson's psychosocial stage centering on the nuclear conflict of Autonomy vs. Shame and Self-Doubt. The toddler who shouts "NO!" and has tantrums is exhibiting normal behaviors as s/he works to develop independence (autonomy). Children developing Initiative (B) vs. Guilt are in a later stage, as are children developing Industry (C) vs. Inferiority. Children developing Basic Trust vs. Mistrust (D) are typically the earlier stage of infancy.

55. B: Maslow conceived of human needs in a hierarchy, and visualized this hierarchy as a pyramid. At the base of this pyramid are physiological needs, which are the most fundamental. Above these are security (C) needs such as shelter and a safe environment. Above these are social needs like feeling loved and belonging to a group. Above these are esteem (D) needs like feeling personal value, social recognition, and accomplishment. At the top of the pyramid are self-actualizing (A) needs, i.e. realizing one's full potential and attaining optimal personal growth. Maslow theorized that lower levels of need must be met before any higher level(s) can be addressed; hence physiological needs must be met first.

56. C: Conditional positive self-regard was Rogers' term for self-esteem that depends on external standards. External locus of control was Julian Rotter's term for attributing one's own success or failure to external factors (e.g. "The teacher didn't explain it to me" for failure or "The teacher helped me" for success). Conditional positive self-regard would be the equivalent in Rogers' theory. Rogers felt that children develop conditional positive self-regard when they are subjected to condition of worth (B), i.e. rewards based not on need but worthiness, as in behaviorism's contingencies of reinforcement. Rogers believed Incongruence (A) between one's ideal self and real self would cause neurosis. Unconditional positive regard (D) was what Rogers believed parents and therapists should give, i.e. unconditional love and acceptance, to children and all individuals.

57. D: This example illustrates the behaviorist principle of negative reinforcement: An aversive stimulus, i.e. something one does not like, is removed contingent on a behavior, increasing the probability one will repeat the behavior. In this example, being rushed by the mother is the aversive stimulus. Positive reinforcement (A) presents a desirable stimulus, i.e. something one likes, contingent on a behavior, increasing probability of repetition. For example, if the mother gave the child a favorite treat right after s/he woke up early, s/he would awaken early again for the treat. Positive punishment (B) presents an aversive stimulus contingent on a behavior to reduce probability of repetition. If the mother yelled at the child for awakening early, s/he would be less likely to awaken early again. Negative punishment (C) removes a desirable stimulus contingent on a behavior to reduce the probability of repetition; e.g. if the mother prohibited TV for awakening early.

58. D: The Montessori Method emphasizes children's self-direction in activities, while teachers make clinical observations and serve as guides; and self-correction via the use of autodidactic equipment. The Montessori Method teaches both practical skills and abstract concepts via physical activities, not just mental tasks (A). Montessori teachers make every effort to engage children's parents in their educations, rather than leaving them uninvolved (B). Learning environments in Montessori schools are adapted to the developmental levels of individual children rather than groups (C).

59. D: In the Bank Street approach, children can learn at different developmental levels appropriate for them. They typically learn multiple subjects together, not one at a time (A); and in groups rather than 1:1 as individuals (B). They engage in physical, cognitive, emotional, and social development through various types of childcare programs, not just one (C).

60. C: Froebel did believe that nature was the heart of all learning. He also believed that the role schools, among other things, was to direct the will of the students (A). He felt that human potential was defined through individual accomplishments (B). He not only believed in, but pioneered, play-based instruction (D) for young children; in fact, Froebel was the person who invented the original concept and practice of Kindergarten. He felt that the goals of education included the development of spirituality and self-control in students. Most of Froebel's philosophy and theory of education remain influential in early childhood education today.

61. B: Siegfried Engelmann collaborated with Carl Bereiter in experiments reexamining Piaget's theory of cognitive development. While Piaget had maintained that the ability to conserve liquid volume depended only on the child's level of cognitive development, Engelmann and Bereiter showed that this ability could also be taught to children before they reached the corresponding Piagetian stage. The Bereiter-Engelmann Preschool Program did not test teaching methods with affluent college faculty children (A); Piaget's case studies used such children, but the Bereiter'-Engelmann Program demonstrated the effectiveness of intensive instruction for enhancing cognitive skills in disadvantaged preschool-aged children. Engelmann did develop the philosophy and methodology of Direct Instruction (C), through his research into curriculum and instruction including children with Down syndrome (D) as well as children from impoverished backgrounds.

62. A: The HighScope Curriculum for preschoolers does include music activities, but these do not include writing musical notation or music composition. They include listening to music, singing, and playing musical instruments. The other choices all represent activities included in each of four other out of 10 main categories of key experiences for preschool children's development and active learning.

63. B: One principle of emergent literacy theory is that young children learn to read and write concurrently, not in sequence, since reading and writing are integrally interrelated and cannot be separated. However, this theory does not find that children's first encounters with written language occur during early childhood (A); but rather that even infants encounter written language.

Emergent literacy theorists also note that young children's scribbles do not all look the same (C) regardless of native language; rather, Egyptian children's scribbles resemble Egyptian writing more, American children's scribbles look more like English writing, etc. While receptive language comprehension develops before expressive comprehension with speech, this does not apply to print (D): preschoolers find early writing activities easier than early reading activities. In this theory, research finds that literacy does not involve abstract, isolated skills learned for their own sake, but rather authentic skills applied for real-life purposes, the same way children see adults use literacy.

64. C: The whole language approach to early childhood literacy instruction has its basis in the philosophy and psychology of constructivism. Hence it is not similar to the analytical nature of teaching phonics (A) or of alphabetical learning (B). It emphasizes the uniqueness of each child's cognitive experience, not similarity (D).

65. D: In the whole language approach, children's overall engagement, comprehension, and appreciation of reading, writing, and literature come before correction of mechanical errors. Therefore, (A) is incorrect. Whole language teachers do not ignore young children's mechanical errors (B). While they do not prioritize correction, they do use formative assessments, not only summative assessments (C) and then design learning activities that give children opportunities and help to acquire mechanically correct linguistic forms.

66. D: Like Darwin describing evolution before him, Piaget referred to adaptation (A) in describing how we adjust to our environment. We adapt not only to survive, but to establish, maintain, and restore equilibrium or balance. Piaget called this natural process of seeking balance equilibration (C). The process of adaptation seeks equilibrium. Components of adaptation are assimilation (B), i.e., fitting new but related information into an existing schema, and accommodation (D), i.e., forming a new schema or changing an existing one to fit new and related but very different information. For example, a young child assimilates a new food into his schema for "things I can eat." Encountering gum, the child accommodates to it by changing that schema to include "things I can chew but not swallow."

67. D: When teachers use the LEA with young children for learning beginning reading, children realize that they acquire knowledge and understanding through their own experiences as well as through instruction. This is because the LEA does connect printed language with the students' own personal life experiences (A). It has the children use their own language and words (B) to describe things. This enables them to interact with text on multiple levels at one time (C).

68. C: Instruction using basal readers goes from the bottom up, moving from smaller subsets of reading skills to larger ones. This helps students make transitions from each part to the whole. Basal readers use texts including children's literature *and* diverse other writing genres (A). Basal reader texts are graded by reading level, and include *both* narrative and expository writing (B). Instructional research finds that using rigid, systematic sequences in teaching from smaller to larger subsets of skills is *more* helpful to students (D).

69. B: All of these are techniques included in the basal reader approach to reading instruction. Young children are aided in decoding text through the precise control of word analysis skills, (A) as well as of vocabulary items (C), and by the use of enlarged "big books" (D).

70. A: During the DRA, teachers prepare students before they read by presenting them with new concepts and vocabulary words they will encounter in the text; and help them become more motivated to read. Only after this preparation by teachers do students read silently, guided by teacher questions and statements (C); they do not read silently first (B). Student reading comprehension is developed not only by teacher actions but also through student discussions (D) of concepts, characters, plots, etc.

71. B: The DR-TA is meant to develop students' ability to read critically by teaching them reading comprehension as a group, not individually (A). It is meant to engage children's active participation in reading, not only by their processing information (C), but also by their asking questions (D) and receiving feedback as they are reading.

72. C: DRA manuals primarily use literal, factual questions that require only convergent thinking of students; whereas DR-TA questions require higher levels of reading comprehension and interpretation of students by demanding they engage in divergent or creative thinking. DRAs, having more specific materials, guidelines, and questions and being more manual-oriented and materials-oriented, are best suited specifically for use with basal readers; however, DR-TAs, having fewer directions and greater teacher flexibility and responsibility, can also be used for other curriculum and lesson planning (A) that involve reading. DRAs feature the pre-teaching of new vocabulary words, while DR-TAs do not (B), instead requiring more realistic during-reading decoding. While DRA manuals specify when to teach which skills, DR-TA approaches do not (D). Thus teachers need more expertise in asking questions and considering varied student answers when using DR-TAs than they do with DRAs.

73. D: Research with early childhood learning devices has proven that manipulatives are effective for helping young children to access abstract math concepts. It is not that they cannot understand these at all (A) or that they can only understand concrete objects (B); but rather that they cannot understand abstract concepts when these are presented only abstractly, but can understand abstract concepts when they are presented using concrete objects that young children can see, feel, and manipulate. Solid objects provide a bridge to abstract ideas for young children. Some early math curricula even require manipulatives (C), such as the Horizons curriculum.

74. B: An activity using non-standard measures to compare something like the weight of apples and grapes is helpful in learning inference skills, since students have to try out different combinations to find the balance. Students improve their inference skills by using the outcome of one attempt to inform their next through inference. Observation skills are also exercised in activities like these, as the students have to observe and operate the scales to find their answer, but it is not such a observationally focused activity as studying and describing physical traits of different objects. Communication would be a key feature if this type of activity were used in a group. Classification is not particularly exercised in this type of activity, since the only classifications would be the type of fruit, which is a given in this type of activity.

75. C: One way to engage preschoolers in scientific inquiry and discovery is to have them compare similarities and contrast differences among various objects, because observation and classification are scientific principles and process skills for children to develop. Exploring the solubility in water of various substances *is* a scientific activity (A) as it involves inquiring and discovering the properties of different forms of matter. Mixing colors is not strictly an art activity (B), but can be used equally well for scientific inquiry and discovery. Preschool teachers can create science centers inexpensively (D) by using common objects like magnets, mirrors, scales, magnifying glasses, prisms; by selecting books, games, puzzles, etc. related to various science themes; and using models, puppets, and other inexpensive, preschool-friendly objects and materials.

76. B: EC experts advise that teachers can and should find science teaching materials in their everyday environments, which cost nothing and appeal to children's natural curiosity and interests.

Preschool children do not learn best from textbooks (A), even age-appropriate books; they enjoy learning with real-world materials. For example, found objects from nature like rocks, loose bird feathers, fallen leaves, etc. make good science materials (C). Teachers can also obtain animal fur from local groomers and turtle shells, snakeskins, etc. from local pet stores (D) are useful teaching materials.

77. A: Preschool children's upper bodies are typically more developed than their lower bodies, giving them higher centers of gravity. This makes them more likely to fall than older children (B). Preschool teachers can help them improve their balance and coordination by encouraging them to hop (C) and balance on one foot. Such exercises, including hopping races, can also enhance children's self-confidence, an emotional benefit (D).

78. B: In instruction about color as an element of visual art, preschool teachers can help children learn color names, sensory discrimination, and classification skills. Teachers can read children a story about colors, or sing/play a song about colors to introduce a lesson (A). Some art museums do offer pre-designed lessons in visual art elements for preschool ages (C), which teachers can use as models. After a story or song, teachers can present a painting or other artwork, which young children can appreciate (D) on their own levels.

79. C: Preschool children's ability to recognize shapes will develop through well-designed lessons focusing on line as an element of visual art. Such lessons will also help preschoolers to improve their ability to make comparisons (A) and expand their ability to recognize symbols (B). Teachers can help children identify different types of lines like straight, wavy, spiral, pointy, zigzag, etc., separately drawn on paper, which is within the abilities of preschoolers, and then ask them to find these line types in a work of art, (D), which they will be able to do after identifying them separately. Teachers can then have children draw the different line types themselves, and experiment with different line-drawing tools.

80. D: Teaching preschoolers about how shape is used in art helps develop their early geometric math skills as well as their understanding of visual art. It also helps them develop their ability to form concepts (A) and to identify discrepancies (B), as well as to stimulate their creative thinking skills (C). For example, teachers can read a story about shapes; then have children point to and name shapes they recognize in the story; then have them identify shapes in a work of art; and then have them arrange solid shapes into formations representing people, animals, houses, flowers, etc.

81. C: Cognitive dissonance is a term coined by psychologist Leon Festinger to describe the discomfort we feel when considering contradictory information. We resolve this discomfort by rejecting certain information, or forming new schemata or changing existing ones to accommodate some information. This term is not related to a disorder (A), sensory overload (B), or incompatible instructional and learning (D) processes.

82. D: Not only is emotional development necessary in itself; but it is also a prerequisite and a support for children's development of social interactions and social skills. Affective learning activities help children to express their emotions, and also to understand them (A). Understanding them will in turn help children to develop emotional self-regulation (B). In addition, affective learning activities can inform teachers about how children feel and which activities most interest them (C).

83. C: Giving preschoolers an activity wherein the teacher prompts them to use different body postures and movements to depict different emotions helps them to understand their own and others' emotions (A); express them as well as understand them (B), get physical exercise and have fun (C), and use creative thinking (D).

84. B: Children's motor skills typically develop sooner than their verbal skills. Hence young children are more likely to use physical aggression like kicking, biting, hitting, and pushing/shoving to get what they want rather than using speech (A). Young children have also not yet developed emotional self-regulation, so preschool teachers must help them learn how to manage their strong emotions constructively (C). Young children do not learn social skills only directly; teachers can help develop their social skills by demonstrating aggressive vs. proactive behaviors using puppets (D), which preschoolers find entertaining as well as concrete representations of emotions they can understand.

85. A: Early childhood education experts recommend providing at least 35 square feet indoors and 75 square feet outdoors of usable play space for learning environments. (B) would not be enough room for typical young children to engage in usual activities and avoid fighting or competing among age groups. (C) and (D) would be excellent but do not reflect the recommended *minimums*.

86. B: Indoor and outdoor spaces in EC learning environments should be arranged to allow individual, small-group, and large-group activities. Children's products and other visual elements should be placed at child eye level, not adult (A) when displayed. Spaces should be organized to allow, not prohibit, children's movement among activities (C) without unduly distracting other students. Spaces should also be arranged to promote children's positive social interactions (D) and behaviors, not to prevent these.

87. C: EC experts say that indoor learning environments for toddlers and preschoolers should have the rooms organized to enable a variety of activities, but not necessarily to limit the activities to certain areas (A). The floors in the rooms should include both hard and carpeted floors (B) to allow crawling, toddling, walking, etc., which should not be limited by insufficient space. Preschool math and science activities might occur in multiple areas of a classroom (D), while the room still should be laid out to facilitate their taking place.

88. C: Positive reinforcement (A) motivates the individuals by presenting something that increases the probability of a behavior's occurrence and/or recurrence. Primary reinforcement (B) is unconditioned, i.e., it naturally reinforces or increases a behavior's probability (e.g., food, water, sleep). Negative reinforcement (C) motivates the individuals by removing something whose removal reinforces or increases a behavior's probability. Secondary reinforcement (D) is conditioned, i.e., it did not originally reinforce the behavior but has been made to do so by pairing it with a primary reinforcement.

89. D: Small inner rooms and partitions in indoor environments provide ways for children to experience privacy and solitude when needed. Adult laps for cuddling (A), pillows and soft upholstery (B) and thickly carpeted floor areas (C) are all related to providing for children's sensory needs for softness, but not for privacy.

90. C: Behavioral principles have proven in many studies that it is more powerful to reward good behaviors than to punish bad behaviors (A); therefore, these are not equally effective (B). Good behaviors should be rewarded consistently, not occasionally (D). Positive reinforcement must be repeated consistently many times for young children to associate their behaviors with the rewards they receive as they will not instantly make this association.

91. B: Behaviors occur for reasons, to meet needs. Thus, one must know what function or purpose they serve before one can change them. An undesirable behavior can be replaced with a more desirable one, but the replacement behavior must serve the same purpose as the undesirable one, so (A) is incorrect. While knowing a behavior's function is necessary, this does not eliminate the need to change it (C). Knowing a behavior's function informs not only the choice of a replacement behavior, but also which consequences to apply to the undesired behavior. The same consequences will not work for every function (D) a behavior can serve. For example, a tantrum behavior the function of which is to get attention will not respond to a certain consequence the same as when its function is to express frustration.

92. A: FERPA provides that schools may furnish student records without prior consent to some researchers if they are conducting certain studies on behalf of the school; by court order or legal subpoena (B); to appropriate personnel in safety or health emergencies (C); and to juvenile justice system authorities, according to specific state laws (D).

93. D: Because of diverse student needs, teachers are required to ensure educational equity by differentiating their instruction accordingly with student abilities (a), offering equal opportunities to all students (b), treating all students fairly (c), and choosing and/or adapting instructional materials to reflect multicultural perspectives (d) to which multicultural students can relate.

94. D: Relative to early childhood behavior management, the "10:1 Rule" means that for every 1 negative comment or correction one gives to a child, the adults should give that child at least 10 positive comments. Positive reinforcement for desired behaviors is proven to be always more powerful than punishment for undesired behaviors.

95. D: When young children follow adults' rules in care and educational settings, the adults should consistently reward them for doing so. Adults should never assume they can do nothing as long as children comply with rules (A): they will not continue without any positive reinforcement. When adults withhold rewards from children who do not follow rules, they cannot assume this needs no explanation (B): they must explain to young children why they did not get the reward by telling them which rule they did not follow. Initially stating the rules is not enough with young children; adults must repeat rules frequently and for a long time (C) before young children can remember and follow them.

96. C: One way EC educators can include families in children's education is to acknowledge the integral part that parents play in supporting their children's learning. Another way is for educators to promote and support parenting skills, their enhancement, and their application by parents (A). To include families, educators should work to achieve reciprocal and regular communication between the school and family (B). All school personnel should not only make parents feel welcome at the school; they should also seek out help and support from parents (D).

97. B: To involve families of diverse backgrounds, EC educators should ask them to develop their own goals for participating in their young children's educations since the family members know better how they are able and willing to participate. EC educators *must* involve families in designing IFSPs for preschoolers (A), since an IFSP is an Individualized FAMILY Service Plan. It is good for educators to create volunteer calendars; however, they should NOT assign parents times for participating (C), but rather should encourage them to collaborate with schools when they are able. If families have difficulty with printed/written English (or any printed/written language), educators should instead speak with them to promote regular communication (D). They should also get an interpreter if needed for parents who speak little or no English.

98. C: EC educators should frequently send communications to diverse families with information about their children (A); about important developmental milestones (A, B, and D); about methods they can use to nurture child growth and development (B and C); and about the content of their classes (D).

99. D: For informal assessments of pre-K classes, teachers can make classroom observations during story or circle times, each observation targeting different skills like math, alphabet knowledge, social-emotional skills, emergent writing, oral language, etc. They can make these observations during both small-group (A) and whole-class (B) activities. They should organize the assessments using around three themes per day (C).

100. D: Formal assessments are typically standardized tests administered to groups of students. They are designed to avoid administrator bias (A) and capture only the children's responses (B). They provide norms for age groups and/or developmental levels for comparison (C). Their data can be scaled and reported in aggregate to school and/or program administrators and policymakers.

101. D: By his term reciprocal determinism, Bandura means that learning involves the individual, the behavior, and the environment, all of which influence and are influenced by one another. This term does not specifically refer only to student and teacher (A), to behavior and environment only (B), or to individual and environment only (C).

102. C: Not all screening and assessment instruments used in EC education programs are appropriate for use with ethnically diverse populations. Depending on their authors and the populations samples used for norming, they may be culturally biased. Screening and assessment instruments used with EC students vary in which developmental domains they measure (A). Different tests are intended for use in different applications (B). The methods of administration also vary across instruments (D).

103. B: While some tests are comprehensive, assessing children's development in multiple domains, not all are (A). Some tests focus on a single domain (C), like language or emotional-social development, while others can even focus on one facet within a domain {(B), (C)}, like attachment or temperament within the emotional-social domain of development. In addition to developmental domains, some tests measure risk and resiliency factors (D) that influence developmental delays and disorders.

104. A: One application of assessment instrument results in ECE programs is for planning curriculum and treatment programs. However, screening instruments are used for identifying children who need further assessments rather than for diagnosing developmental problems (B). Assessment instruments are also applied in developing and/or confirming diagnoses (C) of developmental delays or disorders. An additional important application of assessment instruments is for determining a child's eligibility for a particular program (D).

105. B: It is more advantageous for ECE programs to use tests that cover the entire age range that their programs serve. This is because they not only can assess all ages of children in the program (A) with equal accuracy (D), but also because they are easier to administer and then re-administer later to monitor children's progress in the program than separate, age-specific tests are; they can also be administered during a program for progress monitoring (B); and they are easier to administer at the beginnings and ends of programs for comparison than separate, age-specific tests are (C).

106. C: Self-reporting instruments do have the advantage that they usually take fewer than 20 minutes for parents, caregivers, and teachers to complete. *If* they are self-administered, they must be at the respondents' reading levels and in their native language (A); but some of them *can* alternatively be read to respondents by interviewers who are trained in or familiar with the instrument's administration (B). While ECE program personnel need relatively little training to administer these assessments, they may need more training to score and interpret them (D); or in some cases, trained specialists may score and interpret them instead.

107. D: The interview method for gathering screening/assessment information from adults about infants and young children can involve brief interviews, but they typically still take longer than paper-and-pencil self-reporting questionnaires, surveys, or checklists. Interviews may be conducted in a structured format using the questions given (A); or in a semi-structured format wherein the administrator uses his/her judgment (B) in adding questions to those published to obtain complete enough information. Interview questions can cover not only the child's identified areas of strengths and needs (C), but also parental concerns, parent-child interactions, the child's behavior, and other subjects.

108. D: Instruments that use multiple methods, such as collecting data from a variety of respondents and settings, will yield the most comprehensive information for determining diagnoses and/or developing individualized care or instructional plans for EC populations. Self-reporting questionnaires and surveys (A) are more appropriate for use in screenings because they are usually short, need little administrator training and are easy to administer, are comparatively low in cost, and can be used in different settings like pediatricians' offices, homes, preschools, etc. Formal and informal observational tools (B) and structured and semi-structured interviews (C), while requiring more training, time, and expense, provide more detailed information for assessments to aid diagnoses and planning; however, multiple-method assessments still provide even more comprehensive information than these.

109. D: Test-retest reliability means that a test instrument will yield the same results when administered two or more times to the same child within a short period of time. (Developmental changes in early childhood occur too rapidly for this to apply if testing is done over a longer time period.) (A) is a definition of inter-rater reliability. (B) is a definition of internal consistency reliability. (C) is a definition of content validity.

110. C: If two children take the same test and both score beyond its cutoff score indicating need for assessment, and this results from their scoring the same on mostly the same test items, then the test's individual items correlate with one another and the overall test score, meaning the test has internal consistency. But if two children score past the cutoff but their scores result from completely different test items (A), then the test's items do not correlate with each other (D) or the overall test score (B), meaning the test does not have good internal consistency.

111. B: Content validity means that a test measures the entire content area it claims to measure. If a test does this, it can be used with more confidence to generalize about how its results predict a child's functioning levels in real life. However, if a test to screen for social-emotional development, for example, screens for a child's interactions with caregivers but not with peers (A); or screens for social skills but not communication skills (C); or screens for attention but not for initiation of play (D), the test would have low content validity by not screening for all elements of social-emotional development.

112. A: When a screening tool identifies a potential mental health disorder, and then a complete diagnostic evaluation confirms this prediction by diagnosing an actual mental health disorder, the screening tool has demonstrated good predictive validity. An instrument correctly identifying 6 of 10 children _with_ developmental disorders or delays is said to have a *sensitivity* of 60%, not specificity (B). An instrument correctly identifying 8 of 10 children *without* disorders or delays has

80% *specificity*, not sensitivity (C). Identification of delays/disorders where none exist constitutes false-*positive* errors (D).

113. B: EC educators should make organized outlines of developmentally applicable guidelines for the children they serve. These outlines provide foundations for the anecdotal observations and authentic assessments they will use to track children's developmental progress; hence they are not unnecessary (A). ECE programs must include ample opportunities and activities for children to develop each individual skill, which includes all of the practice and review they need in order to retain what they learn (C). For tracking children's progress, ECE programs should use systems that follow developmental sequences (D). This helps teachers know whether they can advance some children to the next level, or need to reinforce some previously taught skills for other children.

114. C: The law stipulates that EC teachers and other professionals working with children and families are "mandated reporters" who are legally required to report any suspicions of child abuse or neglect. The teacher should report her suspicions to authorities because this law was enacted to stop violence against children, and not just because the law incurs penalties against professionals who do not comply with it (D). Even if the teacher feels sorry for the mother, and/or she cannot prove her suspicions, these are not reasons to refrain from reporting them (A). She should report seeing injuries to the child and hearing from the child that the boyfriend caused them, even though she knows the mother depends financially and emotionally on the boyfriend (B). Avoiding potentially harmful side effects for the mother is no justification for allowing suspected abuse to go unreported.

115. D: EC educators interact positively when they use problem-solving activities and dialogues to help them discover which learning experiences they can make more effective for children, and how to do this. Sharing anecdotal records and observations with other educators within the ECE program for the purpose of improving instruction does not disrespect privacy (A). Communicating with other adults within the ECE setting about the children and families they serve does not violate confidentiality (B) but does constitute positive interaction. EC educators within a program should not only share their observations and records of their students, but should moreover use this shared information to collaboratively plan their instruction (C).

116. D: By law, ECE employees are both required to report suspected child abuse or neglect and are also immune from liability for releasing student records related to such reporting; therefore, (C) is incorrect. The Family Educational Rights and Privacy Act (FERPA) mandates student records confidentiality for every ECE program/facility/agency that receives federal funding, not every ECE program/facility/agency in the country (A): those NOT receiving any federal funding are not subject to this law. The IDEA (Individuals with Disabilities Education Act) is a federal law and hence not superseded by state special education laws (B).

117. D: Because of danger and liability issues, giving medication to children in ECE settings is controversial but often necessary. ECE staff should label children's medications with drug name, child's name, doctor's name and contact information, and dosage and administration instructions to prevent errors. ECE centers/programs must write and follow policies and procedures observing their state government's licensing requirements for medical care and treatment (A). ECE experts advise centers/programs require doctor and parent permission for giving children any prescription/non-prescription medication (B). In addition to keeping written parental consent on file, centers/programs should post separate charts for easy staff access with the child's name, medication, dosage, time to administer, and teacher initials. This does not induce redundancy or errors (C); rather, it documents that teachers follow physicians' and parents' directions, and can prevent errors.

118. C: ECE settings should keep certain things on file for medical emergencies, including detailed emergency treatment procedures; signed, written parent consent, which is necessary (A); parental preferences in doctors and hospitals (B); and information on the health insurance of children's families (C) as well as parent contact information. Notifying parents of emergencies is legally required (D) by licensing regulations; not notifying parents is subject to legal action.

119. B: One issue affecting ECE facilities is if state authorities remove a child from the parents' custody. Another issue that does affect ECE facilities is if two parents not living together are pursuing child custody (C), because parents frequently demand to visit with and/or take the child home even when they do not have custody, so ECE personnel must know this. (A) is the definition of physical custody, not legal custody. (D) is the definition of legal custody, not physical custody. Physical custody does not confer all the rights of full legal custody.

120. A: If an adult without custody or otherwise unauthorized attempts to pick up a child from an ECE facility, the administrator should inform the adult of the center's policies and procedures, including showing them their copy of the court's custody order (A) if needed. If the adult refuses to leave, threatens or shows violence or makes a scene, the ECE should call the police if necessary (B). If the adult leaves, the ECE administrator must not only notify the parents or other adult(s) who enrolled the child of the incident; s/he must also file a written report of it (C), meet with the custodial adult to review and/or update custody arrangements; document the meeting (D) including signatures and dates, and file the documentation in the child's center record.

How to Overcome Test Anxiety

Just the thought of taking a test is enough to make most people a little nervous. A test is an important event that can have a long-term impact on your future, so it's important to take it seriously and it's natural to feel anxious about performing well. But just because anxiety is normal, that doesn't mean that it's helpful in test taking, or that you should simply accept it as part of your life. Anxiety can have a variety of effects. These effects can be mild, like making you feel slightly nervous, or severe, like blocking your ability to focus or remember even a simple detail.

If you experience test anxiety—whether severe or mild—it's important to know how to beat it. To discover this, first you need to understand what causes test anxiety.

Causes of Test Anxiety

While we often think of anxiety as an uncontrollable emotional state, it can actually be caused by simple, practical things. One of the most common causes of test anxiety is that a person does not feel adequately prepared for their test. This feeling can be the result of many different issues such as poor study habits or lack of organization, but the most common culprit is time management. Starting to study too late, failing to organize your study time to cover all of the material, or being distracted while you study will mean that you're not well prepared for the test. This may lead to cramming the night before, which will cause you to be physically and mentally exhausted for the test. Poor time management also contributes to feelings of stress, fear, and hopelessness as you realize you are not well prepared but don't know what to do about it.

Other times, test anxiety is not related to your preparation for the test but comes from unresolved fear. This may be a past failure on a test, or poor performance on tests in general. It may come from comparing yourself to others who seem to be performing better or from the stress of living up to expectations. Anxiety may be driven by fears of the future—how failure on this test would affect your educational and career goals. These fears are often completely irrational, but they can still negatively impact your test performance.

Elements of Test Anxiety

As mentioned earlier, test anxiety is considered to be an emotional state, but it has physical and mental components as well. Sometimes you may not even realize that you are suffering from test anxiety until you notice the physical symptoms. These can include trembling hands, rapid heartbeat, sweating, nausea, and tense muscles. Extreme anxiety may lead to fainting or vomiting. Obviously, any of these symptoms can have a negative impact on testing. It is important to recognize them as soon as they begin to occur so that you can address the problem before it damages your performance.

The mental components of test anxiety include trouble focusing and inability to remember learned information. During a test, your mind is on high alert, which can help you recall information and stay focused for an extended period of time. However, anxiety interferes with your mind's natural processes, causing you to blank out, even on the questions you know well. The strain of testing during anxiety makes it difficult to stay focused, especially on a test that may take several hours. Extreme anxiety can take a huge mental toll, making it difficult not only to recall test information but even to understand the test questions or pull your thoughts together.

Effects of Test Anxiety

Test anxiety is like a disease—if left untreated, it will get progressively worse. Anxiety leads to poor performance, and this reinforces the feelings of fear and failure, which in turn lead to poor performances on subsequent tests. It can grow from a mild nervousness to a crippling condition. If allowed to progress, test anxiety can have a big impact on your schooling, and consequently on your future.

Test anxiety can spread to other parts of your life. Anxiety on tests can become anxiety in any stressful situation, and blanking on a test can turn into panicking in a job situation. But fortunately, you don't have to let anxiety rule your testing and determine your grades. There are a number of relatively simple steps you can take to move past anxiety and function normally on a test and in the rest of life.

Physical Steps for Beating Test Anxiety

While test anxiety is a serious problem, the good news is that it can be overcome. It doesn't have to control your ability to think and remember information. While it may take time, you can begin taking steps today to beat anxiety.

Just as your first hint that you may be struggling with anxiety comes from the physical symptoms, the first step to treating it is also physical. Rest is crucial for having a clear, strong mind. If you are tired, it is much easier to give in to anxiety. But if you establish good sleep habits, your body and mind will be ready to perform optimally, without the strain of exhaustion. Additionally, sleeping well helps you to retain information better, so you're more likely to recall the answers when you see the test questions.

Getting good sleep means more than going to bed on time. It's important to allow your brain time to relax. Take study breaks from time to time so it doesn't get overworked, and don't study right before bed. Take time to rest your mind before trying to rest your body, or you may find it difficult to fall asleep.

Along with sleep, other aspects of physical health are important in preparing for a test. Good nutrition is vital for good brain function. Sugary foods and drinks may give a burst of energy but this burst is followed by a crash, both physically and emotionally. Instead, fuel your body with protein and vitamin-rich foods.

Also, drink plenty of water. Dehydration can lead to headaches and exhaustion, especially if your brain is already under stress from the rigors of the test. Particularly if your test is a long one, drink water during the breaks. And if possible, take an energy-boosting snack to eat between sections.

Along with sleep and diet, a third important part of physical health is exercise. Maintaining a steady workout schedule is helpful, but even taking 5-minute study breaks to walk can help get your blood pumping faster and clear your head. Exercise also releases endorphins, which contribute to a positive feeling and can help combat test anxiety.

When you nurture your physical health, you are also contributing to your mental health. If your body is healthy, your mind is much more likely to be healthy as well. So take time to rest, nourish your body with healthy food and water, and get moving as much as possible. Taking these physical steps will make you stronger and more able to take the mental steps necessary to overcome test anxiety.

Mental Steps for Beating Test Anxiety

Working on the mental side of test anxiety can be more challenging, but as with the physical side, there are clear steps you can take to overcome it. As mentioned earlier, test anxiety often stems from lack of preparation, so the obvious solution is to prepare for the test. Effective studying may be the most important weapon you have for beating test anxiety, but you can and should employ several other mental tools to combat fear.

First, boost your confidence by reminding yourself of past success—tests or projects that you aced. If you're putting as much effort into preparing for this test as you did for those, there's no reason you should expect to fail here. Work hard to prepare; then trust your preparation.

Second, surround yourself with encouraging people. It can be helpful to find a study group, but be sure that the people you're around will encourage a positive attitude. If you spend time with others who are anxious or cynical, this will only contribute to your own anxiety. Look for others who are motivated to study hard from a desire to succeed, not from a fear of failure.

Third, reward yourself. A test is physically and mentally tiring, even without anxiety, and it can be helpful to have something to look forward to. Plan an activity following the test, regardless of the outcome, such as going to a movie or getting ice cream.

When you are taking the test, if you find yourself beginning to feel anxious, remind yourself that you know the material. Visualize successfully completing the test. Then take a few deep, relaxing breaths and return to it. Work through the questions carefully but with confidence, knowing that you are capable of succeeding.

Developing a healthy mental approach to test taking will also aid in other areas of life. Test anxiety affects more than just the actual test—it can be damaging to your mental health and even contribute to depression. It's important to beat test anxiety before it becomes a problem for more than testing.

Study Strategy

Being prepared for the test is necessary to combat anxiety, but what does being prepared look like? You may study for hours on end and still not feel prepared. What you need is a strategy for test prep. The next few pages outline our recommended steps to help you plan out and conquer the challenge of preparation.

STEP 1: SCOPE OUT THE TEST

Learn everything you can about the format (multiple choice, essay, etc.) and what will be on the test. Gather any study materials, course outlines, or sample exams that may be available. Not only will this help you to prepare, but knowing what to expect can help to alleviate test anxiety.

STEP 2: MAP OUT THE MATERIAL

Look through the textbook or study guide and make note of how many chapters or sections it has. Then divide these over the time you have. For example, if a book has 15 chapters and you have five days to study, you need to cover three chapters each day. Even better, if you have the time, leave an extra day at the end for overall review after you have gone through the material in depth.

If time is limited, you may need to prioritize the material. Look through it and make note of which sections you think you already have a good grasp on, and which need review. While you are studying, skim quickly through the familiar sections and take more time on the challenging parts.

Write out your plan so you don't get lost as you go. Having a written plan also helps you feel more in control of the study, so anxiety is less likely to arise from feeling overwhelmed at the amount to cover.

STEP 3: GATHER YOUR TOOLS

Decide what study method works best for you. Do you prefer to highlight in the book as you study and then go back over the highlighted portions? Or do you type out notes of the important information? Or is it helpful to make flashcards that you can carry with you? Assemble the pens, index cards, highlighters, post-it notes, and any other materials you may need so you won't be distracted by getting up to find things while you study.

If you're having a hard time retaining the information or organizing your notes, experiment with different methods. For example, try color-coding by subject with colored pens, highlighters, or post-it notes. If you learn better by hearing, try recording yourself reading your notes so you can listen while in the car, working out, or simply sitting at your desk. Ask a friend to quiz you from your flashcards, or try teaching someone the material to solidify it in your mind.

STEP 4: CREATE YOUR ENVIRONMENT

It's important to avoid distractions while you study. This includes both the obvious distractions like visitors and the subtle distractions like an uncomfortable chair (or a too-comfortable couch that makes you want to fall asleep). Set up the best study environment possible: good lighting and a comfortable work area. If background music helps you focus, you may want to turn it on, but otherwise keep the room quiet. If you are using a computer to take notes, be sure you don't have any other windows open, especially applications like social media, games, or anything else that could distract you. Silence your phone and turn off notifications. Be sure to keep water close by so you stay hydrated while you study (but avoid unhealthy drinks and snacks).

Also, take into account the best time of day to study. Are you freshest first thing in the morning? Try to set aside some time then to work through the material. Is your mind clearer in the afternoon or evening? Schedule your study session then. Another method is to study at the same time of day that you will take the test, so that your brain gets used to working on the material at that time and will be ready to focus at test time.

STEP 5: STUDY!

Once you have done all the study preparation, it's time to settle into the actual studying. Sit down, take a few moments to settle your mind so you can focus, and begin to follow your study plan. Don't give in to distractions or let yourself procrastinate. This is your time to prepare so you'll be ready to fearlessly approach the test. Make the most of the time and stay focused.

Of course, you don't want to burn out. If you study too long you may find that you're not retaining the information very well. Take regular study breaks. For example, taking five minutes out of every hour to walk briskly, breathing deeply and swinging your arms, can help your mind stay fresh.

As you get to the end of each chapter or section, it's a good idea to do a quick review. Remind yourself of what you learned and work on any difficult parts. When you feel that you've mastered the material, move on to the next part. At the end of your study session, briefly skim through your notes again.

But while review is helpful, cramming last minute is NOT. If at all possible, work ahead so that you won't need to fit all your study into the last day. Cramming overloads your brain with more information than it can process and retain, and your tired mind may struggle to recall even previously learned information when it is overwhelmed with last-minute study. Also, the urgent nature of cramming and the stress placed on your brain contribute to anxiety. You'll be more likely to go to the test feeling unprepared and having trouble thinking clearly.

So don't cram, and don't stay up late before the test, even just to review your notes at a leisurely pace. Your brain needs rest more than it needs to go over the information again. In fact, plan to finish your studies by noon or early afternoon the day before the test. Give your brain the rest of the day to relax or focus on other things, and get a good night's sleep. Then you will be fresh for the test and better able to recall what you've studied.

STEP 6: TAKE A PRACTICE TEST

Many courses offer sample tests, either online or in the study materials. This is an excellent resource to check whether you have mastered the material, as well as to prepare for the test format and environment.

Check the test format ahead of time: the number of questions, the type (multiple choice, free response, etc.), and the time limit. Then create a plan for working through them. For example, if you have 30 minutes to take a 60-question test, your limit is 30 seconds per question. Spend less time on the questions you know well so that you can take more time on the difficult ones.

If you have time to take several practice tests, take the first one open book, with no time limit. Work through the questions at your own pace and make sure you fully understand them. Gradually work up to taking a test under test conditions: sit at a desk with all study materials put away and set a timer. Pace yourself to make sure you finish the test with time to spare and go back to check your answers if you have time.

After each test, check your answers. On the questions you missed, be sure you understand why you missed them. Did you misread the question (tests can use tricky wording)? Did you forget the information? Or was it something you hadn't learned? Go back and study any shaky areas that the practice tests reveal.

Taking these tests not only helps with your grade, but also aids in combating test anxiety. If you're already used to the test conditions, you're less likely to worry about it, and working through tests until you're scoring well gives you a confidence boost. Go through the practice tests until you feel comfortable, and then you can go into the test knowing that you're ready for it.

Test Tips

On test day, you should be confident, knowing that you've prepared well and are ready to answer the questions. But aside from preparation, there are several test day strategies you can employ to maximize your performance.

First, as stated before, get a good night's sleep the night before the test (and for several nights before that, if possible). Go into the test with a fresh, alert mind rather than staying up late to study.

Try not to change too much about your normal routine on the day of the test. It's important to eat a nutritious breakfast, but if you normally don't eat breakfast at all, consider eating just a protein bar. If you're a coffee drinker, go ahead and have your normal coffee. Just make sure you time it so that the caffeine doesn't wear off right in the middle of your test. Avoid sugary beverages, and drink enough water to stay hydrated but not so much that you need a restroom break 10 minutes into the test. If your test isn't first thing in the morning, consider going for a walk or doing a light workout before the test to get your blood flowing.

Allow yourself enough time to get ready, and leave for the test with plenty of time to spare so you won't have the anxiety of scrambling to arrive in time. Another reason to be early is to select a good seat. It's helpful to sit away from doors and windows, which can be distracting. Find a good seat, get out your supplies, and settle your mind before the test begins.

When the test begins, start by going over the instructions carefully, even if you already know what to expect. Make sure you avoid any careless mistakes by following the directions.

Then begin working through the questions, pacing yourself as you've practiced. If you're not sure on an answer, don't spend too much time on it, and don't let it shake your confidence. Either skip it and come back later, or eliminate as many wrong answers as possible and guess among the remaining ones. Don't dwell on these questions as you continue—put them out of your mind and focus on what lies ahead.

Be sure to read all of the answer choices, even if you're sure the first one is the right answer. Sometimes you'll find a better one if you keep reading. But don't second-guess yourself if you do immediately know the answer. Your gut instinct is usually right. Don't let test anxiety rob you of the information you know.

If you have time at the end of the test (and if the test format allows), go back and review your answers. Be cautious about changing any, since your first instinct tends to be correct, but make sure you didn't misread any of the questions or accidentally mark the wrong answer choice. Look over any you skipped and make an educated guess.

At the end, leave the test feeling confident. You've done your best, so don't waste time worrying about your performance or wishing you could change anything. Instead, celebrate the successful completion of this test. And finally, use this test to learn how to deal with anxiety even better next time.

> **Review Video: Test Anxiety**
> Visit mometrix.com/academy and enter code: 100340

Important Qualification

Not all anxiety is created equal. If your test anxiety is causing major issues in your life beyond the classroom or testing center, or if you are experiencing troubling physical symptoms related to your anxiety, it may be a sign of a serious physiological or psychological condition. If this sounds like your situation, we strongly encourage you to seek professional help.

Thank You

We at Mometrix would like to extend our heartfelt thanks to you, our friend and patron, for allowing us to play a part in your journey. It is a privilege to serve people from all walks of life who are unified in their commitment to building the best future they can for themselves.

The preparation you devote to these important testing milestones may be the most valuable educational opportunity you have for making a real difference in your life. We encourage you to put your heart into it—that feeling of succeeding, overcoming, and yes, conquering will be well worth the hours you've invested.

We want to hear your story, your struggles and your successes, and if you see any opportunities for us to improve our materials so we can help others even more effectively in the future, please share that with us as well. **The team at Mometrix would be absolutely thrilled to hear from you!** So please, send us an email (support@mometrix.com) and let's stay in touch.

If you'd like some additional help, check out these other resources we offer for your exam:
http://MometrixFlashcards.com/PraxisII

Additional Bonus Material

Due to our efforts to try to keep this book to a manageable length, we've created a link that will give you access to all of your additional bonus material:

mometrix.com/bonus948/priiintereced